# Red Money for the Global South

*Red Money for the Global South* explores the relationship of the East with the "new" South after decolonization, with a particular focus on the economic motives of the Council for Mutual Economic Assistance (CMEA) and other parties that were all striving for mutual cooperation.

During the Cold War, the CMEA served as a forum for discussions on common policy initiatives inside the so-called "Eastern Bloc" and for international interactions. This text analyzes the economic relationship of the East with the "new" South through three main research questions. Firstly, what was the motivation for cooperation? Secondly, what insights can be derived from CMEA negotiations about intrabloc and East–South relations alike? And finally, which mutual dependencies between East and South developed over time?

The combination of analytical narrative and engagement with primary archival material from former CMEA states, and India as the most prestigious among the former European colonies, makes this text essential reading for students and instructors of Cold War history, Economic History, and international relations more generally.

**Max Trecker** is at the Leibniz Institute for Contemporary History, Munich, Germany. He is currently working on privatization in Eastern Europe in the 1990s.

# Routledge Studies in Modern History

**Reforming Senates**
Upper Legislative Houses in North Atlantic Small Powers 1800–present
*Edited by Nikolaj Bijleveld, Colin Grittner, David E. Smith and Wybren Verstegen*

**Unsettled 1968 in the Troubled Present**
Revisiting the 50 Years of Discussions from East and Central Europe
*Edited by Aleksandra Konarzewska, Anna Nakai and Michał Przeperski*

**Marginalized Groups, Inequalities and the Post-War Welfare State**
Whose Welfare?
*Edited by Monika Baár and Paul van Trigt*

**Union and Disunion in the Nineteenth Century**
*Edited by James Gregory and Daniel J. R. Grey*

**Intellectuals in the Latin Space during the Era of Fascism**
Crossing Borders
*Edited by Valeria Galimi and Annarita Gori*

**The Co-opting of Education by Extremist Factions**
Professing Hate
*Sarah Gendron*

**Alcohol Flows across Cultures**
Drinking Cultures in Transnational and Comparative Perspective
*Edited by Waltraud Ernst*

**Red Money for the Global South**
East–South Economic Relations in the Cold War
*Max Trecker*

For a full list of titles, please visit: www.routledge.com/history/series/MODHIST

# Red Money for the Global South

## East–South Economic Relations in the Cold War

**Max Trecker**

Routledge
Taylor & Francis Group
LONDON AND NEW YORK

First published 2020 by Routledge

2 Park Square, Milton Park, Abingdon, Oxon OX14 4RN

605 Third Avenue, New York, NY 10017

*Routledge is an imprint of the Taylor & Francis Group, an informa business*

First issued in paperback 2021



Publisher's Note

The publisher has gone to great lengths to ensure the quality of this reprint but points out that some imperfections in the original copies may be apparent.

*British Library Cataloguing-in-Publication Data*
A catalogue record for this book is available from the British Library

*Library of Congress Cataloging-in-Publication Data*
Names: Trecker, Max, author.
Title: Red money for the global South : East-South economic relations in the Cold War / Max Trecker.
Description: Milton Park, Abingdon, Oxon ; New York, NY : Routledge, 2020. | Series: Routledge studies in modern history | Includes bibliographical references and index.
Identifiers: LCCN 2019049967 (print) | LCCN 2019049968 (ebook) | ISBN 9780367244750 (hardback) | ISBN 9780429282683 (ebook)
Subjects: LCSH: Council for Mutual Economic Assistance—History. | Europe, Eastern—Foreign economic relations—Developing countries. | Cold War—Economic aspects.
Classification: LCC HC243.5 .T74 2020 (print) | LCC HC243.5 (ebook) | DDC 337.470172/409045—dc23
LC record available at https://lccn.loc.gov/2019049967
LC ebook record available at https://lccn.loc.gov/2019049968

ISBN: 978-0-367-24475-0 (hbk)
ISBN: 978-1-03-217361-0 (pbk)
DOI: 10.4324/9780429282683

Typeset in Times New Roman
by Apex CoVantage, LLC

# Contents

# Acknowledgment

Scholarly writing
is like mining radium.
For every gram
you work a year.

For the sake of a single word
you waste
a thousand tons
of verbal ore.

But how
incendiary
the burning of these words
compared with the smoldering
of the raw material.

These words
will move
millions of hearts
for thousands of years.
(Based on V.V. Maiakovski)

Mining radium is a serious business. So is scholarly writing. This book could be cited as proof that planned economies actually can work, since the research and the first draft of the manuscript were finished on time, as promised in the original research agreement. However, such a statement would conceal the ups and downs and changes the project lived through during this period and thereafter. Nevertheless, what remained stable, was the institutional umbrella of this work. Without the support of the Graduate School for East and South East European Studies in Munich and Regensburg, this project would not have been possible, as I profited significantly by the intellectual environment of the Graduate School and the intellectual exchange with my fellow PhD students.

I want to thank foremost my two supervisors Martin Schulze Wessel and Martin Aust. Many people have helped me with their advice on the way. Without their help, this work could not have been concluded in such a short time. Among them are Amit Das Gupta, Guido Hausmann, Andreas Hilger, Ravi Ahuja, Madhavan K. Palat, Hari Vasudevan, and Jun Fujisawa. I also want to thank the employees at the archives I have visited for this project. The head of the KfW company archives, Lysanne Goldbach, kindly provided me with the contact details of a former East German banker, Dr. Erich Klober, who was ready to answer my questions on inter-bloc and East–South financial relations and economic cooperation to clarify my own views. Boris Ganichev and Matthias Golbeck helped me to avoid the most serious mistakes in the manuscript. All remaining deficiencies are entirely my fault and will be fixed during the next five-year plan.

Berlin, September 2019

# Introduction

In the summer of 1959, an unscripted verbal exchange evolved between the then General Secretary of the CPSU, Nikita Khrushchev, and the American Vice President, Richard Nixon. The debate between the two occurred in Moscow at the 1959 American exhibition at Sakolniki Park, where, among other appliances and consumer goods, a "typical" American kitchen could be seen; hence, the name "kitchen debate".[1] The General Secretary of the CPSU used the opportunity to praise the achievements and the promising future of Soviet society:

> This is what America is capable of? And how long has she existed? 300 years? 150 years of independence and this is her level? We haven't quite reached 42 years, and in another 7 years, we'll be at the level of America. And after that, we'll go farther. As we pass you by, we will wave "hello" to you – Nikita S. Khrushchev to Richard M. Nixon during the "kitchen debate" on 24 July 1959.

This short extract of the improvised debate can be interpreted in two ways: to begin with, Nikita Khrushchev boasted of the dynamism and successes of the Soviet economy in comparison to lower growth rates in the US. Therefore, it seemed statistically possible that the Soviet economy could overtake the American one somewhere in the future, if the high growth rates proved sustainable. Despite its negative long-term consequences, the Virgin Lands Campaign led to a rapidly increased agricultural output in the late 1950s. This coincided with strong growth in manufacturing. Furthermore, Soviet prestige received a boost by the successful launch of the first Sputnik.[2] These developments led to Khrushchev's remark at the exhibition in Moscow that the Soviet economy would overtake the American one within a matter of years.

But Khrushchev's remarks contained another promise, as well. One that could resonate outside of the direct confrontation between two perceived superpowers and which is important for the topic of this book. Khrushchev drew a direct connection between the economic success and development of the US and the years passed since independence. In his talk with Nixon, he interpreted the October Revolution as the Independence Day of the people inhabiting the former Russian empire freeing them from the shackles of "colonial" oppression. According to Khrushchev's view of Soviet history, the country had achieved remarkable success in only 42 years of independence and was on target to achieve in less than 50 years what had taken the US more than 150 years. This statement was nurtured by the radical social and economic transformation the Soviet Union had lived through. While being predominantly agricultural in its early years, the Soviet Union had become an industrialized country by the late 1950s and outlived the Second World War. This resilience and the rapid economic development had the potential of becoming desired export products in the Cold War, as the focus of the Cold War turned away from Europe towards the Global South, where the former European colonial empires were being dismantled. The economic side of East–South relations during the Cold War constitutes the topic of this book.

Since the beginning of decolonization when the former colonies had been released into independence, the socialist countries had tried to get in touch with them. This relationship of the East with the "new" South originated mainly in the Khrushchev era.[3] Most of the new regimes that established themselves either by force or public consent in the former colonies promised their citizens some form of economic development and industrialization to overcome poverty and improve the prevailing living conditions. Both East and West competed for influence in the Global South and could not afford to ignore the changes on the world map. What they had on offer was military as well as economic aid. This book focuses on the latter, since the Cold War was in reality more often fought in the sphere of the economy and of ideas than with weapons in a literal sense.[4] The more so, as the abrupt end of the Cold War came without a shot being fired.

As concerned economic aid the industrialized countries of Western Europe and North America had far greater resources on hand and could offer more sophisticated technology. However, the countries of the so called Eastern Bloc could compete with them for several reasons, despite their – on average – inferior economic capabilities: as evidenced by Khrushchev's remarks, the Soviet Union, and with her the countries of the Eastern Bloc, could offer a path to rapid industrialization and transformation of former "backward" peasant societies into capable industrial societies that could produce all basic goods by themselves without relying on their former colonial overlords for this transformation. Furthermore, the socialist East could promote its own version of "international solidarity." The countries that made up the Eastern Bloc had no colonial past of their own in Africa, Latin America, and South Asia.[5]

They could therefore present themselves as friends of the oppressed peoples of the South more easily than the British or the French or even the Americans after they had associated themselves with the European colonial empires despite their uneasiness with European rule outside of Europe. The Eastern Bloc even had an organization for regional economic development that promised to kickstart the transformation of formerly "backward" societies, the Council for Mutual Economic Assistance (CMEA). The CMEA was founded in 1949 as a counterweight to the Marshall Plan and comprised the countries that were occupied by the Red Army at the end of the Second World War. Its beginnings were therefore an exclusively European affair. Besides this, the practical relevance of the CMEA despite its huge promises was limited in the Stalin years. However, by the mid-1950s, after Khrushchev's accession to power, the CMEA played an increasing role for intrabloc cooperation as well as for cooperation with the outside world of the Eastern Bloc. For this reason, the documents of the CMEA play a central role in this book.

## Research questions

This work focuses on three main research questions: first, what motives were present for the parties involved to cooperate with each other? More often than not there is little value in a strict separation of economic and political motives, as these were frequently intertwined in different compositions. The CMEA countries embarked on cooperation schemes with the emerging independent states of the Global South to push the influence of the former imperial powers and to use the political vacuum to advance their own political and ideological system. Simultaneously, they found new markets for their own products in these societies which partially absorbed manufactures of dubious competitiveness that could not be sold, or not as easily, in Western markets by the CMEA countries. For the South, cooperation with the East could underpin the new-found independence economically and thus served political purposes as well.

Second, what can be said about the web of intrabloc relations by looking at the CMEA files on East–South economic cooperation? One direction this question is aiming at concerns the role of the Soviet leadership in CMEA negotiations. The second aspect are differences among the smaller member states of the CMEA which were on different economic levels. The Western periphery of the CMEA was more developed in economic terms than its Southern periphery when the CMEA was founded and remained so, even if the gap narrowed during the 1950s and 1960s. It could be assumed that the Soviet Union, due to its dominant position inside the Eastern Bloc and vast raw power, could easily command the smaller CMEA member states which were entirely dependent on the Soviet Union for survival. Rather, the reverse is true.

The Soviet leadership proved unable to push through the negotiation results they desired. What the Soviet delegates to the CMEA could achieve was to ensure that the agenda for discussions inside the CMEA looked the way they wanted it to be. The smaller members of the organization rarely defied Soviet demands openly but they could obstruct Soviet plans by simply refusing to put them into practice which equaled a no. As concerns the relationship between the smaller European members of the CMEA, the economic planners of the developed Western periphery often relied on, e.g., Romanian or Bulgarian partners, as providers of goods and services of low added value when it came to economic cooperation with the Global South. This contradicted the pattern of cooperation prevailing in intrabloc cooperation where the structure of the CMEA proved quite effective to level economic differences between the member states, even if they couldn't be eliminated completely.

Third, how did the exchange and mutual cooperation between East and South develop over time? This question has multiple dimensions and is strongly connected to looking at archival documents on concrete cooperation schemes that were executed by CMEA countries in the Global South from the perspective of the CMEA actors and of the receiving party. At the most basic level this question relates to problems in the field and persisting patterns of failure and achievement that can be observed for several independent cooperation projects scattered over different decades. Connected to this is the search for learning processes and reflections by the parties involved.

A focus is laid on the agency of actors from the Global South and their power in the field as well as in negotiations with members of the CMEA. As the European state socialist countries were delivering relatively advanced technology, it could be expected that they were also able to shape the relationship as they desired. Therefore, it is necessary to look at mutual dependencies and emerging patterns of division of labor between East and South. On a more abstract level, this means to search for pillars of a "socialist world system" as an alternative to the Western model of cooperation and the Western notion of the capitalist world market and its institutional foundations.

The leadership of the CMEA countries promised to offer an alternative to capitalism as embodied by Communist ideology. This coincided with mentioning an emerging "socialist world system" occasionally. The economic system prevailing inside the CMEA differed in important aspects from the rules prevailing on the world market dominated by the West, as economic planning, the dominance of bilateral barter trade, and the absence of important market mechanism made the intrabloc CMEA world somewhat different from the Western economic system. There were endeavors by the CMEA countries to expand this system to include countries from the Global South. Actually, the CMEA expanded its membership in the 1960s and 1970s by taking up Mongolia, Cuba, and Vietnam as full members. During the 1970s and 1980s, the CMEA concluded several multilateral cooperation treaties with countries from the Global South that could have led to full membership. Nevertheless, these attempts can't conceal the fact that the CMEA countries relied heavily on the Western economic order and Western national and international financial institutions for conducting the bulk of their trade with the Global South.

## Important terms and their analytical application

The "principal agent" of this book is the CMEA. It is therefore mandatory to define in which ways the CMEA is perceived and used for the research agenda of this book. The CMEA never constituted a supranational organization. For this reason, the CMEA is better regarded as an umbrella organization that hosted discussions and negotiations on a multitude of issues considered relevant by its members. The majority of these issues settled intrabloc affairs but some were encompassing (economic) relations between the CMEA and the outside world. These will be looked at in this book to analyze the economic side of East–South relations during the Cold War. Since the Secretariat of the CMEA itself could not make decisions on its own in the name of all members, the official material of

CMEA negotiations is supplemented by complementary documents drawn from national archives of the former member states to trace back the evolution of decisions that shaped the economic relations between East and South. The fact that the Secretariat of the CMEA didn't make decisions of its own is therefore irrelevant, since the protocols of the meetings that took place in its name deliver important insights into intrabloc affairs and plans to interact with countries from the Global South as well as reflections on such cooperation schemes conducted in the past.

Some remarks on central terms are necessary. These concern the concepts of "economic aid" and the "Global South." "Economic aid" is a heavily loaded term that looks well on the surface but becomes ever more dubious, the closer one analyzes it. Aid can be split up in three categories: humanitarian aid, charity-based aid, and systematic aid. Humanitarian or emergency aid is usually employed as immediate disaster relief. Its aim is short-term to prevent people from starving after an earthquake, flood, or similar events. Charity-based aid is handed out to people on the ground or to specific local agencies by private organizations. Systematic aid means aid transferred by one government to another government. This can be done bilaterally or by an international institution like the World Bank which would then qualify as multilateral aid.[6] This book deals with the third form of aid, systematic aid. What qualifies as (systematic) economic aid is a matter of definition and the differences between aid and trade are often blurred.

In its guidelines for official development aid (ODA), the OECD, to make a case in point, demands a grant element of 25 % for projects to qualify as economic and development aid.[7] In a fact sheet titled "Is It ODA?" the OECD gives more details on its definition.[8] Therefore, ODA includes, among others, certain peacekeeping operations, civil police work, assistance to refugees, the promotion of the peaceful use of nuclear energy, and funding of research relevant for the target country, like research on tropical diseases. This short overview exemplifies a certain randomness of the criteria employed. According to the OECD loans can classify as aid, if they are handed out at an interest rate below the level the recipient would otherwise be able to achieve on the international financial market.[9] Therefore, contrary to common connotations of economic and development aid in the wider public, aid is not for free and often comes with strings attached. The concept of economic and development aid beyond immediate disaster relief has come under heavy fire for causing more harm than good and perpetuating extreme poverty by leading scholars. Among them William Easterly and Angus Deaton, who was awarded the Nobel Memorial Prize in Economic Sciences in 2015, to name a few.[10]

For the purpose of this book, the terms economic and development aid are avoided, because they conceal more than they expose. Instead, this book is about economic cooperation in a broader sense without the moral connotations of the term "aid." Economic cooperation comprises such projects of the members of the CMEA that were deemed essential for the advancement of national economic interests by the receiving countries in the Global South confined to the civilian sector. Therefore, this book is mainly about industrial investment schemes executed by state socialist countries in the Global South. Although these schemes often contained some grant element, they were in general not executed on a pro bono basis but with the assumption that both sides were to gain something in economic as well as political terms. Analyzing these investment schemes can therefore tell something about general patterns of trade between East and South during the Cold War. "Development" is used in the sense it was applied by contemporaries, mainly economic experts and planners, during the time period under investigation in this book. However, this book is about practices, not discourses of "development." For this reason, dissertations and articles on economic cooperation with the South written at academic departments of state socialist universities and research institutes are included in this work only insofar, as they are mentioned in ministerial or CMEA documents.

If one talks about development in a broad sense, immediately the terms "developing country" and "Third World" come to mind. These terms are very handy but are solely Western creations as they mesh up a vast array of totally different countries under one defining category. They are therefore "guilty" of oversimplification and of not accounting for societies that in essence have not much more in common than any other sample of states, except for them being labeled poor and in need of (Western) caretakers. However, most of the countries belonging to the "Third World" have in common that they were colonized by European societies sometime in their past.[11] Unfortunately, some of the terms prove hard to pass by. But it is important to know their deficiencies and connotations. Some of these problematic terms are also used in the sources and were deemed totally appropriate during the Cold War. In this book, the phrase "Global South" is used in a majority of cases. The term encompasses by and large the same societies defined as belonging to the "Third World" during the Cold War with the colonial heritage being an important commonality for the issue of this book. Nevertheless, Global South has not (yet) acquired the same moral baggage and is more neutral.

The use of theory is kept to a minimum in this book. Authors that have touched on some of the topics talked about in this book have employed several theories for their analyses. These are mentioned and explained where appropriate like the use of the works of Karl Polányi. In the latter part of this book, Wallerstein's concept of core, semi-periphery, and periphery is used to highlight interdependencies between East and West at the end of the Cold War and the relativity of these categories, as one country could occupy different positions in such a hierarchy depending on the point of view. However, Wallerstein himself has not written extensively on the potential role of the socialist East and the CMEA countries in the Capitalist World System of the 20th century. An exception to this is an early paper by him published in 1974.[12] As concerns the question of the role of the Soviet Union in intrabloc affairs and economic cooperation schemes, Alexander Motyl's theory is used as a base.[13]

## Archival sources

The core material used here is constituted by documents of the CMEA. The bulk of these documents were translated into all official languages of the member states. Therefore, the same documents can be seen in the respective national archives outside Moscow, where the former headquarters of the CMEA were located, as well. This applies to all official documents like protocols of meetings or letters exchanged between the delegations in advance of meetings and conferences. During its existence, many so called "Permanent Commissions" were formed inside the CMEA which dealt with specific branches of the economy or other broad economic issues. One of these Permanent Commissions, the Permanent Commission for Technical Assistance (PCTA), was responsible for coordinating the economic activities of the CMEA member states with the Global South. Its material therefore takes center stage in this book.

Archival research in the archives of former CMEA member states has been conducted in the RGAE in Moscow, the Federal Archives (Bundesarchiv) in Berlin, and the MNL (Magyar Nemzeti Levéltár) in Budapest. While the personnel of all the archives visited were very helpful in general, there were certain limits to what could be accessed. In the RGAE, the most valuable accessible documents belonged to the Fonds 302 and 561 and comprised protocols of the Permanent Commissions as well as the documents of the Permanent Representative of the Soviet Union to the CMEA, often including reports on meetings between the Secretary of the CMEA and foreign dignitaries. On the downside, it proved difficult to see documents on concrete cooperation projects with the Global South, particularly for the late 1970s and 1980s. The same is true for the Hungarian National Archives, where documents on economic cooperation with the Global South were primarily accessible until the late 1970s. An overview over the different fonds used for this project is given at the end of the book.

There is a certain "home bias" towards East German documents present in this book. This has several reasons, some of them of pragmatic nature: due to the proximity of the Berlin archives and the low travel costs, it was possible to conduct much longer archival stays in Berlin than would have been possible in more distant locations. Since the bulk of material of the CMEA was translated into all official languages, it would have been rather inefficient and not economical to read all the material in Russian or Hungarian, as using German documents allowed for many more documents to be processed per input unit of time. The more so, since the translations are as identical as possible. More problematic is the focus on East German documents when it comes to elaboration on the evolution of decisions inside the CMEA. Nevertheless, East German documents are the best ones available for this purpose as well, because in contrast to the archives in Moscow and Budapest, nearly all archival documents filed till the late 1980s were accessible. The reason for this is most likely that there is no continuation of the former GDR. The majority of the population of the Federal Republic of Germany and most of its leading politicians have no ties with the GDR which is therefore to a much greater extent "history" than is the case of the former Soviet Union and the Hungarian People's Republic.

It is the aim of this book to combine several perspectives by including not only documents from within the Eastern Bloc but also from countries of the Global South taking their view on economic cooperation with the East into consideration. This was the main motivation to conduct intense archival research in India, namely in the National Archives of India (NAI) in New Delhi. Although foreigners are allowed in general to work in Indian archives, a far lower number of documents on the history of independent India is open to the public than is the case for post-war Germany in the Federal Archives in Berlin. There is no reliable practical rule on which documents Indian ministries give to the NAI at what point in time. This is to a certain degree decided by chance.[14] However, the material available was sufficient enough to provide an asset for this research project.

The decision on which archive(s) to choose to broaden the horizon of this work was a difficult one. The CMEA countries entertained strong mutual relations with the Arab countries of the Middle East during the 1960s and 1970s. Therefore, conducting research in Damascus, Bagdad, or Cairo would have been theoretically interesting. In practice, this was impossible due to missing language skills, missing access to archives, and security issues. Among countries where English is one of the official languages, that had strong relations with the CMEA countries and are accessible for foreign researchers, only India and Ghana seem promising destinations. The choice fell on India as it enjoyed strong relations with the Soviet Union but also ever improving relations with the smaller members of the CMEA from the mid-1950s on. This makes economic cooperation with India an interesting issue to ask for changes induced by the Gorbachev administration, as well. With Ghana, on the other hand, relations cooled down significantly after the ouster of Kwame Nkrumah in 1966 and gained steam in the 1980s again without approaching their level of cooperation prevailing in the early 1960s.

## Literature

The importance of the Global South as a hotspot of the Cold War period has received growing scholarly attention.[15] Still, there is a certain disparity compared to the bulk of literature following the classical narrative of an "East–West conflict" or – more extreme – of a conflict between two superpowers. This bias applies in particular to economic relations where it is often explicitly or implicitly assumed that all eyes are turned primarily to Western donors and Western technology. It is hardly recognized that the Global South played a significant role for the East – not just to gain political prestige – and that by the late 1970s economic interdependencies had emerged.[16] Nevertheless, there is a noticeable positive dynamic at work with more recent literature focusing on the agency of allegedly "weaker" actors.[17]

The picture looks more grim when it comes to the CMEA. Initially, the CMEA had no significant practical meaning but was revived under Khrushchev. Its structure expanded with time, next to two socialist international banks, many committees were formed to deal with specific areas. It thus became an important forum for discussions of common problems and endeavors which would make it an interesting organization to study. The CMEA was a topic on the research agenda of political scientists during the latter half of the Cold War. But, naturally, these authors relied on interviews, declassified Western intelligence material, and newspaper articles. The hitherto best accounts of the CMEA were published in the late 1980s by a political scientist, Jozef van Brabant, and a former Polish banker,

Adam Zwass.[18] Fortunately, there are articles on the PCTA which dealt with the coordination of economic relations between East and South. The early phase of its existence has been the topic of articles by Sara Lorenzini.[19]

The CMEA has received only marginal attention after the dissolution of the Eastern Bloc and of the CMEA itself in 1991. The literature that was produced after 1991 on the CMEA has mainly left the research tableau unaltered, didn't go any further than the authors of the late 1980s, and didn't include a noticeable amount of archival sources, although the archival revolution after 1989 provided ample opportunity to do so. There are some exceptions to this rule but these apply to authors who focus on the role of a certain member state of the CMEA inside the organization and therefore operate in the realm of national history.[20] One can only speculate about the reasons for the absence on a profound corpus of research literature on the CMEA.[21] The CMEA was operating behind the scenes when it came to relations with the outer world of the Eastern Bloc. However, it was a frequent topic in state newspapers, televised news programs, and school books, particularly during the 1970s and 1980s.[22] From a Western perspective, the CMEA was a "loser" topic, since the organization embodied everything that went wrong inside the planned economies of the East. Coupled with its complexity, it made for no interesting research object.

With regards to the political economy of the Eastern Bloc comments on two books published after the dissolution of the Eastern Bloc are needed: "Satellites and Commissars" by Randall Stone, published in 1996, and "Red Globalization" by Oscar Sanchez-Sibony, published in 2014. Sanchez-Sibony argues that the Soviet leadership never pursued autarky but actually sought to integrate the Soviet Union in international trading patterns. This applied to Stalin as well as to the Khruchshev administration. According to him, Soviet foreign trade was to maximize economic gains not to forward any ideological agenda. Sanchez-Sibony's views are scrutinized in this book. It is one central assumption of this research project that trade needs some form of cultural and ideological underpinning which is demonstrated by looking at several economic cooperation schemes of the 1970s and 1980s.[23] Besides this, it must be kept in mind that autarky is a goal not a state. There never was an entirely closed economy in modern history and even the war economy of Nazi Germany which was supposed to be autarkic, at least according to the Four-Year Plan supervised by Goering, was highly dependent on foreign trade. The statement that the Soviet Union was no autarkic country is busting a popular Cold War myth and is therefore an important one, but is of limited analytical value.

Sanchez-Sibony does not rely on sources from other former members of the Eastern Bloc nor from countries in the Global South despite making claims on intrabloc as well as on East–South trade alike. This choice of archival sources is in line with the bulk of research published in the 1990s and 2000s, when scholars focused on one particular national archive. This approach leads to a neglect of intrabloc learning processes facilitated by CMEA meetings starting in the Khrushchev era.[24] This manuscript tries to fill the gap for the post-Stalin years. However, there are substantial similarities between this book and Sanchez-Sibony's as well, like the emphasis on the importance of foreign trade and the agency of leaders from the Global South as well as the disaffirmation of bipolarity as a useful analytical concept. For his statements on intrabloc trade Sanchez-Sibony mainly relies on Randall Stone's "Satellites and Commissars." One central argument Stone makes in his book is that Soviet foreign trade officials were constantly outsmarted by their peers from the smaller bloc and CMEA countries and the Soviet Union thus disadvantaged by CMEA trade.

While the findings of this book support Stone's claim that the grip of Soviet leaders on the smaller bloc members' affairs was rather weak, at least in the post-Stalin period, there is no hard evidence to assume that Soviet foreign trade officials were less capable or institutionally more impaired than their state socialist colleagues. If the foreign trade framework of the Soviet Union was more byzantine than that of the smaller countries, there were certainly factors at work that counterbalanced such tendencies. One could think of the information advantage the Soviet Union could rely upon due to its vast intelligence network and its political prestige as the "motherland of the revolution" which granted the Soviet Union some form of gravitational power. Stone relies to a large degree on interviews he conducted which is a totally valid approach considering that he wrote "Satellites and Commissars" in the early 1990s. However, one can't deny the impression that interviews conducted in the early 1990s say more about the attitudes of the interview partners prevailing after the dissolution of the CMEA and the Eastern Bloc than they say about the real state of affairs of intrabloc trade in the 1970s or 1980s.

This book does not cover discussions inside the UN bodies. The discussions taking place inside the United Nations Conference on Trade and Development (UNCTAD) were touched upon inside the PCTA to coordinate the views of the CMEA member states. Nevertheless, they constituted a side issue inside the PCTA and other CMEA organs. Furthermore, the negotiations inside the UN and inside the CMEA constitute totally different forums. The discussions that took place inside the CMEA were never meant to be completely public or published. UNCTAD sessions, on the other hand, took place on the world stage in public and therefore contained much more of a performance element not inherent in most CMEA negotiations that more closely resembled expert meetings behind closed doors. UNCTAD is more closely covered by authors like Johanna Bockman.[25] More comments on the most relevant pieces of literature are made in the respective chapters of this book which rely on these works or argue against them.

## Structure of this book

This book is divided in four parts, each containing between two and three chapters. The first part deals with the inner economic integration taking place in the Eastern Bloc in the period following its formation and with the first contacts between East and South. Reform attempts initiated by the Khrushchev administration to create more economic cohesion inside the Eastern Bloc coincided with attempts to take advantage of decolonization, a process that was already underway in the late Stalin years but had played no important role in the early phase of the Cold

War. This began to change after Stalin's death. The first part of the book therefore shows how domestic intrabloc reforms and events taking place outside the bloc intermingled with each other.

Part two is titled "The Complex-Program" and elaborates on the role of the CMEA reform initiatives embarked on by the Brezhnev administration in the late 1960s and early 1970s. This reform program has often been described as a failure. This particular view is scrutinized in part two. The "real" state of affairs of economic cooperation between East and South in the 1970s is investigated by dissecting a concrete cooperation scheme in the form of East German and Bulgarian endeavors to build a cement industry from scratch in Syria. The last chapter of part two focuses on the power relations inside the CMEA and asks from the viewpoint of the CMEA documents, if the Soviet Union actually constituted the heart of an empire or if such a term is insufficient to describe the web of relations prevailing inside the Eastern Bloc.

"Red Globalization" copes with the expansion of the CMEA in the 1970s which was not confined to taking up new full members like Cuba and Vietnam. The 1970s saw a series of cooperation treaties concluded between the CMEA and several countries from the Global South. The aim of part three is to take a look at these treaties and similar endeavors to increase the global outreach of the CMEA by encompassing the perspective of the European CMEA member states as well as the perspective of the prospective partners in the Global South where possible. This is achieved by including letters and reports on meetings between the Secretary of the CMEA and foreign dignitaries.

The last part of the book focuses on the 1980s. It is argued for that the CMEA countries were hit not only directly by the policies of the West – due to their role as capital importer – but also indirectly via the Global South which could not repay its loans and therefore aggravated the impending crisis of the socialist countries in the 1980s. Furthermore, the members of the CMEA found it increasingly difficult to sell their equipment and economic model in a changing political and economic environment. The relations with India were an exception to this. Therefore, the last chapter of part four takes a look at the economic cooperation between the CMEA and India and combines this issue with economic intrabloc reforms during the Gorbachev period. A multilateral project to build a steel plant at Visakhapatnam is taken to investigate the problems of cooperation in the 1980s. One last note on transliterations from Cyrillic: these follow the guidelines provided by the Library of Congress.[26]

## Notes

1 See on the event "The Cold War's Hot Kitchen," *New York Times*, 23 July 2009, 25.

2 See on these developments Taubman, *Khrushchev*.

3 Westad, *The Global Cold War*, 67–8.

4 This is not to ignore the millions of people killed in so-called proxy wars. These proxy wars were a particular issue during the latter half of the Cold War when the Global South took clear center stage of the Cold War. However, this doesn't change the fact that the Cold War didn't end by force, neither in the Global South nor in Europe. The

wars were the accompanying symptoms but not the primary causes for the development of the Cold War.

5 The Soviet Union is a certain exception to this and for most scholars constituted an empire of its own. However, since neither the Russian empire nor the Soviet Union had directly controlled India, Africa, nor Latin America, the claim of socialist leaders had some kind of credibility, even if the peoples of Siberia, Central Asia, the Caucasus, the Baltics, and Ukraine, among others, could claim to have been colonized with some justification. As these peoples had no strong independent voice on the world stage during the Cold War, the fact that the Soviet Union could be regarded as an empire by itself was overshadowed by its anti-imperial promise. Another exception is East Germany, since Germany had owned colonies prior to the First World War. But contrary to the FRG, the GDR repudiated any legal continuation with former German states.
6 Differentiation according to Moyo, *Dead Aid*, 7.
7 "Official Development Assistance – Definition and Coverage – OECD."
8 OECD, "Is It ODA?"
9 OECD.
10 See Deaton, *The Great Escape*; Easterly, *The White Man's Burden*.
11 See on the background of the terms discussed here Mason, *Development and Disorder*, 2–19.
12 Wallerstein, "The Rise and Future Demise."
13 Motyl, *Imperial Ends*.
14 This information is derived from personal experiences in Delhi as well as from email exchanges and meetings with Amit Das Gupta, Madhavan K. Palat, and Hari Vasudevan.
15 One valuable book in this respect is Westad, *The Global Cold War*.
16 See as newer examples for the prevalence of this bias Kotkin, "The Kiss of Debt"; Gaidar, *Collapse of an Empire*.
17 See e.g., the contributions in McMahon, *The Cold War in the Third World*.
18 Brabant, *Economic Integration in Eastern Europe*; Zwass, *Der Rat Für Gegenseitige Wirtschaftshilfe*.
19 See Lorenzini, "Modernisierung Durch Handel."
20 See Ahrens, *Gegenseitige Wirtschaftshilfe?*
21 See Müller, "Der RGW Als Schlüssel."
22 This is clear by taking a look at newspapers like Pravda, Neues Deutschland, and Népszabadság. For an example on how the CMEA was integrated in teaching pupils see *Geschichte in Übersichten*.
23 It is interesting that Sanchez-Sibony separates economics strictly from ideology and culture, despite being an adherent of Polányi.
24 Sanchez-Sibony dismisses the CMEA as insignificant. See Sanchez-Sibony, *Red Globalization*, 72.
25 Bockman, "Socialist Globalization Against Capitalist Neocolonialism."
26 Library of Congress, "Romanization Tables Russian," accessed March 12, 2017. www.loc.gov/catdir/cpso/romanization/russian.pdf.

# Part I

# Inner integration and first contacts with the South

# 1 The dawn of the CMEA

## Out of the ashes of the past?

When the Soviet troops finally had taken Berlin, the former capital of European fascism, the future of Europe and of Eastern and Central Europe in particular was unclear. What was clearly visible, however, was the devastation caused by war. Four years of severe fighting had hardly left any bigger settlement between Magdeburg and Moscow untouched by war. The Soviet Union had suffered most by the atrocities of the war with approximately 27 million of its 1939 population dead, the most important industries having been transferred behind the Urals, and its Western part laying in ruins.[1] Over one-fourth of its capital stock had been destroyed during the war.[2] The production level of the Soviet Union in 1945 was at less than 80 % of its 1940 value. The economy of the US, on the other hand, had greatly expanded during the war.[3] The Land-Lease aid given by the US to the Soviet Union had contributed decisively to the Soviet war effort and had helped to sustain the population despite a big drop in agricultural output.[4] With the end of the war, these funds were soon drying up.

The Soviet economy was in need of reconstruction. The situation in the territories occupied by the Red Army showed different shades of war destruction. While certain areas like the industrial parts of what later became the German Democratic Republic were heavily bombed during the war and afflicted by street-fighting, other parts like Czechoslovakia were relatively unharmed with regard to the industrial base of the country. A few areas had even experienced an industrial buildup during the war, often on the basis of forced labor, while others had been systematically plundered to fuel the German war machine.[5] Some of the occupied regions like Saxony, Berlin, and Bohemia were historically on par with other industrialized regions in Europe. Big parts of Romania, Bulgaria, and Poland, on the other hand, belonged to the least developed European regions and were dominated by agriculture. Their respective countryside's were marked by overpopulation and underemployment.[6]

During the war the economies of those countries occupied by the Red Army had been centered on the German Reich, an empire that had ceased to exist in May 1945.[7] A continuation of the economic policies of the past was therefore – even in theory – impossible. This made Soviet interference inevitable. The future of Central and East-Central Europe thus depended upon the Soviet designs for that region, which were themselves reliant on how long the Soviets intended to stay in East-Central Europe and how cordial their relations with their wartime Western allies would turn out to be.

The Cold War was as much a military and political confrontation as it was a contest of ideas.[8] While Soviet ideology was marked by collectivism, determinism, and belief in revolutionary change, the ideology of the "West", as an ideal type in a Weberian sense, relied on individualism, liberal freedom, and evolutionary progress. Ideological opposition alone did not necessarily have to lead to the Cold War as it unfolded first in Europe, then soon in the rest of the world. It was the messianic impetus inherent to both mindsets that made conflict in one form or another hardly avoidable, as each side – at least in theory – offered a genuine path to mankind's salvation.[9]

Still, in Summer 1945, there was room for further negotiations and the possibility of defusing future conflicts.[10] Soviet post-war occupation policies can be separated in two phases with the first one lasting from 1945 to 1947 and the second one from 1947 till Stalin's death in 1953.[11] The two years after the Potsdam Conference were characterized by a flexible and moderate Soviet policy, as a set of coalition governments was formed in most countries with the exception of the Soviet occupation zone in former Germany that gained statehood in October 1949. Elections were held that produced a variety of outcomes ranging from communist-dominated governments in Bulgaria to an inclusion of domestic communists as junior partners in government as in Hungary.[12]

The second phase of Soviet occupation policies between 1947 and Stalin's death was marked by the forced Sovietization of East-Central Europe that coincided with the first "hot phase" of the Cold War taking place in Korea and former Germany, and thus on the fringes of the "Eastern Bloc." "Eastern Bloc" became the common name for the region between the river Elbe and the Korean Peninsula. At the beginning of 1947 though, Communist parties held a monopoly of power only in Yugoslavia and Albania. By mid-1948 all Central Eastern European countries with the exception of Greece and Finland were governed by Communist governments.[13]

## The Soviet Union as an "Imperial Scavenger?"

An important event that finally led to drawing the boundaries of the future two blocs in economic terms was the Marshall Plan. In theory, the American offer was open to both the European States under Soviet control and to the Soviet Union itself.[14] The Soviet leadership had tried to gain access to American loans to rebuild the Soviet economy since as late as 1943. They were still interested in such a loan in 1946 but were told by US officials that the Soviet Union would have to join the Bretton Woods institutions as a prerequisite, namely the World Bank and the International Monetary Fund (IMF). Thus the country would have had to embrace American free trade.[15] This condition was impossible to accept for the Soviet leadership, since it would have meant – at least in Stalin's view – to go back to the economic order of the Belle Époque in which the role of Eastern Europe was mainly characterized by supplying agricultural goods and raw materials for the world market. In Soviet ideology, protectionism on the verge of autarky and forced industrialization were unnegotiable key characteristics of its development model.

Since the Soviets were not inclined to see the Soviet economy being absorbed into the capitalist world economy, they refused to participate. The Soviets subsequently forced the Central-European countries within their sphere of influence to follow suit. There were voices inside the Soviet leadership, like foreign trade minister Anastas Mikoyan, who argued in favor of the American proposal, because the Soviet Union would be more independent, if it were strong, and to be strong, it needed the most sophisticated Western technology.[16] His view, however, was not shared by Stalin, although the same debate reemerged in the 1970s in the Eastern Bloc. Mikoyan's view by then had become the majority position. Eventually, the Americans granted $14 billion in Marshall Plan aid – mostly in the form of credits – to their European allies. This was in itself not a large sum for such a vast area but proved enough to revive transatlantic trade.[17]

The rejection of the Marshall Plan imposed upon Central Eastern European states made an economic integration of Central Eastern Europe with the Soviet Union inevitable. How this integration would be designed was unclear and depended heavily on Soviet goals. The fact that the Soviets had played with the idea of obtaining American loans for themselves up to 1947, suggests that no master plan was in existence. The Soviet leadership had to choose between strategies that provided short-term gains and strategies that would prove beneficial in the long term. A possible short-term strategy could be the extraction of as many resources and capital goods as fast as possible out of East-Central Europe, transfering them to the Soviet Union thereby crippling the production capacity of the area severely and delaying the economic recovery of East-Central Europe. Such a strategy did not require complex integration measures and could be improvised.

However, such a strategy would prove detrimental to Soviet interests, if the area was to be considered to become a vanguard of Communism, as strong allies needed strong economies. Any long-term strategy worthy of that name thus had to be grounded in complementary economies profiting from specialization. Such a path demanded complex and well-designed integration measures. In the absence of any market mechanisms, it would have been up to the state planning agencies to coordinate their plans and negotiate specialization agreements. This would require a fair amount of administrative capability and mutual trust to ensure that such a coordination provided benefits for every one of the participants involved.

The US historian Austin Jersild has put forward the idea of the Soviet Union as an "Imperial Scavenger."[18] He states that particularly during the Stalin period Soviet policies toward Central Eastern Europe were one-dimensional and short-sighted, since they were mainly behaving as if the war hadn't stopped and as if their grip on the region was still unsecure.[19] Soviet "imperial scavenging," according to Jersild, followed the purpose to transfer technologies and expertise in industrial organization from East-Central Europe to the Soviet Union to enable the Soviet economy to compete with the West. As Jersild points out, this was not a very appropriate behavior for an imperial center with vested interests in the region but was more in line with the behavior of an aggressively modernizing state that grasps at every opportunity.[20]

As the Soviet attempts to garner unconditional financial assistance from the US failed, they had to search for compensation elsewhere. Nowhere was this set of "scavenging" policies more vigorously executed than in the Soviet occupation zone in former Germany that became the GDR in October 1949. This area had already been highly industrialized before the war and saw its industrial base expand significantly during the war.[21] It had been highly integrated into the former German economy and depended upon imports of resources and products for its sophisticated industries. With the annexation of East Germany by Poland and the breakup of relations between the victors of the Second World War, the economy of the Soviet occupation zone was in trouble anyway.[22]

All in all, the Soviets extracted goods worth more than 14 billion US dollars in 1938 prices between 1945 and 1953.[23] This was the equivalent of about one-sixth of the GNP of the entire US in 1938.[24] The sum more than compensated the Soviets for the refusal of the Western powers to grant them access to reparations from the industrial heart of the later FRG. The Soviet leadership didn't limit "imperial scavenging" to their occupation zone between the rivers Elbe and Oder. Countries like Romania and Hungary also had to pay reparations worth several hundred million US dollars each. But former Central Germany was the most valued prize.

The Western powers meanwhile relied on a much more elaborate and long-term oriented set of policies. The flagship project of their approach was the Marshall Plan. This didn't mean that they refused to extract reparations out of their occupation zone but they focused more on intellectual property and leading scientists, taking care to foster a kind of exchange that consisted to a large degree of win-win situations. Starting in the late 1940s they even allowed companies like Volkswagen to prosper that were highly discredited by fascism and at the same time able to pose a threat to their Western competitors in a free market. This divergence of occupation policies in the late 1940s would come back to haunt the Soviets, since they stayed in East-Central Europe and had to form long-time allies out of a scavenged region.

## The founding of the CMEA

The concept of the Soviet Union as "Imperial Scavenger" proves useful to analyze Soviet policies in the Stalin period. In contrast to Jersild though, it will be argued that the 1950s saw a significant change in the Soviet approach that is not adequately described by calling it more of the same just without the bluntest forms of exploitation.[25] In fact, one can trace hints at a different policy to the late 1940s, even if the path of developing a long-term plan for the region had never been rigorously pursued by the Soviets during Stalin's reign.

The creation of the Council of Mutual Economic Assistance in 1949 was a first nod in this direction. The origins of the CMEA are still a matter of debate and remain mysterious in a certain sense, since the documents on its foundation in the late 1940s have not been worked through up to now and it remains doubtful, whether the background of its creation can be reconstructed in detail. The most likely explanation is that the CMEA was primarily an idea of the head of Gosplan, Nikolai Voznesensky, and his supporters who were in favor of developing an activist long-term development strategy for the region under Soviet control West of the Soviet borders.[26]

Such reasoning by the head of Gosplan is not surprising, since – in an economic sense – the strategy of scavenging the region, despite a high probability of remaining in close contact with it for an unlimited time, was not very rational and not in the Soviet Union's own interest. By transforming Central Eastern Europe into an economic powerhouse, the Soviet elites could have built up strong allies and profited from mutual specialization. This could have offset the effects of the Western economic sanctions following the Berlin blockade and could have contributed to the isolation of renegade Yugoslavia in a best case scenario.[27] The fact that some voices advocating a more sophisticated line of economic thinking actually existed is further underlined by the comments of Anastas Mikoyan on using American credits in 1947. It is likely that the creation of the CMEA was accompanied and followed by a policy struggle inside the Soviet leadership.[28] In the end, the "Imperial Scavenger" prevailed until Stalin's death but alternative paths were popping up on the way.

There are two founding dates that can be cited for the creation of the CMEA: on 25 January 1949, the foundation of the CMEA was announced in all major party newspapers.[29] The official proclamation of its creation was preceded by a joint conference of the heads of the planning agencies of the prospective members and some party leaders in Moscow between 5 January and 8 January 1949.[30] Thus, 8 January 1949, can also be taken as the founding date of the CMEA. The supposed founding document defines the far-reaching tasks of the CMEA. It was to formulate a common economic plan for the entire region with the aim to diversify the region's economies and make them much more complementary. The CMEA should help its members in exploring and developing the resources needed for fast industrialization. By coordinating the national development plans, the CMEA was to encourage cooperation, standardization, and economies of scale. Mass production by specialized companies for the whole Eastern Bloc in theory should drive down production costs per unit of output immensely. According to the plans of early 1949, encouraging scientific cooperation was also one of the tasks of the CMEA.[31]

A secretariat was set up in Moscow to function as the executive arm of the council sessions which formed the highest organ of the CMEA. The members agreed to pay into a common fund worth 100 million rubles by 1 April 1949.[32] This sum would not have been sufficient for big investment projects all over the whole Eastern Bloc, but it would have been enough to found a kind of Eastern Monetary Fund as a regional equivalent of the IMF to multilateralize trade among its members by balancing trade deficits.[33] The promised sum was never paid in full, and the CMEA was not able to function along the lines intended in the founding document – at least not in the early years of its existence. The reason for this could be that Nikolai Voznesensky fell in disgrace and was removed from his post as head of Gosplan in March 1949. Being a close associate of Andrei Zhdanov, he was shot one year later, following the Leningrad Affair. The secretariat began to conduct preliminary works on how a harmonization of the Central Eastern European and the Soviet economies could be reached but no general plan was worked out.[34] However, there is evidence in the Hungarian state archives that far-reaching policy proposals were still discussed on the second meeting of the CMEA in August 1949.[35]

On 25 June 1950, the Soviet Union stopped its active participation in the CMEA's Bureau without warning.[36] This doesn't mean that the CMEA didn't exert any influence at all, but following a subsequent tightening of Soviet control and interference in Central Eastern Europe after the outbreak of hostilities on the Korean peninsula, the CMEA completely ceased to develop in the direction of becoming an instrument of integration and discussion. The national planning commissions were directly instructed and controlled by Soviet advisers on the ground.[37] Yet, the secretariat of the CMEA in Moscow was not shut down but continued to operate on a low level.[38]

## The fundamentals of economic integration

Before moving on to the post-Stalin period, it is worthwhile to look at the scholarship on economic integration which will prove helpful in analyzing the steps of integration taken post-1953. Although the focus in the literature is clearly on the integration of capitalist economies, in particular of the transatlantic economies after the Second World War, many of its principles hold true for any kind of economic and political integration process as integration in its basic sense means the gradual elimination of economic frontiers between differing entities with the final aim to make these entities function as one.[39] Economic integration thus serves a higher goal that is more than merely economical, since making different entities function as one also has severe political implications and demands a political harmonization, too.[40]

Seen from a Western perspective, the political aims that coincided with economic integration in Western Europe and in the transatlantic region were the prevention of a future war, fostering and stabilizing democracies in Western Europe, and promoting human rights. The more welfare a democracy could provide for its citizens, the more stable it would be.[41] This was the reasoning behind the Marshall Plan and behind the first steps of cooperation between France and West Germany in the heavy industries sector. From a purely economic angle, the argument for economic integration is that bigger markets allow for more specialization and economies of scale, thus enhancing productivity growth and generally raising the living standards of all people involved.[42]

There are three stages of market integration: free trade zones, customs unions, and common markets with the first one being characterized by the free movement of goods within the free trade zone, while its members can set customs at any rate they like for non-member states. Within a customs union its members also give up the right to set tariffs on their own for non-member countries. A common market allows for the free movement of goods and capital in addition to common regulations for products.[43] Political integration can accordingly be defined in three stages: economic union, monetary union, and political union. An economic union is defined by a common market plus a coordination of economic policies. Monetary union implies a common currency and a common set of economic policies, while a political union encompasses the coordination of domestic and foreign policies other than economic policy.[44] It is clear that each of these steps demands the member states to give up sovereignty.[45]

According to textbook literature the first step of integration is market integration that – in its early stages – doesn't require a significant amount of political interference or coordination.[46] Indeed, this holds true for Western Europe and the transatlantic economy which were already experiencing a surge in mutual trade for centuries before heading into the 20th century. This, as has been stated previously, was not the case for Eastern and Central Eastern Europe in the same way. Thus, applying the textbook approach, that is almost exclusively centered around Western experience, to the Eastern half of the European continent proves difficult. Many authors who analyzed the CMEA in the 1980s, have made it clear from the start that they regarded the effort undertaken within the realm of the CMEA as a total failure.[47] This seems to be unfair to a certain extent as the Eastern Bloc is by definition hard to analyze by using a framework that was derived from a reality comprised of advanced capitalist market economies.

What the Soviets and their Central Eastern European allies or clients did, was turning the whole model of integration upside down. Economic integration was to follow – or at least to coincide with – political integration. Rather than dismissing this seemingly unorthodox attempt right from the start, it should be analyzed for what it was: a serious experiment whose chances of being successful are hard to judge, since history doesn't allow for repetitions. The political aims of integration in the Communist realm were – on an abstract level – not that much different from the Western one as the Soviets aimed at homogenizing politics, too, just not in order to foster democracies but so called "People's Democracies" and the rule of the proletariat in the way they understood it. In a pure quantitative sense, the secretariat of the CMEA – especially at the end of the 1950s – hardly deployed much less people than the predecessor of the European Commission, the headcount of which stood at 1000 in 1960.[48]

The violent leveling of old political elites and domestic communists between 1948 and 1953 provided the ground for creating common political institutions in every state within the Soviet sphere of control. In theory, this situation could have been used to enact any "grand design" ideas on East-Central Europe. This opportunity was obviously taken into consideration by the Soviet leadership in early 1949 but dismissed a few months later. When Stalin died on 5 March 1953, the same set of institutions was still in operation in the Eastern Bloc and provided his successors with a second chance not only for political but also for economic reforms within the bloc.

However, the "imperial scavenging" of Central Eastern Europe and the Sovietization of its economies had detrimental effects not only for the countries and regions that were to pay directly for the war damages in the Soviet Union. The introduction of planned economies modeled after the late-Stalinist Soviet Union reduced the competitiveness and efficiency particularly in the most developed regions under Soviet control. Thus, both the GDR and the CSSR suffered from the change in socioeconomic ideology, even though the CSSR didn't have to pay reparations.[49] In fact, although the economies of the CMEA member states were Sovietized, this didn't actually lead to sprawling trade among them, although compared to the interwar period, trade between the economies of Central Eastern and Eastern Europe had increased indeed and was centered around the Soviet Union. The reason for the limited volume of mutual exchange lies not only in them becoming more competitive than complementary to each other, but also that trade was under strict Soviet surveillance and took place mainly via bilateral agreements. Nevertheless, the CMEA provided a framework that could be used for integration attempts in the Post-Stalin period.

## New endeavors

By the time of Stalin's death, the Soviet Union was more powerful than ever before but diplomatically rather isolated.[50] Its power ended mainly at the borders of its Central Eastern European zone of control and it was facing a hostile bloc on its Western borders that was organized militarily by NATO. Despite the uneasy relations at the top of the Soviet leadership following Stalin's death, reforms were initiated that encompassed all levels of society.[51] The execution of Beria signaled a shift in the style of government as his death reestablished the primacy of the party over the security apparatus. The Soviet government turned from an autocracy to a bureaucratic oligarchy that set out to demonstrate its right to rule not by terror but rather by competence and the increase of living standards.[52] The changes of the mid-1950s thus significantly shaped the accepted ways in which future Soviet leaders could rule.

As concerned inter-bloc relations, the triumvirate – and later on particularly Khrushchev – were ready to accept a bigger slice of domestic autonomy and diversity as long as the foundational structures of the bloc were not questioned or threatened.[53] Although the Soviets eventually intervened in Hungary in 1956, the acceptance of a transfer of power to Gomułka in Poland was a clear sign that the system of tight Soviet control over the Eastern Bloc, as exercised in the last years of Stalin's rule between 1948 and 1953, was about to change. The relaxation of political control and the willingness of the Soviet elites to interact more actively with other bloc leaders widened the opportunities for cooperation. This was still meant to be cooperation under Soviet auspices but events like the founding of the Warsaw Pact in 1955 offered a new forum for multilateral discussions rather than bilateral talks or dealing with Soviet demands via the respective Soviet embassies. It also became possible for the smaller members of the bloc to communicate directly with the People's Republic of China after 1953.[54] Such developments indicated change and pointed at a new quality and quantity of intrabloc relations. This was underlined by the joint conference of Communist parties in Moscow in November 1957, whose participants – at least on paper – agreed on the possibility of "peaceful coexistence" and multiple paths to socialism.[55]

It is self-evident that the new policies and changed political environment of the mid-1950s also provided a good opportunity for the revitalization of the CMEA, as it could still be reformed and used to improve the economic performance of the socialist bloc by complementing the bilateral system of economic negotiations established after 1945. It could thereby also serve to increase cohesive powers inside the bloc. Khrushchev most likely had this already in mind when he presented Mao with the idea that the People's Republic of China (PRC) could join the CMEA while visiting Beijing in 1954.[56] This proposal was not totally detached from reality, since the PRC conducted roughly two-thirds of its foreign trade with the Soviet Union in the mid-1950s and an additional part of its foreign trade with the smaller bloc members.[57] 1954 was also the year when the CMEA resumed its activities again. While the year 1949 had featured two CMEA meetings, only one meeting had taken place in 1950. The following meeting turned out to be in 1954.[58]

Nevertheless, at the time of Stalin's death, the CMEA countries were still conducting the bulk of their trade with each other and hardly with any other region of the world despite the failure of the CMEA to support mutual exchange. The proportions of intrabloc bloc trade differed from 70 % for Romania to up to 86 % for Bulgaria.[59] This was as close to regional autarky as it could get. Trade inside the CMEA in the mid-1950s was still organized bilaterally, but so was trade in Western Europe. The convertibility of the Western currencies and multilateral trade in Western Europe were accomplished in the late 1950s.[60] The CMEA, however, still had no real set of rules and conduct nor any precisely defined policy aims when it met for the first time after Stalin's death in March 1954.[61]

Nevertheless, many institutional reforms were initiated in 1954: the Secretariat of the CMEA was reformed and expanded, and the Conference of Representatives of Member States founded.[62] Its main task was to supervise the Council Sessions and to monitor the implementation of the policy programs agreed upon inside CMEA in between the subsequent Council Sessions. The Conference of Representatives of Member States was renamed as the Executive Committee in 1962. It comprised one representative of each member state. Each of them had to hold the position of vice head of government to ensure that the delegates to the CMEA had enough political gravitas.[63] The Executive Committee was scheduled to meet four times a year.[64] In addition, the first production specialization agreements were drawn up in 1954 and successively expanded in the following years to make the economies of the bloc more complimentary.[65]

The next set of reforms was implemented following the Council Session in 1957 when first steps were taken to establish a form of multilateral clearing[66] of trade transactions inside the CMEA via Soviet banks.[67] These were first steps towards a common socialist capital market that coincided with similar but eventually more successful attempts in Western Europe.[68] Nevertheless, an internal credit market emerged which enabled the more developed members of the bloc to finance development projects in basic industries and resource extraction in the less developed members states. This possibility was used on a modest scale in the late 1950s and early 1960s.[69] The efforts taken culminated in the creation of the first common bank inside the CMEA, the International Bank for Economic Cooperation (IBEC) in 1964.

The late-1950s were also the time when the CMEA member states agreed upon a common set of policy guidelines concerning "Socialist Economic Integration" (SEI). Up to 1959 no such document existed. The first attempt to formalize what economic cooperation and integration in the Eastern Bloc meant at least in broad terms was the publication of the Charta of the CMEA in 1959.[70] The Charta called for a more efficient use of natural resources and an accelerated development of the economies of the bloc by a coordination of the national development plans and combining the strengths of several socialist economies to solve problems of mutual interest. Originally, the Charta restricted membership exclusively to European countries. However, this rule proved short-lived, as Mongolia gained full membership in 1962.[71] Although Mongolia had been dependent on the Soviet Union since the 1920s, Mongolia was the first "developing country" that became a member of the CMEA.

The efforts to reform the CMEA culminated in the formulation of the "Basic Principles of the International Socialist Division of Labor" (ISDL) in 1962.[72] The ISDL was implemented as a common policy guideline in the preamble of the Charta of the CMEA to ensure the realization of a socialist and later communist society.[73] Its aim was to create stable markets in the Socialist Hemisphere and to ensure the optimal utilization of comparative advantages concerning costs and production efficiency inside the region.[74] The ISDL was referring to this Socialist Hemisphere represented by the CMEA as "socialist world system."[75] Since the CMEA had dropped its membership limitation, the "socialist world system" could theoretically encompass the whole world, indeed. The methods to achieve the stipulated goals involved supranational planning and thus threatened to curtail the sovereignty of the individual members of the CMEA, even though the protection of national interests was mentioned in the document.

This was the kind of grand design that promised to eliminate bilateralism by creating a supranational planning institution at the top of the CMEA with the authority to formulate a common five-year plan for all members of the CMEA. Multilateralism, a reformed pricing model, and a supranational planning institution should overcome Stalinist autarky in the shortest time period possible and transform the economies of the region from competitive to complementary ones by forcing them to specialize and differentiate their economies but also by specialization to cooperate with each other.[76] The implementation of the ISDL should also result in a renunciation of extensive growth in favor of intensive growth by focusing on productivity gains and not so much on generating more economic output by simply increasing the input factors.

The implementation of the ISDL failed. Hardly any of the proposed measures were taken. Part of the reason was the reluctance of the Communist leaders in the smaller CMEA countries to yield essential elements of their newly acquired autonomy to a prospective, powerful agency based in Moscow. Since the national five-year plan was the most important policy document in a Communist country indicating the future flow of national resources and administrative capacity, giving up the right to formulate the five-year plan themselves, would have meant a severe loss of power for the respective socialist elites in the smaller member states of the CMEA. On the other hand, it is quite possible that some Soviet leaders also feared to be taken hostage by the demands of the smaller members of the bloc and feared to be dependent on them for deliveries of essential machineries and consumer goods.

The fears of autonomy loss and dependence on potentially unreliable partners were not solely responsible for the failure. When the ISDL was announced, it hardly contained any detailed implementation mechanisms. It was unclear how plan coordination, production specialization, independent trade pricing, and regional multilateralism should be achieved exactly and which methods should be used.[77] Finding ways to achieve the goals formulated in the ISDL required a great leap forward in mutual trust and cooperation between the smaller and bigger, the less and more developed members of the CMEA that was not about to materialize soon. The fiercest resistance against a supranational planning authority at the core of the CMEA was articulated by the Romanian leadership but it was not the only one that had reservations.[78]

The diligent work and long-term engagement required to radically alter the way the Eastern Bloc countries were cooperating with each other didn't suit the approach of the Khrushchev administration in particular. The way he tried to implement reforms concerning the CMEA resembled his style of doing politics at home and was strongly connected to it. In 1957, the Khrushchev administration enacted economic reforms in the Soviet Union that aimed at reducing the power of the central ministries in Moscow. Handing power to the regions should foster economic cooperation among them and unleash efficiency reserves. The reforms were implemented almost overnight and rather led to more particularism than increased economic efficiency. Instead of trying to fix the reforms, which were promising in theory, Khrushchev pledged a few weeks later to overtake the US in agricultural production in the near future.[79]

His mercurial style was also visible in the preparations for the 22nd Congress of the CPSU in October 1961 and his proclamation that a Communist society will be built in the Soviet Union by 1980. It is most likely no coincidence that he embarked on radically transforming the CMEA and thereby intrabloc relations a few months later.[80] His hands-on approach mixed with some utopianism had its political merits yet eventually proved unsuitable to convince the bloc leaders to reform their planned economies radically at once and in short time. This conduct was in particular unproductive, if Khrushchev didn't want to resemble Stalin who would have simply ordered the Communist elites of the bloc to subordinate to a central planning agency in Moscow. However, Khrushchev's more subtle attempts to reform the institutional framework of the CMEA proved also more successful. One of those, next to the Executive Committee, was the formation of the Permanent Commissions which dated back to the mid-1950s.

## The permanent commissions

Expanding trade and the revival of the CMEA increased demand for additional institutional structures inside the CMEA which could respond more quickly to the needs of specific industries than the Council Session or Executive Committee could. Thus, the Permanent Commissions[81] of the CMEA were founded in 1956 to replace the temporary committees that emerged during the "New Course" to coordinate sectoral economic activities.[82] They were organized along ministerial lines or encompassed whole industries. The Permanent Commissions soon became the real working organs of the CMEA.[83] Twelve of them were constituted in 1956 but their number gradually increased in the late 1950s. Among the first ones to be created were the Permanent Commissions for agriculture, coal, ferrous metals, and engineering.[84] They were chaired by Soviet ministers or at least high-ranking Soviet officials and summoned in general twice a year. As was true for the Soviet delegations, the delegations of other member states also had to be led by the respective ministers or senior officials.[85]

One of the original Permanent Commissions that was not strictly organized along a certain branch of the economy was the Permanent Commission for Foreign Trade. On its agenda were issues of common interest concerning trade inside the bloc – which was the main issue – but also concerning trade with other world regions. It encompassed regular meetings of the ministers for foreign trade of all member states who headed their delegations for the meetings. However, the ministers for foreign trade soon considered it inconvenient to mingle East–East, East–West, and East–South trade together. They thus decided to form another Permanent Commission that should focus solely on East–South economic relations. The political background and implications of this measure as well as the first years of its existence are covered in the next chapter. The rest of this chapter deals with the formal process of its inauguration. It is worth noting, though, that a special CMEA institution on East–South trade preceded any such creation on East–West trade which by definition had a very strong attraction of its own.

## The permanent commission for technical assistance

The Permanent Commission for Technical Assistance (PCTA) was rather a latecomer among the Permanent Commissions, since it was founded in 1961. Interestingly, its existence remained unnoticed by Western scholars working on the CMEA during the Cold War.[86] The PCTA had a predecessor in a working group that had operated inside the Permanent Commission for Foreign Trade. This working group was founded in September 1957 following a Soviet proposal. Its task was to foster relations with the "economically less developed capitalist countries."[87] The working group was renamed several times thereafter and christened "Commission for Complete Plants" in November 1959. This already emphasized the means by which stronger ties between East and South should be accomplished – by exporting factories to the newly independent states.[88]

The founding of the PCTA took place on the 14th Session of the CMEA that lasted from 28 February to 3 March 1961 in East Berlin.[89] Next to the full members of the CMEA, guest delegations from the People's Republic of China, the Democratic People's Republic of Korea, and the Democratic Republic Vietnam participated in the Council Session and thus were present when the PCTA was founded.[90] The idea to transform the already existing working group into a Permanent Commission was put forward by the East Germans and Soviets already in advance of the 14th Session.[91] This action by the CMEA roughly coincided with similar developments inside the OECD.[92] In September 1961 the OECD agreed on coordinating the bilateral development aid initiatives of its members by forming the Development Assistance Committee (DAC). The DAC was a step in the direction of multilateral coordination.

The 14th Session of the CMEA was chaired by Bruno Leuschner, who was head of the East German planning commission, deputy head of government, and member of the Politburo of the Central Committee of the Socialist Unity Party (SED) in early 1961.[93] It is interesting to note that Bruno Leuschner gave up his post as head of the East German equivalent of Gosplan[94] to become the first permanent representative of the GDR in the newly founded Executive Committee of the CMEA one year later, while keeping his post as a member of the Politburo. He had already been responsible for CMEA affairs as head of the planning commission but gave up national posts to focus on his responsibilities as central figure for GDR-CMEA relations.[95] This indicates that posts in the realm of the CMEA could be attractive for the national nomenclature from the early 1960s on. It also illustrates the increasing importance of the CMEA.

The founding of the PCTA was subsumed under topic three of the Council Session titled "Coordination of activities of the member states of the Council concerning technical assistance for building factories in economically less developed countries."[96] The report on its creation gave explicit ideological reasoning on why a new Permanent Commission was needed. The report states:

> The Session of the Council of Mutual Economic Assistance asserts that the coordination of the activities of the member states of the CMEA as concerns the support of the economically less developed countries in fostering their economic independence gains special importance under the current circumstances of the collapse of colonial slavery in Africa, Asia, and Latin America under the mounting pressure of national liberation movements.[97]

The authors of the document put the collapse of the "colonial regimes" in the common ideological context of the bloc:

> It was pointed out in the historic declaration of the meeting of representatives of Communist and Workers Parties that the imperialists, with the USA as principal supporter of modern colonialism, try desperately to maintain the colonial exploitation of the former colonies under the disguise of "economic aid."[98]

This statement was referring to a meeting that took place in Moscow in November 1960 and succeeded the corresponding meeting in Moscow three years before. Its purpose was mainly to resolve the looming Sino-Soviet conflict on which a fragile peace could be reached.[99] These negotiations took place behind the scenes, as the final statement of the meeting tried to paint the future of Marxism-Leninism in bright colors and emphasized the relevance of the events that had taken place in the Global South. It is interesting that the report on the CMEA Council Session emphasized that political independence didn't automatically lead to economic independence. The authors of the document thus proceeded to formulate guidelines for "genuine" economic aid:

> The economic aid and technical assistance which the member countries of the CMEA grant are not tied to any political or other conditions which affect the sovereignty of the economically less developed countries, nor are they tied to the acquirement of any kind of economic privilege, especially not to the extraction of profits from their involvement in constructing factories. This aid is granted to the economically less developed countries for creating their own industry. . . . In most cases long-term credits at special conditions will be granted to pay for the delivered equipment and materials, the design works, and the technical assistance.[100]

The contrast was postulated clearly: while the capitalist Western countries, foremost the US, were giving "economic aid" to keep the former colonies in a system of unequal exchanges, the CMEA countries were promising to respect the sovereignty of the former colonies or so they claimed. Economic aid thus was a weapon in the struggle with the West to win over the peoples of the Global South. Furthermore, the members of the CMEA offered a path to economic independence by helping the former colonies to build their respective economy from scratch, be it in the field of agriculture by developing irrigation schemes and building dams, or industry. Nevertheless, this aid was not to be delivered for free. Every delivery had to be paid in the end, since granting credits, even if at favorable terms, meant only a deferment of payments.

The founding document of the PCTA also gave some thoughts on how this should be achieved and offered pieces of self-criticism concerning the way things were hitherto handled in the bloc. The exchange of information was a centerpiece of the new Permanent Commission. The current level of information exchange was deemed insufficient.[101] The institutions designated to handle the mutual exchange were the foreign trade organizations. A pure information exchange can be regarded as the most basic form of cooperation. That it figures so prominently in the founding document of the PCTA indicates the real state the CMEA was in during the late 1950s and early 1960s. Working jointly in the CMEA to design and manufacture equipment and whole factories in addition to sending international teams of experts is also mentioned but in a more vague way. The founding document gives the impression that information exchange was the main task in getting the multilateral coordination of development efforts started. Actually executing development projects together seemed to be the second, more distant step.

The Council Session concluded the following:

> 4 [The Council has decided] to define the following main tasks for the Permanent Commission of the CMEA for the coordination of technical assistance:
>
> Coordinating the actions of the member countries of the CMEA in granting economic aid and technical assistance for the economically less developed countries with regards to building factories and other objects on the basis of studying the economies of these countries to determine the most suitable forms, directions, and conditions of economic aid and technical assistance for the economically less developed countries . . .
>
> Coordinating the activities of the foreign trade organizations of the member countries of the CMEA . . . with regards to prices for supplying equipment, and designing plans, for the reimbursement of technical assistance, for the conditions of delivering equipment . . .
>
> 5 [The Council decided] to authorize the Permanent Commission of the CMEA for the coordination of development assistance to revise the recommendations on questions of granting economic aid and technical assistance adopted earlier . . . thereby relying on the following guidelines:
>
> a) economic aid and technical assistance for the economically less developed countries should contribute to the creation of a national economy and should strengthen the political independence of these countries;
>
> b) long-term credits will be granted to the economically less developed countries on conditions prior agreed upon by the CMEA member countries which will differentiate between economically less developed countries that belong to aggressive blocs, and economically less developed neutral countries that don't belong to those blocs;
>
> c) necessary measures will be anticipated to raise the technical level of projects and equipment deliveries as well as to maximally standardize the conditions for design and production of equipment on the basis of joint studies by the member countries of the Council of the peculiarities of using this equipment in economically less developed countries;[102]

The tasks set by the Council Session for the newly founded Permanent Commission emphasized the important role attached to the standardization of rules of conduct. This clearly aimed at reducing the detrimental effects of "aid-shopping." By informing each other about their ongoing negotiations with developing countries, the members of the CMEA couldn't be played off against each other. While this would benefit exclusively the member states of the CMEA, the task to help the developing countries to become economically independent would suit the recipients of Eastern development aid. The same applied to using the PCTA to increase the technological level of the deliveries of the East and to increase the usefulness of the delivered equipment under local circumstances. At least in theory, the development projects should fulfill a real need in the economies of the recipients.

The needs of the donors are not mentioned in the document with the exception of them striving for unified price levels to avoid rock-bottom competition among them. It is interesting to note that the socialist countries agreed on discriminating against certain developing countries collectively. Those which were deemed too close to the US or other Western powers should pay higher interest rates on loans, while those that were defined as being neutral should be rewarded for their neutrality with more favorable interest rates. The members of the CMEA didn't define a third category for developing countries they considered friendly. There is no clear explanation for that missing category in the files. One explanation could be that the countries of the Eastern Bloc had just started to make friends in the Global South in early 1961 as becomes clear in the following chapter.

## Conclusion

Stalin's death brought rapid changes not only to the Soviet Union but to the whole bloc. The policies of his successors and of the bloc's leaders had a profound impact on the economy in particular. The "Imperial Scavenger" was dismantled. The "new course" led to higher investment in the consumer goods sector and shifted resources away from heavy industries. The Stalinist policy goals of simply emulating Soviet industrialization and attempted autarky of the 1930s were abandoned. Thus, the economies of the bloc began to become more complimentary – or at least tried to do so. This opened the possibility of specialization to increase production efficiency and use comparative advantages. It also made trade as a source for growth more attractive.

At the same time, the Soviet leadership under Khrushchev embarked on "building communism" and raising the living standards and consumption levels significantly to match the US consumer and to eventually "burry" the capitalist West with the means of peaceful coexistence. The revitalization of the CMEA has to be seen within this context. It is connected inseparably with the policies of Khrushchev and his leadership.[103] His administration tried to use the CMEA to urge the smaller bloc members to cooperate with each other thereby abandoning the methods employed by Stalin to command and to punish the Central Eastern European socialist leaders. The ghosts Khrushchev had summoned himself hindered him from completing his reforms of the CMEA. Supranational planning was rejected. But the institutional framework of the CMEA created in the 1950s and early 1960s remained stable till the end.

There was, however, at least one significant downside to the developments of the 1950s: while the economic reforms of the 1950s on the one hand strengthened the socialist economies, made them gradually more consumer-oriented, and encouraged cooperation across the bloc, they also restricted trade on the other hand, since the reforms were not the same in each of the socialist countries. Some, like Hungary after 1956, were keener to implement market mechanisms than others who relied more on central command structures. This divergence of the socialist economies increased in the 1960s and made it more difficult to conclude far-reaching agreements, as their planning and decision-making processes had become less complimentary and more mutually exclusive.

A look "behind the scenes" will be taken in the next chapter, as the founding document of the PCTA and the official protocol will be put aside to look at the consultations on the national level and the respective reasoning and expectations connected with forming the PCTA that were not expressed during the Council Session but in national meetings in Budapest and East Berlin. Furthermore, the early years of the PCTA up to the late 1960s will be analyzed, which projects were started, and if the discussions inside the commission actually yielded any tangible results. This will be placed within the context of decolonization and the general reaction of the Socialist East to these global developments.

## Notes

1 Maier, "The World Economy and the Cold War," 55–6.
2 Pechatnov, "The Soviet Union and the World 1944–1953," 90.
3 Maier, "The World Economy and the Cold War," 55–6.
4 Suny, *The Soviet Experiment*, 322.
5 See on German wartime economic policies Tooze, *The Wages of Destruction.*
6 Brabant, *Economic Integration in Eastern Europe*, 13.
7 Brabant, 14.
8 Westad, "The Cold War," 13.
9 Engerman, "Ideology," 22–3.
10 Mastny, *The Cold War and Soviet Insecurity*, 21.
11 Suny, *The Soviet Experiment*, 339.
12 Suny, 349.
13 Suny, 358–9.
14 Suny, 353.
15 Suny, 350–1.
16 Suny, 353–4.
17 Maier, "The World Economy and the Cold War," 57–9.
18 See Jersild, "The Soviet State as Imperial Scavenger."
19 Jersild, 112.
20 Jersild, 112.
21 Steiner, *Von Plan Zu Plan*, 21–2.
22 Steiner, 23–4.
23 Steiner, 36.
24 National Bureau of Economic Research, "Gross National Product in Constant Dollars for United States."
25 Jersild describes Stalin's death as an important marker but regards the policies of his successors as only gradually different. See Jersild, "The Soviet State as Imperial Scavenger," 115.
26 Brabant, *Economic Integration in Eastern Europe*, 10.
27 Brabant, 12.
28 Brabant, 10.
29 See "K sozdaniiu Soveta Ekonomicheskoi Vzaimopomoshchi," *Pravda*, 25 January 1949, 2.
30 Brabant, *Economic Integration in Eastern Europe*, 19.
31 Brabant, 20.
32 Brabant, 21.

33 Brabant, 23–4.
34 Brabant, 22.
35 "A KGST szerveiben folyó túdományos és müszaki együttmüködés megszervezésének kérdéséhez," dated 1962, MNL Budapest XIX-A-90-c 88. doboz.
36 Brabant, *Economic Integration in Eastern Europe*, 39.
37 Brabant, 22.
38 Brabant, 40.
39 Molle, *Economics of European Integration*, 4.
40 Molle, 4.
41 Molle, 8.
42 Molle, 4.
43 Molle, 10–1.
44 Molle, 11.
45 Molle, 13.
46 Molle, 9–10.
47 See Sobell, *The Red Market*; Brabant, *Economic Integration in Eastern Europe*.
48 Molle, *Economics of European Integration*, 340.
49 Müller, "Der RGW Als Schlüssel," 38–9.
50 Pechatnov, "The Soviet Union and the World 1944–1953," 111.
51 Taubman, *Khrushchev*, 263.
52 Suny, *The Soviet Experiment*, 390.
53 Taubman, *Khrushchev*, 342.
54 Lüthi, "China and Eastern Europe," 235–6.
55 See Shen and Xia, "Hidden Currents During the Honeymoon."
56 Zhang, "The Sino-Soviet Alliance," 358.
57 Lüthi, *The Sino-Soviet Split*, 37.
58 Zwass, *Der Rat Für Gegenseitige Wirtschaftshilfe*, 16.
59 Zwass, 24.
60 Zwass, 10.
61 Brabant, *Economic Integration in Eastern Europe*, 48.
62 Brabant, 54.
63 Adebahr and Maennig, *Außenwirtschaft*, 396–7.
64 Zwass, *Der Rat Für Gegenseitige Wirtschaftshilfe*, 35.
65 Brabant, *Economic Integration in Eastern Europe*, 47.
66 Clearing ensures that no trade partner accumulates a significant trade surplus nor deficit.
67 Brabant, *Economic Integration in Eastern Europe*, 57.
68 Brabant, 65–6.
69 Brabant, 59.
70 Brabant, 55.
71 Brabant, 56.
72 Brabant, 66–7.
73 Brabant, 56.
74 Brabant, 67–8.
75 Brabant, 67.
76 Brabant, 67–9.
77 Brabant, 68–9.
78 Brabant, 69–72.
79 Taubman, *Khrushchev*, 303–5.
80 Taubman, 508–13.
81 They have occasionally also been translated as Standing Commissions.
82 Brabant, *Economic Integration in Eastern Europe*, 54.
83 Brabant, *Socialist Economic Integration*, 190.

84 Brabant, 190.
85 Brabant, 190–1.
86 It is not mentioned by the standard textbooks. See Brabant, *Socialist Economic Integration.*
87 Lorenzini, "Modernisierung Durch Handel," 223.
88 Lorenzini, 223.
89 "Protokoll der XIV. Tagung des RGW," Barch Berlin, DE 1/39184–39187.
90 Ibid.
91 Lorenzini, "Modernisierung Durch Handel," 224.
92 Lorenzini, 224.
93 "Protokoll der XIV. Tagung des RGW," Barch Berlin, DE 1/39184–39187.
94 Staatliche Plankommission (SPK).
95 Bundesstiftung Aufarbeitung Biographische Datenbanken, "Leuschner, Bruno Max."
96 "Protokoll der XIV. Tagung des RGW," Barch Berlin, DE 1/39184–39187.
97 Ibid.
98 Ibid.
99 Lüthi, *The Sino-Soviet Split*, 187–94.
100 "Protokoll der XIV. Tagung des RGW," Barch Berlin, DE 1/39184–39187.
101 Ibid.
102 Ibid.
103 Zwass, *Der Rat Für Gegenseitige Wirtschaftshilfe*, 34.

# 2 Decolonization and the reaction of the East

## Embracing the colonial world

The era associated with Nikita Khrushchev as the General Secretary of the CPSU was not only marked by significant change inside the Eastern Bloc and its domestic affairs but also by changes in foreign policy. The international position of the USSR in 1953 had been very tenuous as the nascent Eastern Bloc had already been eroded by the Soviet–Yugoslav split. In economic and military terms, it was not on equal footing with the West. Outside Central Eastern Europe and parts of East Asia, the Soviet Union could neither project power nor exert substantial levels of influence.[1] The same was true for its allies, be it Mao's China or the Communists of Poland or Czechoslovakia.

The most visible foreign policy initiatives of the Eastern Bloc in the mid and late 1950s were directed at the West, leading to the first phase of détente that culminated in Khrushchev's visit to the US in 1959. Détente came to an abrupt halt when one of the U-2 planes spying on the Soviet missiles program was shot down over Soviet skies on 1 May 1960 as Khrushchev's handling of the incident made any reconciliation in the near future impossible.[2] Tensions subsequently began to rise again with the building of the Berlin Wall in 1961 and the Cuban Missile Crisis one year later that almost led to a nuclear war between the two blocs. It could be argued, though, that the more conciliatory tone between East and West in the mid and late 1950s was an attempt to relate to the spirit of the alliance against Nazi Germany. The new attitude towards the peoples of the colonial empires, however, was a more radical departure from Stalinist policies.

Stalin had been very skeptical of the chances of Communist-inspired liberation movements in the colonies. The policies of the Comintern towards the Global South had been one of its few unshakable pillars in the interwar period.[3] This didn't mean that the consequences of this stubborn policy were beneficial for spreading Communism. They often proved detrimental for regional Communist parties. When the Comintern condemned Gandhi and his ideas as being reactionary in nature, the Indian CP suffered a severe setback. It was reduced to not much more than 20 members.[4] Stalin had also been critical of Mao's chances and provided considerable assistance to the Kuomintang before eventually backing Mao and forming an alliance with the emerging People's Republic of China.[5]

Deviating from Stalin's policies towards the Global South thus provided ample opportunities for his successors as the results could only get better. The ways in which the new Soviet leadership altered the old set of policies were twofold: the Soviet Union and the Eastern Bloc should pursue a much more activist line than in the interwar period in which the Soviet leadership had remained rather passive. Furthermore, ideological dogmatism should be reduced accepting multiple paths to socialism and in particular nationalist movements to avoid any future disasters like the almost total collapse of Communist influence in India.[6]

With hindsight, the Second World War had set a process in motion that eventually led to the dissolution of colonial rule and independence for the peoples living in the former colonial territories.[7] Back in 1953, though, it was not clear for contemporaries neither in the East nor in the West, which turn the colonial empires of the West would take. The European empires had taken a severe blow in the Second World War but didn't collapse immediately. The British and French Mandate countries had been released into independence in the late 1940s, as had been Dutch Indonesia. Undoubtedly the biggest prize of all countries that became independent in the late 1940s had been British–India, the former backbone and crown jewel of the British Empire.

But in other parts of the world like Africa, the colonial empires seemed to be quite stable still, with no European colonial power showing any intention to leave the continent soon. The retreat from India, parts of the Middle East, and South East Asia were of a more tactical nature, as the remaining colonies were deemed essential for the economic recovery of their respective "mother countries" in the 1950s. Their resources fueled British, French, and Belgian industries and provided dollar export earnings to balance the trade deficit with the US.[8] For maintaining imperial rule, the colonial powers relied heavily on American support.[9] While the Roosevelt administration had been very critical of European colonialism, its successor had a more pragmatist approach. The Truman administration supported the fight of the colonial regimes against insurgents it suspected being left-leaning or even Communist.[10] The American government was underwriting the checks that kept the imperial economy gaining momentum. The benefits of American support outweighed the losses in India and other parts of Asia and constituted a new imperial system that differed from the one practiced in the interwar years.[11]

The limits and fragility of this new colonial system became visible when the US government withdrew its support in the wake of the Suez Crisis in 1956. The triumph of the Egyptian leader, Gamal Abdel Nasser, and the humiliation of France and Britain, didn't necessarily mean the end of colonial rule in Africa. The direct consequences of the Suez Crisis on colonial policies were intangible.[12] But the costs of maintaining the colonial regimes were slowly outrunning its benefits as the 1950s proceeded. A report commissioned by the British government came to the conclusion in 1957 that the colonies were not needed anymore for British prosperity. Quite on the contrary, an informal empire, which allowed the former center to keep considerable parts of its economic privileges, would be much more beneficial than a formal empire with ever increasing costs for policing and administering the colonies.[13] However, if the colonial centers wanted to establish an informal empire, they had to ensure that the transition of political power was evolving peacefully.[14]

Almost immediately after Stalin's death Soviet diplomats did try to foster relations with the colonies that had already become independent. Since decolonization was still in the making, this meant to focus primarily on India, the Arab countries, and Indonesia.[15] One of the first countries of the Global South with which the Soviet Union concluded a trade deal was Egypt. In exchange for cotton, the Soviet Union provided kerosene. Already at this early stage, the Soviet Union cooperated with the smaller bloc members, in this case with Romania.[16] This occurred at least partially out of necessity, since the Soviet oil industry was still struggling in the early 1950s.[17]

## The short-lived spirit of Bandung

The example of Nasser's Egypt illustrates well the difficulties the emissaries of the Eastern Bloc were facing in the Global South. Nasser was regarded a close ally of the Eastern Bloc in the 1960s but in fact nationalist regimes like his were very reluctant to embrace the offers the East could make. He was very cautious to accept more than limited trade with the Eastern Bloc in the mid-1950s and a kind of first breakthrough occurred when the Soviets were selling weapons to Egypt at a discount.[18] Nevertheless, Nasser would have preferred to strike the same deal with the US in the first place.[19] Nasser, as well as other leaders of the Global South, tried to play East and West against each other to achieve the best possible results for himself.

Even when Nasser had concluded an arms deal and an ordinary trade deal with the Soviet Union this didn't mean that he was inclined to accept large quantities of economic aid by the Eastern Bloc as envisaged in the CMEA a few years later. In late 1955 Nasser and his administration tricked the US and UK into helping him execute the Aswan High Dam project, his most favorite big-scale development project, by supplying them with forged intelligence hinting at an imminent Soviet move to take over financing the project worth more than 420 million US dollars.[20] The decision of the Eisenhower administration against financing the project in July 1956 largely contributed to Nasser's move to nationalize the Suez Canal a few weeks later.[21] Eventually, Nasser became an uneasy ally of the Eastern Bloc as were many other colonial leaders like Indonesia's Sukarno or Ghana's Kwame Nkrumah.[22]

For many countries outside the Western Hemisphere, decolonization was a much more defining trait of their times than the Cold War, at least in the years immediately following the end of the Second World War.[23] Apart from the Middle East, and East Asia, large parts of the Global South took center stage of the Cold War only beginning in the 1970s.[24] They focused more on their domestic goals, securing their power internally, and trying to increase the often dismal living standards in the former colonies. Most of the newly independent states were very fragile, as many of them didn't possess a "historic" identity in the sense that their borders and internal compositions of society relied on artificial lines drawn up by European colonial bureaucrats.

Despite their differences, some of them tried to form a unified voice independent from the Eastern and Western Bloc. The representatives of 30 newly independent states met in the Indonesian town of Bandung in 1955, among them leaders from the two biggest countries of the Global South: India and the People's Republic of China. The participants were discussing anticolonial ideologies as much as different forms of regional, class-based, or racial solidarity.[25] They opted to stay neutral, although the People's Republic of China already had concluded an alliance with the Soviet Union and was a core member of the Eastern Bloc. But most of the participants of the Bandung Conference, which can also be described as the first large postcolonial summit, were not bound by an alliance with the Soviet Union.

The meeting of the "Third World" in Bandung bore connotations of the "Third Estate" in prerevolutionary France that was populous but underrepresented politically as were the former colonies.[26] Their meeting and common discussions also implied to look for a "third way" that was neither Communist nor capitalist and allowed them to develop independently.[27] However, the actual results of Bandung apart from the signal a common conference by political leaders from the Global South was sending to the world public sphere, were marginal. The spirit of Bandung dissipated soon, as the political differences between the countries of Asia, Africa, and Latin America were too great to work closely together; this was due to mainly three reasons: their economies were not complementary enough, Western banks refused to finance big economic projects outside the Western Hemisphere in the 1950s, and since Southern governments insisted on barter trade, South–South trade didn't develop very fast.[28] Finally, the war between India and the People's Republic of China, the most powerful participants of the movement, in 1962 had mortally wounded the spirit of Bandung.[29]

## Differing development models?

The Soviets and their allies in the Eastern Bloc were mainly bystanders as events unfolded in the 1950s and early 1960s. Up until 1960 the possibility of a Soviet intervention in the former colonial empires was rather prospective than actual.[30] The Soviets had tried to deliver a small amount of weapons to Guatemala in 1954 but this had made the situation of the more social democrat than socialist government of Jacobo Árbenz only worse as it tipped the balance in the US government in favor of an intervention.[31] At the height of the Suez Crisis Nikita Khrushchev tried to influence events by threatening to use atomic weapons, if the French and British didn't stop their intervention against Nasser's regime.[32] This threat did not influence the outcome of the crisis, since the British and French had already decided to skip their intervention after the Eisenhower administration had refused to support them.

A different pattern began to emerge in 1960 with the twin crises in Cuba and in the Congo.[33] The Soviets tried to interfere in both cases but could not significantly alter the events in the Congo when a covert operation by the CIA together with an intervention by Belgium and the backing of the British contributed to the fall and violent death of Patrice Lumumba.[34] When the Soviet leadership tried to strengthen the Cuban military against a possible intervention and to simultaneously use the Cuban island to intimidate the US by assembling an atomic arsenal, the subsequent crisis almost triggered a new world war, but the Castro regime remained in place. It is at this time, between the uproar in the Congo and the Cuban Missile Crisis, that the Permanent Commission for Technical Assistance was founded and the CMEA thus expanded to reach out to the former colonial world in an attempt to underpin the political efforts by the leaders of the Eastern Bloc with an economic fabric. Next to political and military support, the advancing economies of the East, which began to experience their own small post-war economic miracles, were to contribute to the new efforts in the Global South.

They were not the first ones to come up with such an idea. Actually, the late interwar period already saw first attempts in the imperial centers of Paris and London to work out development plans for the colonies which had to be postponed during the Great Depression.[35] In the post-1945 era the economic subdiscipline of development economics began to expand rapidly. One of its first most prominent figures was W. Arthur Lewis who stated that differences between "developed" and "underdeveloped" countries could be explained by different saving rates.[36] He published his main works in the mid-1950s, at a time when the diplomats and economic experts of the Eastern Bloc were just beginning to look in earnest for opportunities in the Global South.[37]

Shortly after the end of the Second World War the US Senator from Arkansas and chairman of the Foreign Relations Committee J. William Fulbright had called for the internationalization of development aid to dismantle it as a weapon of the Cold War and transform development aid into an instrument of West–East cooperation.[38] His efforts failed, not least because the leaders of the Eastern Bloc could claim with some justification that they were not responsible for colonialism. However, aid became partially internationalized subsequently in the East and in the West, via the OECD and CMEA, respectively. It could finally be argued that Fulbright's idea was illusory, since the Eastern Bloc and the West offered two very distinct versions of, and paths to, modernity that were incompatible with each other.

This view is underlined by looking at the most prominent advocates in the field of development economics and their participation in public discourses. In his most famous and most influential book, "The Stages of Economic Growth: A Non-Communist Manifesto," the American economic historian and political advisor Walt Whitman Rostow, who was also referred to as the "Wernher von Braun of developmentalism,"[39] envisioned a master plan for the advancement of "underdeveloped" nations. His vision was modeled on his perception of the Western, mainly British and American, experience and advancement along the different stages of industrialization and consumerism.[40] Unfortunately, there were no such influential voices participating in public discourse in the post-Stalin East. This does not, however, diminish the fact that the experts and politicians of the Eastern Bloc regarded their policies as being entirely different from the West, as was pointed out in the founding document of the PCTA.

The view that the United States and the Soviet Union each were offering genuine and conflicting paths to modernity can still be found in recent scholarship, like in the works of Odd Arne Westad.[41] This view is both right and wrong, depending on the perspective. It holds true as concerns ideological intentions, public declarations, and the discourses of contemporaries. However, the picture becomes much more blurred by looking at the practices of development aid and economic cooperation in East and West, at least for the better part of the Cold War. Though both blocs had competing visions of the role of free markets or agricultural development, in practice they often competed for the same kind of projects. This will be shown in the subsequent chapters of this book that connect the practices of development aid as discussed inside the CMEA with the execution of concrete projects.

But even on a more abstract, theoretical level, the approaches taken by East and West were not sufficiently different from each other as to justify their description as being antagonistic. Coming back to W. Arthur Lewis, as mentioned, one of the founders of development economics: he himself started working for the Ghanaian government in 1957 where he helped to draw up the first Five-Year Development Plan of Ghana that took effect starting in 1959.[42] At this time, it was already clear that Kwame Nkrumah, the Ghanaian strongman, was seeking close political and economic ties with the Eastern Bloc, foremost with the Soviet Union. This didn't mean that Lewis had changed his views and had suddenly become an adherent of Soviet economics.

When Lewis stipulated his claim that the differences in development can be explained by different rates of domestic saving, the conclusion was imminent that if the countries of the Global South achieved higher rates of domestic saving than the Western countries, the "development gap" between them would be narrowing and eventually closing. This fit well into post-war Keynesian growth models as developed by the economists Harrod and Domar.[43] They stressed the importance of a country's capital stock. The bigger the capital stock, the more developed and richer a country would be. The higher the domestic rate of saving, the faster the respective capital stock would increase yielding economic growth on the way, as higher savings enabled higher investments in the capital stock.

Increasing the domestic rate of saving, though, to accelerate industrial development and capital formation could be stated as an almost exact definition of Stalinist forced industrialization which was in essence a high forced rate of domestic saving that could be channeled by the state into industrial development projects like Magnitogorsk. This policy, which suppressed consumption in the present, yielded high growth rates as much in the Soviet Union as it did in the Eastern Bloc after 1945 when the countries of Central Eastern Europe emulated this set of policies.[44] In their concentration on the formation of a country's capital stock, neither Western nor Eastern economics were behaving antagonistically towards each other.

Developing countries as defined by policy-makers and economists were thus starving for capital. The question that development economists were posing as early as in the late 1940s and 1950s was, if the former colonial countries were able to close the perceived capital gap on their own or if they needed support by the international community. A group of UN experts that used the Harrod-Domar model to estimate the gap concluded in 1951 that the "underdeveloped areas" needed an annual input of 20 billion US dollars to reach a per capita growth rate in national income of 2 %.[45] The UN experts concluded further that the countries of the Global South could come up with only 5 billion US dollars annually for investments in their capital stock.[46] This meant that 15 billion US dollars had to come from the international community or the gap between rich and poor would never start to narrow. This was the scholarly underpinning and justification for development aid. It was not born out of mere altruism, as policy-makers in the West could easily be convinced that providing development aid by helping poor countries build up their capital stock would simultaneously boost production and employment at home.[47]

Building up one's country's capital stock meant primarily investing in infrastructure and heavy industries as the backbone of industrialization. This was another point where Western and Eastern experts and policy-makers were not as far apart from each other as could be concluded by following their rhetoric. They could agree on another issue as well: the importance of planning for realizing a set of projects on the ground. The vast majority of Western development economists agreed that economic development could not merely be left to market forces, it had to be planned, or at least thoroughly supervised by the state.[48] This explains why Lewis could work on Ghanaian development plans.

The buildup of a capital stock under the auspices of the state also implied in practice strict trade controls and protectionism. In fact, most countries of the Global South up to the 1980s tried to industrialize and expand their capital stock by import substitution. This meant to substitute imports by expanding the respective industries at home.[49] It is easy to find documents and directives on trade in the archives of the CMEA member countries that use the language of industrialization by import substitution. An internal document of the GDR's Council of Ministers titled "The Tasks in the Field of Foreign Trade" and drafted in May 1963 reads as follows:

> Volume and structure of imports and exports of the perspective plan [Perspektivplan] from 1964 to 1970 have to be in line with the demands of the highest possible economic utility. . . . All organs of the economy of the GDR are responsible that imports, in particular from non-socialist countries, are solely employed, where substitutes out of own production can't be used. . . . Unnecessary imports are to be stopped already at the stage of research, development, and design. The influx of economically unnecessary imports is prohibited.[50]

The authors of this trade directive of the Council of Ministers were arguing for exports of sophisticated machinery and other high-end products the East German industry was able to produce to earn the foreign currency needed for importing the goods and resources that couldn't be produced in the GDR. Such lines as cited previously illustrate why representatives of the CMEA countries and of the countries of the Global South could find common ground in economic debates without necessarily copying the entire socio-political system of the Eastern Bloc. This not only shows the common ground but also the possible fault lines: like the GDR, countries such as India or Ghana and their respective representatives would have liked to produce and to export the most sophisticated machinery in the world, too. The following trade directive on imports from 1963, however, demonstrates that the countries of the CMEA were not necessarily producing cutting-edge technologies themselves:

> The task in the field of importing machines and equipment in 1964 is to create new sources of supply on top of the plan by concluding trade agreements (goods allocated by quota) for high-tech products that are mainly produced in the capitalist countries of Europe, among them the European Economic Community countries.[51]

This illustrates that the CMEA countries and the countries of the Global South shared another commonality: although they wanted to minimize their imports, they needed access to new technologies which they had to import with hard-earned convertible currency for which they had to export something in return. The point is that the CMEA countries obtained a peripheral position as seen from the West. Eastern products were hardly competitive and the East was striving for Western technology. However, seen from the perspective of the South, the East was not the periphery of the world economic system, but could appear to be center stage, as it had something to offer that was resembling the potential proposals of the West.

As long as the CMEA member states were able to stay ahead of the Southern countries on the technological ladder by at least one step, East and South could embark on promising cooperation schemes. The moment they were starting to compete for the same scarce resources or for the same export markets, their relationship could turn sour. Since this was becoming an issue of increasing importance over the years, it will be covered more closely in the last third of the book. Moreover, it is interesting to note that the GDR trade directive mentioned previously was making a clear exemption for intra-CMEA trade. Trade within the CMEA should not work according to the framework of import substitution, on the contrary a more pronounced internal division of labor and increased cooperation among the member states were called for.[52]

An emphasis on the significance of accumulating physical capital was the most important and widely accepted development pattern during the 1950s.[53] It is clear that the respective set of policies could easily be reconciled with and appropriated by the socialist East. However, this development pattern was increasingly challenged in the 1960s by economists who pointed at the missing human component. They argued that the more efficient organization of work processes, better education, and training of the work force were more essential for growth and development than the mere accumulation of capital, as the efficiency of machines strongly depended on the skills of their inventors and applicants.[54] Investment in education, workers' skills, and measures to avoid a "brain drain" were termed "technical assistance" in contrast to "capital aid."[55]

In a general context outside of development economics, economists were also talking about "human capital." Scholars like Robert Merton Solow developed models of development that included physical as well as human capital in their calculations as both were needed for long-term growth. The equation of growth of per capita income with development was not challenged in the 1960s.[56] However, the fact that the Permanent Commission for Technical Assistance bore the name "Technical Assistance" in its name indicates that the socialist policy-makers and planners of development aid were familiar with the Western concepts. The founding document of the PCTA states that its task was to advance both capital aid and technical assistance granted by the Eastern Bloc.

## Differing motivations?

The founding of the PCTA can be seen as a sign of strength, on the one hand. The international situation of the Eastern Bloc was improving rapidly since Stalin's death as was its economic power, even if on a much more modest scale than its international influence. Therefore, the PCTA was founded to fix some minor issues and to advance cooperation schemes that were already proving to be successful. Such a narrative, however, would be way too flattering. The founding document of the PCTA already reveals some cracks in the façade as cooperation in economic terms among the CMEA countries in the Global South was deemed too little, too inefficiently executed. A deeper look at the archival sources dealing with the circumstances of the founding of the PCTA points at additional factors that were forcing the CMEA member states to find a common line and to improve their cooperation.

One of these factors was the People's Republic of China. The intrabloc relations between Mao's China and the Soviet Union were deteriorating from 1958 on with the start of the Great Leap Forward.[57] After the removal of the Soviet advisers in 1960, the Chinese leadership tried to play off the smaller members of the bloc, in particular the CSSR and GDR, against the Soviet Union. This increased intrabloc cohesion and cooperation and thus didn't lead to the desired benefits for the Chinese.[58] The leadership of the GDR formed a special commission in September 1964 that was to combine and coordinate the efforts taken by the different ministries and state agencies. It was named "Permanent Commission for uniform Control and Steering of the political, economic, and cultural Measures for Developing the Relations with Nation States." It provides insights into the background motives of development cooperation insight the CMEA.

The name indicates that this commission was strongly connected to the PCTA to ensure the execution of the measures agreed upon in the CMEA. Its chairman was none other than Bruno Leuschner, the former head of the East German equivalent of Gosplan who had headed the founding session of the PCTA and who had taken up a new post as the main representative of the GDR in the CMEA. He could therefore act as a broker, since he knew what was going on in the GDR as well as in the other countries of the CMEA. Due to his information advantage he was one of the best-informed GDR officials with regards to internal bloc affairs. According to the protocol of its first session Bruno Leuschner said the following on Mao's China:

> The relations with national states are increasingly gaining importance. The developing countries pose an important force in international relations today. We know that East and West are struggling to influence the developing countries. This [struggle] is intensified by conflicts with the People's Republic of China. Her [the PRC's] peculiar efforts in these countries against the political and economic interests of the other socialist countries are known.[59]

The Sino-Soviet Split that was evolving in the early 1960s, was a push factor for the other members of the bloc to double their efforts and to increase their mutual cooperation in the Global South, as the PRC started to work against their interests. The PRC had – at least implicitly – promoted the interests of the Eastern Bloc before, since it was according to its self-description a Communist country and a former colony that had gotten rid of its colonial oppressors.[60] Even if it was an economically weak country, it lent its unique prestige to the other members of the Eastern Bloc during the 1950s.

The fact that the GDR was forming a special commission on the cooperation with the former colonies was no coincidence. Neither was its purpose limited to the implementation of policy measures drafted in CMEA negotiations. The reason for its founding lay as much in a perceived weakness of the GDR of which the East German leadership was convinced. They had the impression that their competitors from inside the CMEA were far more advanced than them in doing business with the Global South and forging new economic ties.

This self-perception becomes visible in the archival documents. The protocol of a meeting of GDR trade officials on economic cooperation with South and South East Asia that took place in 1964 stated bluntly:

> We don't work according to our resolution. Instead of going ahead, we are having stagnation, even decline in economic and political relations. The foreign trade volume with these countries is shrinking relatively. But it is supposed to double till 1970. We have huge programs – but those exist only on paper. No one is abiding by them in his practical work. . . . I say it with distinct clarity at the beginning of the meeting to prepare the right ground for the reports of the respective comrades. We don't need no general declarations here. Relate precisely to such questions:
>
> - How could it happen that our trade with the majority of these countries is stagnating, being even less in 1964 than in 1963?
> - Who is responsible? Is it the fault of the foreign trade [organizations]? Is it the fault of the industry? What is the MAI [Ministry for Foreign

> and inner-German Trade] intending to do to catch up partially till the end of the year?[61]

The author of these words was most likely Bruno Leuschner. But criticism with regard to the economic achievements of the GDR was not limited to him. A letter to Gerhard Weiß, then deputy minister for foreign and inner-German trade, about forming joint ventures with Southern governments reads as follows:

> We regard such methods and forms as very important to improve our sales organization, the more so since the GDR has an immense loss of time in this area compared with other socialist countries. . . . Furthermore, I regard it as essential that the increased risk-taking by forming such companies [is counterbalanced] by highlighting the greater economic utility associated in general with taking the risks. Therefore, the experiences, in particular of the CSSR but also of the PR Poland, should absolutely be analyzed in the draft for the Council of Ministers.[62]

This letter to Gerhard Weiß about his views on economic cooperation with the Global South is of particular importance, since Weiß was promoted in 1965 to deputy head of the Presidium of the Council of Ministers and in 1967 to serve as the Permanent Representative of the GDR for the CMEA, thereby taking up the post of Bruno Leuschner who had died in 1965. Weiß remained in that position till 1986. He was also Vice Head of the German–Arabic Society and had written his dissertation on socialist economic integration.[63]

The perceived inferiority of the GDR with regard to its economic ties with the emerging nations in the Global South was not restricted to forming joint ventures. It also comprised building objects like entire factories on a turnkey basis by granting credits. However, a conference in Budapest in late November 1962 had shaken this view of the East German officials. The representatives of Poland and Hungary in this CMEA expert meeting on "technical assistance for economically less developed countries by building turnkey plants" were behaving quite frankly by admitting that they had learned their lessons the hard way and that their projects often were on the brink of failure. In advance of this and succeeding conferences, the GDR experts and officials had thought that their Hungarian and Polish counterparts already were on a winning streak.[64] This episode on the one hand illustrates how insufficient the knowledge of their respective partners and close allies was inside the Eastern Bloc in the 1960s. On the other hand, it shows the dynamic inside the Eastern Bloc and the CMEA to increase cooperation, to advance information exchange and to learn from each other's experience.

## The early years of the PCTA

In between the regular meetings of the PCTA the representatives of the CMEA member states used the opportunity to exchange information via the Secretariat of the CMEA. The respective state agencies were also sending material on the actual value of their economic assistance granted to the Global South to Moscow. These numbers were then forwarded to all other member states. Till 1 January 1963 the Soviet Union had – according to the CMEA material – granted economic assistance worth 778.9 million rubles. The CSSR came second with 258.6 million rubles followed by Poland with 88.1 million rubles. The volume of the GDR's economic aid amounted to 56.3 million rubles and the south eastern member states of the CMEA, Bulgaria, Romania, and Hungary, were forming the bottom half with 20.7, 20.0, and 17.0 million rubles, respectively.[65]

What is astonishing about these numbers is the "success" of the CSSR in forging economic ties with the former colonies and the last place of Hungary, although the difference with Bulgaria and Romania was only marginal. Thus, the CSSR trade officials must have done something right in comparison with the other smaller members of the bloc by offering a relatively attractive mix of advanced technology, "customer" service, and credit conditions. They proved much more able in this early phase than their more populous neighbors, the GDR, and Poland. The numbers shared by the Secretariat of the CMEA also help to put the perceived weakness of the GDR officials into perspective.

In addition to exchanging information, the CMEA member states were also sending cooperation requests for projects they could not manage alone, often already stating their preferred partners in the requests. One such request sheet was sent by the Hungarian Permanent Representative to his colleagues in the CMEA. The Hungarian foreign trade officials expressed in this document that they were looking for partners for two projects in India, one project in Guinea, and one in Cuba. For all of the projects they were stating either the Soviet Union, the CSSR, or the GDR as preferred partners. The other members were not mentioned.[66]

This was a looming problem. Romania and Bulgaria were hardly mentioned as preferred partners in the documents of the early 1960s. If a country like the CSSR was to choose its partners relatively free of political considerations, it would hardly turn to the least developed of the CMEA countries. In the year 1965 the USSR had reported to the Secretariat of the CMEA to have concluded 42 treaties related to economic cooperation with the Global South, followed by the CSSR and Hungary with 31 and 29, respectively. While the GDR and Poland could claim to have signed 19 and 14 such agreements, the number amounted to 13 for Romania and merely 2 for Bulgaria.[67] Although the numbers only give indications about the quantity and quality of economic cooperation with the Global South, it is clear when they are combined with the value of the economic aid granted by the CMEA member states that at least Bulgaria, but also Romania and Hungary, had not really been able to jump on the bandwagon yet. This picture is only slightly altered when their relative economic strength and the share of "developing countries" within their foreign trade is taken into account.[68]

The written exchange sent via the channels of the CMEA concerning economic relations with the Global South also indicates that remnants of the Stalinist period of the early 1950s and of Stalinist autarky in particular were still present in the 1960s. In a letter to the Secretariat of the CMEA on opportunities for potential cooperation with other partners from within the bloc the export organization of Skoda stated in early August 1967:

> The CSSR is in no need to cooperate with regards to planning whole factories, because the strength of our organization lies in the completion of any metallurgical factory. As concerns equipment we are forced to cooperate, because our factories produce 70% of the equipment themselves. For that reason, we are interested in a cooperation with the USSR, GDR, Poland, and Hungary.[69]

This statement still expressed the spirit of the time of the Korean War. It had a certain arrogant connotation and presented the ability to plan and build factories without anyone's help as a desirable ability. Where Skoda was "forced" to cooperate they also didn't mention Bulgaria and Romania but their immediate neighbors which in the case of Poland and the GDR happen to be much more successful in forging economic ties with the Global South. However, this "spirit," as expressed in this letter, proved detrimental rather than beneficial for expanding mutual trade inside the Eastern Bloc and between the CMEA and the Global South.

The early discussions that took place between the ministers for foreign trade during the PCTA meetings aimed at harmonizing certain rules and remunerations for skilled personnel working in the recipient countries of economic assistance. In its third session in September 1962 the PCTA adopted two resolutions. One was titled "General conditions for sending specialists of the CMEA member states to countries which are economically less developed to give all kinds of support" and the other "Methodology to determine the export value of planning plants and objects which are being built in economically less developed countries." The participants of the fourth session of the PCTA that took place in April 1963 drafted two resolutions on general conditions for training cadres from the Global South in the CMEA member states.[70] The titles of the adopted resolutions already show that the first years of the PCTA were used to agree on very basic issues.

In addition to discussing general procedures on sending experts and receiving students, the delegates to the PCTA were also discussing credit relations in the mid-1960s. The member countries of the CMEA were using credits for their development aid granted to the Global South thereby emulating Western practices to bridge the development gap with the Global South. The experts assembled in the PCTA exchanged information on the conditions of their issued credits. The material of the 12th session of the PCTA reads as follows:

> The PRP [People's Republic of Poland] encouraged the discussion of certain basic questions at the beginning of the expert consultation. . . . The CSSR experts declared that a review of their credit policy is currently taking place and that it can be expected that the CSSR will grant more commercial credits out of economic reasons. . . . The GDR experts issued a declaration during bilateral consultations and [general] consultations stating that the peculiar situation of the relations of the developing countries with the GDR (missing normalization of relations, retreat of the developing countries before the

> exclusive agency [Alleinvertretungsanspruch] of West Germany, attempts of West Germany to discriminate against the GDR in its relations to developing countries) necessitates the GDR to use its limited means to grant technical assistance primarily for solving political tasks.[71]

This extract shows how different the aims of individual countries of the Eastern Bloc could be when they were dealing with the Global South. While the CSSR was focused on maximizing its economic gains, the leadership of the GDR pursued different goals. Because of its precarious diplomatic position outside the Eastern Bloc it had to use credits and thus development aid to gain diplomatic recognition by the former colonies to counter West German policy measures to perpetuate the isolation of the GDR. The more countries had recognized the GDR, the more likely it was to ameliorate its position and to align it more to the Czechoslovakian one. But in the mid-1960s this was a luxury the GDR trade officials couldn't yet afford.

## The Resource-Program

The most important issue and concrete policy proposal discussed during the mid and late 1960s was the so-called Resource-Program. The first attempts to use the PCTA to discuss the import of raw materials from the former colonies occurred in late 1962. During 1962 and 1963 the respective member states were sending their draft versions for such a program via the Secretariat of the CMEA.[72] These draft versions were containing proposals to import copper, cotton, and natural rubber. The underlying idea was to conclude trade agreements on a barter basis. The CMEA countries would invest in the capital stock of selected partners in the Global South by building turnkey factories and importing resources in exchange. Thus, the "developing countries" would receive "capital investment" without paying the investment back with capital in the form of foreign exchange. The CMEA countries in return would either save rubles for intrabloc trade or convertible currencies, if they imported the respective resources on the world market.

The individual CMEA member states were sharing information on projects they thought could be arranged by them because of their good contacts and the available resources in the country concerned. The country that thought that it could successfully conclude a treaty took the lead and offered the other members of the CMEA to join. If a CMEA member state could not offer a project but was in need of importing certain resources like copper, it wrote a request to the Secretariat of the CMEA that would then inform the other member states in return. According to the planned procedure the countries which had less sophisticated relations with the Global South had the opportunity to join their colleagues and to profit from their already successful efforts. In return, they had to contribute to the development efforts by assembling factories or building infrastructure.

The Resource-Program took center stage during several PCTA meetings, e.g., on the 7th session of the PCTA in Moscow in June 1965.[73] To make a case in point, the GDR together with the CSSR joined a project for geophysical prospecting of copper and nickel in Burma. The endeavor was led by Soviet trade officials and conducted by Soviet geologists that were joined by East German and Czechoslovak experts in their work. The GDR also participated in a project under Bulgarian auspices to search for copper in Chile and led a project in Ceylon to import natural rubber in which it was joined by Bulgarian experts as junior partners.[74]

The fact that the discussions concerning the Resource-Program were occurring from 1962 on was not necessarily a good sign as archival documents show. The directive for the East German delegation that was to take part in the 8th session of the PCTA in Moscow in early June 1965 read:

> The delegation of the GDR has made its viewpoint clear concerning the mentioned issues of cooperation with
>
> - Burma to the delegation of the USSR on 8.4.1965 and to the delegation of the CSSR on 9.4.1965
> - Chile to the delegation of the PRB [Bulgaria] on 9.4.1965.
>
> The delegation of the GDR has received no material from these delegations. The proposal of the GDR to conduct joint consultations between the experts of these countries has not been realized. Neither the delegation of the GDR nor the delegation of the PRB has prepared any material concerning the cooperation with Ceylon
>
> The delegation of the GDR is emphasizing its view again that the studies, as envisioned in the working plan related to questions of securing deficit resources, have to be conducted jointly by the country delegations involved. In relation with this, it [the delegation of the GDR] is informing the session that its proposals for joint expert consultations remain unanswered by the delegation of the USSR due to missing material and by the delegation of the PRB.[75]

The cooperation between the members of the CMEA was not working according to the plan. Most – if not all – of the projects were behind schedule and yielded few tangible results in the 1960s. The Resource-Program was meant to galvanize multilateral cooperation inside the bloc but suffered from shortages of the CMEA member states which were either not willing or not able to realize such projects requiring well-developed management skills on both the ministerial level and the level of state combines and foreign trade organizations involved. The situation as described in internal documents of the GDR written in 1965 didn't change till the end of the decade:

> The 8th session reviewed information on the cooperation with certain developing countries. This material gave an overview on the situation, but didn't lead to a reinforcement of the cooperation of the member states. The protocol stated commodities for import, in particular copper, nickel, zinc, tin, lead, bauxite, iron ore, oil, natural rubber, cotton, mineral fertilizer and others, and

> [stipulated] an agreement that the member states should concentrate on chosen developing countries.[76]

The situation seemed unaltered when the delegations to the PCTA met for the 15th session in December 1968 in Moscow and noted that

> critical remarks have to be made that the plenary session was confined to demonstrating single points of view and [that] a real exchange of opinions didn't take place.[77]

## Conclusion

Concerning concrete multilateral development projects, the CMEA member states didn't achieve much during the 1960s as becomes clear from the PCTA documents on the Resource-Program. The discussions between late 1962 and late 1968 didn't lead to the comprehensive program originally envisioned as the goal of the mutual consultations. Instead, discussions were prolonged indefinitely and delegations were unprepared or not authorized to make serious commitments for the proposed cooperation projects.

However, despite this failure, the achievements of the 1960s were great compared to the previous decade. During the 1950s no policy coordination worthy of that name with regard to the Global South had existed in the Eastern Bloc. While the Khrushchev administration was trying to avoid the mistakes of the Stalin period and to take advantage of the post-war anticolonial movement, many of the smaller members of the bloc were not ready to do so due to their limited means and international status. The Soviet Union eventually succeeded in forging ties with the former colonies, the vast majority of which had become independent in the 20 years following the end of the Second World War.

By the late 1950s the smaller members of the bloc were consolidated enough to follow the Soviet Union. The internal documents of the CMEA member states show that they were almost entirely unaware of the measures taken and methods employed by their respective neighbors. But this was to change in the 1960s and the CMEA, the PCTA in particular, proved to be the main forum of information exchange. This was the CMEA's main asset during this decade. Its achievement with regard to multilateral policy programs were modest at best, but it was important in harmonizing policies and learning from the experiences of the other member states, even if these learning processes concerned mainly basic issues such as the education of young people from the Global South and the formation of joint ventures.

It is interesting to note that, while reading the reports and documents on the PCTA in chronological order, the language becomes less ideologized from 1963 on. While the early reports on sessions of the PCTA were similarly structured to the report on its founding session, regularly making statements on the fight against imperialism, the rhetoric gradually changed and became more technocratic with fewer and fewer ideological statements as the 1960s proceeded. The fight against imperialism was replaced by discussions on import quotas for deficit resources and geophysical prospecting in the Global South.

In the next chapter the efforts to reform the CMEA in the late 1960s and early 1970s will be reviewed with a special focus on the PCTA and the coordination of development aid. This reform program was termed "Complex-Program". It will be asked how the discussions surrounding the Complex-Program influenced the PCTA. The Resource-Program will play an important part in analyzing the effectiveness of the reforms, since it remained prevalent during the 1970s.

## Notes

1 Fursenko and Naftali, *Khrushchev's Cold War*, 540.
2 Taubman, *Khrushchev*, 464–8.
3 Westad, *The Global Cold War*, 54–5.
4 Westad, 54–5.
5 Bernstein, "Introduction," 5–6.
6 Westad, *The Global Cold War*, 67–8.
7 Shipway, *Decolonization and Its Impact*, 12–3.
8 Darwin, *After Tamerlane*, 435.
9 Darwin, 436–7.
10 Maier, "The World Economy and the Cold War," 61.
11 Louis and Robinson, "The Imperialism of Decolonization," 72.
12 Shipway, *Decolonization and Its Impact*, 201.
13 Louis and Robinson, "The Imperialism of Decolonization," 68.
14 Louis and Robinson, 66–7.
15 Fursenko and Naftali, *Khrushchev's Cold War*, 58.
16 Fursenko and Naftali, 58.
17 Painter, "Oil, Resources and the Cold War 1945–1962," 489–90.
18 Fursenko and Naftali, *Khrushchev's Cold War*, 66–7.
19 Fursenko and Naftali, 64–5.
20 Fursenko and Naftali, 80.
21 Fursenko and Naftali, 83.
22 See e.g., on the uneasy Soviet-Indonesian relationship in the late 1950s and early 1960s Boden, "Das Scheitern."
23 Darwin, *After Tamerlane*, 439–41.
24 Lüthi, "The Non-Aligned," 97.
25 Bradley, "Decolonization," 479–80.
26 Westad, *The Global Cold War*, 2.
27 Westad, 2.
28 Westad, 104.
29 Westad, 107.
30 Louis and Robinson, "The Imperialism of Decolonization," 67.
31 Fursenko and Naftali, *Khrushchev's Cold War*, 60–1.
32 Taubman, *Khrushchev*, 359.
33 Fursenko and Naftali, *Khrushchev's Cold War*, 294–5.
34 Louis and Robinson, "The Imperialism of Decolonization," 70–1.
35 See Cooper, "Modernizing Bureaucrats."
36 Arndt, *Economic Development*, 54.
37 Lewis received the Nobel Prize in Economics for his work in 1979.
38 Unger, "Histories of Development and Modernization," 1.
39 Mason, *Development and Disorder*, 20.

40 Mason, 20.
41 Westad, *The Global Cold War*, 4–5.
42 Tignor, *W. Arthur Lewis*, 163–80. Lewis left Ghana in disagreement with Nkrumah to take up a new post at the UN. However, the reason for his disillusionment with Nkrumah was not rooted in ideological disagreement on the role of the state but on the role of political patronage and prestige projects in spending the scarce Ghanaian resources.
43 Arndt, *Economic Development*, 2–3. Note that Keynes himself wrote "Indian Currency and Finance" at the beginning of his career. Unfortunately, he didn't cope with the economic framework of the colonies afterwards anymore.
44 Growth rates in the Eastern Bloc in the early fifties were as high as 8.5 % in Hungary or 11 % in Poland. Suny, *The Soviet Experiment*, 376–7.
45 Arndt, *Economic Development*, 55.
46 Arndt, 55.
47 Arndt, 55–6.
48 Arndt, 57–8.
49 Frieden, *Global Capitalism*, 305, 351–4.
50 "Die Aufgaben auf dem Gebiet des Außenhandels," dated 03 May 1963, Barch Berlin, DC 20/2798.
51 "Konzeption für die Durchführung von Verhandlungen mit den kapitalistischen Ländern über die gegenseitigen Warenlieferungen," dated 21 August 1963, ibid.
52 "Die Aufgaben auf dem Gebiet des Außenhandels," dated 03 May 1963, ibid.
53 Arndt, *Economic Development*, 60.
54 Arndt, 60–1.
55 Arndt, 60, 64–6.
56 Arndt, 70.
57 Jersild, *The Sino-Soviet Alliance*, 22.
58 Jersild, 164–7.
59 "Ausführungen des Gen. Leuschner," dated 25 September 1964, Barch Berlin, DC 20/18353.
60 Bradley, "Decolonization," 481.
61 Annex titled "Zu den Berichten: 'Südostasien'" to the document "Notiz für Genossen Leuschner," dated 20 October 1964, Barch Berlin, DC 20/18353.
62 "Brief des Genossen Hofmann an Genossen Weiss," dated 13 November 1963, Barch Berlin, DC 20/2799.
63 Bundesstiftung Aufarbeitung: Biographische Datenbanken, "Weiss, Gerhard." The identity of Mr. Hofmann, the author of the letter cited previously is not clear. It is probably Artur Hofmann who was heading the department of the economy inside the secret service and was working for the Central Committee.
64 "Bericht über die Expertentagung zur Frage der technischen Unterstützung gegenüber den in ökonomischer Hinsicht schwachentwickelten Ländern beim Bau von schlüsselfertigen Betrieben und bei der Beteiligung an Bau- und Montagearbeiten vom 20. – 24 November 1962 in Budapest," without date, Barch Berlin, DE 1/51310.
65 "Ob"em obiazatel'stv i fakticheskogo okazaniia tekhnicheskogo sodeistviia stranami-chlenami SEV slaborazvitym stranam," early 1963, RGAE, Fond 561 op. 26s/pp d. 3 l. 35.
66 "Perechen' ob"ektov, po kotorym BNP prosit uchastiia v postavkakh v slaborazvitye v ekonomicheskom otnoshenii strany v poriadke kooperatsii so stranami-chlenami SEV v 1963–7 gg.," early 1963, RGAE, Fond 561 op. 53 d. 3 ll. 17–20.
67 "Kolichestvo torgovykh i plateinikh soglashenii, a takzhe soglashenii ob ekonomicheskom i tehnicheskom sotrudnichestve i torgovle mezhdu stranami-chlenami SEV i razvivaiushchimisia stranami, postupivshikh v Sekretariat SEV v 1965 godu," early 1966, RGAE, Fond 561 op. 53 d. 18 ll. 90–1.
68 "Kapcsolataink A Fejlődő Országokkal," dated 12 October 1965, MNL Budapest, XIX-A-90-c 153. doboz.

69 Letter by Skodaexport to the Secretariat of the CMEA, dated 01 August 1967, RGAE, Fond 561 op. 53 d. 32, l. 15.

70 Letter from the head of the department for economic cooperation of the Ministry for Foreign and inner-German Trade, dated 23 August 1963, Barch Berlin, DC 20/2799.

71 "Information über die Ergebnisse der Beratung von Experten der RGW-Länder zur Vorbereitung eines Entwurfs von 'Empfehlungen über die Prinzipien der gemeinsamen Gewährung von Regierungskrediten durch interessierte RGW-Länder an Entwicklungsländer im Falle der gemeinsamen Erweisung ökonomischer und technischer Unterstützung an diese Länder' (Moskau, 27. – 29.9.1967)," dated 19 October 1967, Barch Berlin, DC 20/10027.

72 "Informatsiia v sootvetsvii s protokolom 3-ei sessii Postoiannoi kommissii Soveta ekonomicheskom vzaimopomoshchi po koordinatsii tekhnicheskoi pomoshchi, soztoiavshei v Moskve s 21 po 22 sentiabria 1962 goda," dated 04.01.1963, RGAE, Fond 561 op. 53 d. 4, ll. 43–5; and "Vozmozhnosti uchastii stran-chlenov SEV v organizatsii i rasshirenii proisvodstva medi, nikelia, kautchuka i khlopka v slaborazvitykh stranakh," dated 21 January 1963, ibid., ll. 47–51.

73 Protocol of the 7th session of the PCTA that took place between 2–4 June 1965 in Moscow, in particular point 2 of the protocol "ob izuchenii vozmozhnostei sotrudnichestva otdel'nykh stran-chlenov SEV s nekotorymi razvivaiushchimisia stranami putem okazaniia ekonomicheskogo i tekhnicheskogo sodeizstviia s cel'iu rasshireniia proizvodstva defitsitnykh tovarov i uvelicheniia ikh importa stranami-chlenami SEV," RGAE, Fond 561 op. 26s/pp d. 5, ll. 1–41.

74 Directive for the 8th session of the PCTA between 3–5 June 1965 in Moscow, Barch Berlin, DL 2/22815.

75 Ibid.

76 "Direktive für das Auftreten der DDR-Delegation auf der 9. Tagung der Ständigen Kommission für die Koordinierung der Technischen Unterstützung," without date, Barch Berlin, DL 2/22839.

77 "Bericht über die 15. Tagung der Ständigen Kommission des RGW für die Koordinierung der Technischen Unterstützung 18. – 20.12.1968 in Moskau," 15 January, 1969, Barch Berlin, DE 1/54932.

# Part II

# The Complex-Program

# 3 The reforms of 1971

## The road to the Complex-Program

The reform attempts of the early 1960s vanished with Nikita Khrushchev's demise. The new Soviet administration under Brezhnev and Kosygin didn't show much initiative with regards to policy proposals to reform the CMEA. Neither did the smaller members of the CMEA which were in many cases experimenting with new economic reforms on a national level.[1] The one exception was the introduction of the so-called interested-party principle in 1967.[2] This meant that two or more members of the CMEA could officially agree to pursue specific cooperation measures under the umbrella of the CMEA without the consent of its other members. Thus, the principle of unanimity was reduced in meaning but still remained the official guideline of the CMEA. This didn't change the fact that the CMEA could still only draft recommendations, the implementation of which was up to the member states.[3]

This did not prove a very radical reform in practical terms, as the CMEA had no authority to urge its members to implement or to reject a certain set of policies, since every member state was guarding its own autonomy. On the other hand, as far as reforming the CMEA was concerned in the mid-1960s, neither of the smaller members nor the Soviet leadership interfered and scaled back the activities of the CMEA returning to the situation of 1953. Many of the reforms enacted in the early 1960s still had to show how they would play out. As the example of the PCTA demonstrates, the newly formed working organs of the CMEA had to find new ways of cooperation and were often occupied with basic forms of information sharing and studying the experiences of the other members of the organization before they could embark on huge policy schemes.

This changed in the late 1960s. It is often stated in the literature written in the late 1980s by political scientists that the new reform process of the CMEA institutions that started in 1969 was highly connected with the incidents in Czechoslovakia one year before. Since the Soviets had crushed the "Prague Spring" by force, so the narrative goes, they had to offer a "piece of candy" in return. This "sweetener" to increase the internal cohesion of the bloc that had been threatened before was supposed to be a long-term investment and integration program for the CMEA.[4] This program was termed "Complex-Program." The negotiations on this program started in 1969, a few months after the invasion of the CSSR. Furthermore, 1969 also happened to be the year of the 20th anniversary of the CMEA.

However, this narrative that emphasizes the role of the Prague Spring is doubtful. It was written at a time when political analysts interested in the affairs of the Eastern Bloc had to rely on (non-)socialist newspapers, interviews, publicly available intelligence, and rumors. It is hard to find any strong archival evidence for a direct connection between the Soviet invasion of the CSSR in 1968 and the reform initiatives in the CMEA that started to be discussed publicly in 1969. It makes sense that the events in Czechoslovakia played at least an indirect role in the decision-making process but they didn't dominate the negotiations and reform discussions of the CMEA.[5]

The structure and statutes of the CMEA needed amendments anyway in the late 1960s and 1970s, since many of the programs initiated during the Khrushchev period were blocked or slowed down by the smaller members of the CMEA like Romania. Although new working organs like the Permanent Commissions and the Executive Council were successfully established, the idea of grand-scale supranational planning had died as an infant. This meant that the CMEA contained some kind of institutional carcass but this institutional frame was operating without a clear agenda and long-term goals. Such goals had been expressed in the "Basic Principles of the International Socialist Division of Labor" (ISDL) in 1962. Yet, the ISDL became increasingly obsolete as time was commencing. It was possible to develop mutual cooperation along pragmatic lines for some time, but not indefinitely.

Therefore, it is safe to state that new Council Sessions concerned with the long-term future of the CMEA were bound to take place sooner or later. The events in Czechoslovakia may have accelerated this process but they hardly caused it. The national economic reforms undertaken by most CMEA member states were an additional strong factor urging new negotiations inside the CMEA, since they threatened to further erode the compatibility of the respective planning processes, thereby hindering the expansion of trade inside the CMEA. Another factor that necessitated reforms of the CMEA was détente which enabled the CMEA member states to expand their economic ties with the West. On the other hand, lowered tensions between East and West made it possible for the Eastern Bloc to increase its cooperation with the Global South.

## The content of the reforms

On 27 July 1971, the so called "Complex-Program for a further Consolidation and Perfection of the Socialist Economic Integration of the CMEA Member Countries" was approved by the 25th Council Session that took place in Bucharest.[6] The Complex-Program was meant to define the goals of the CMEA and of Socialist Economic Integration (SEI) for the next 15 to 20 years.[7] It was accompanied by discussions inside the CMEA on what SEI could mean, to what extent market elements and regional planning were advisable and needed for the future development of the CMEA, and more regional integration. The strongest advocate for market mechanisms as guidelines for intrabloc integration was the Hungarian delegation.[8] The opposite view was represented by the Soviet delegation that was still arguing for supranational planning like at the beginning of the 1960s. However, by the end of the decade, the Soviet experts were arguing for supranational planning on a much more modest scale. The new form of supranational planning envisioned most prominently by them was supposed to leave the bulk of day-to-day decision making to local subsidiaries.[9]

Neither of the two sides could push through its agenda entirely. The result was some sort of compromise that included a common declaration to strive for more integration but avoided formulating a rigorous master plan for achieving more cooperation. Thus, the internal cracks didn't break open as every delegation could live with a compromise that was not binding its autonomy tightly.[10] The experts and policy-makers of the CMEA agreed to focus their efforts on the branches of agriculture, machine building, logistics, and raw materials. Some forms of joint economic planning were introduced but these were limited to long-term plan coordination. They comprised cooperation in the fields of forecasting supply and demand for goods and commodities and conducting long-term studies on the future of selected branches of industry.[11]

An important part of the Complex-Program was the proposed encouragement of joint investment projects by several CMEA member countries on the territory of another member. This could be defined as a kind of proposed "capital" mobility, even if no currencies were exchanged but investment goods on a barter basis. The investment possibilities were in theory not limited to any particular member state. However, in practice most investment schemes were envisioned to take place on the territory of the Soviet Union and Mongolia.[12] Most of these investment projects concerned the extraction of resources, in the case of Mongolia all of them. Nevertheless, some of them focused on other branches of the economy, too, like the development of the chemical industry in the Soviet Union.[13]

In contrast to the ISDL and the attempts of the Khrushchev administration to push through wide-ranging reforms in record time, the SEI promised only limited immediate consequences. It left a lot of room for improvisation and further adjustment. Its achievement was to formulate – however vaguely – a common set of goals as policy guidelines. It was up to the respective planning agencies to develop tools and forms of cooperation that would realize these goals in practice. Therefore, the reform program that was evolving between 1969 and 1971 can be seen from two different angles: on the one hand, it can be regarded as a realistic hands-on approach taking into account the realities of intrabloc relations and differing opinions. It provided an umbrella for the practitioners. On the other hand, it can be viewed as a failure, since nothing really new came out of the negotiations, neither supranational planning nor – alternatively – market mechanisms guiding economic integration. Although negotiations inside the CMEA were multilateral, trade still continued to be organized mainly on a bilateral level.

## Revisions

The reform momentum began to fade in the mid-1970s as many of the envisioned projects and investment schemes were only advancing slowly.[14] Therefore, revisions were needed and the 29th Council Session that assembled in Budapest in 1975 focused on reworking the Complex-Program. The delegations agreed to focus their coordination efforts on a certain branch and chose the energy sector to accomplish a breakthrough in the form of big joint investment projects.[15] This approach pushed the needle more in favor of the advocates of regional, if not supranational, planning since it missed any market or other economic mechanisms to direct economic integration in the realm of the CMEA. It also meant strengthening barter trade inside the bloc.[16]

However, the focus on the energy sector led to the realization of the Mir and Druzhba projects in the 1970s as the most visible milestones of economic integration in the East. The Mir energy network, started in 1975 and finished in 1979, connected the Soviet power grid with the other European CMEA member states, while the Druzhba pipeline system, or to put it more precisely, the extension of the already existing pipeline system, during the second half of the 1970s increased the supply of Soviet oil and gas to the smaller socialist countries of Central Eastern Europe and allowed the Soviet Union to export some of its oil and gas resources more easily to Western Europe, mainly West Germany.[17]

These measures agreed upon in the Council Sessions were accompanied by a more pronounced plan coordination inside the CMEA that started in 1974. Its members consented to the idea of a so-called Concerted Plan, the first of which had been worked out in 1975. This plan contained all priority projects of Socialist Economic Integration and was thus of common interest for two or more CMEA member states. It was drafted every five years and supplemented by the Target Program which had a longer planning horizon.[18] The Concerted Plan offered numbers and targets in several categories: the first being the material, financial, and labor input transfer needed for common integration projects; the second dealt with how the objects relate to already concluded production specialization agreements. Other categories of interest concerned the development of the new members of the CMEA that joined in the 1960s and later, and the influence of integration projects on third countries outside the CMEA.[19]

## The IIB

One reason no dramatic takeoff in economic cooperation took place in the CMEA following the enacting of the Complex-Program was the Eastern Bloc's rudimentary financial system. The first bank of the CMEA, the International Bank for Economic Cooperation (IBEC), had already been founded in 1964, following the reforms of the early 1960s inside the CMEA. The role of the IBEC was to function as a clearing bank for the internal CMEA trade using the new currency of the Transferable Ruble (TR) for this purpose. The problem was that, although the TR was transferable, it was not convertible[20] and thus couldn't function as an international currency outside the CMEA.[21] In theory, the IBEC would have been able to hand out credits for joint investment projects, as its statute allowed such measures. But the bank executives hardly made use of this opportunity.[22]

Nevertheless, the financial system and credit relations inside the CMEA played a huge role since at least the late 1950s in mutual consultations. They continued to do so during the discussions and negotiations of the Complex-Program. This led to the creation of the second bank of the CMEA, the International Investment Bank (IIB). The creation of the IIB took effect on 1 January 1971. The discussions to create a new bank had already evolved in 1969. Its creation was connected to the experiments with small-scale market reforms that had taken place inside most of the CMEA member states and the common will for a deeper intrabloc integration.[23]

Since the economic reforms enacted by the CMEA countries during the 1960s differed more or less from country to country, the traditional bilateral trade suffered from the increasing incompatibility of the planning and allocation mechanisms. The foundation of the IIB was part of the compromise between those countries in favor of planning coordination and those which would have liked to see more integration led by market mechanisms.[24] The task of the IIB was to facilitate an "international socialist division of labor" by granting credits on a multilateral basis.[25] Thus, its creation was to please the adherents of more market-oriented reforms.

The IIB was not allowed to invest in projects, the benefit of which would only suit a single member country. All projects had to be multilateral.[26] The chief executive of the bank was Soviet but the rest of the personnel was mixed and came from all members who had underwritten stakes in the IIB, which totaled one billion TR.[27] The stakes ranged from roughly two-fifths of the capital for the Soviet Union to less than 0.5 % for Mongolia. However, every member state of the executive council had only one vote. Some decisions needed to be adopted unanimously, the rest required at least a three-fourths majority.[28] Every member of the IIB was free to make investment proposals.

During the first year of its existence, the IIB financed 16 projects worth 181 million TR and 50 million US dollars in five different member states. The growth continued in the following years. The money for its loans was taken on the international credit market.[29] Since the IIB issued loans in convertible currencies, it received many proposals that it could scrutinize on its own without relying on national cadres. The projects were then monitored by the bank's personnel to ensure the right usage of the money.[30] The lending practice of the IIB changed with the renegotiations of the Complex-Program in 1975. From then on till the early 1980s the bankers of the IIB were occupied with obtaining the loans needed for the expansion of the oil and gas pipeline system in the Eastern Bloc. Projects in the energy sector which had played no role in the early years of the IIB were responsible for nearly 80 % of its credit portfolio at the end of the 1970s.[31]

## Effects on the PCTA

One of the most important changes that occurred in the 1970s for the economic cooperation between the Eastern Bloc and the Global South was the accession of two countries of the Global South to the CMEA. Cuba became a full member of the CMEA in 1972, Vietnam joined six years later. To make a case in point, Cuba had already established close political and military ties with the Eastern Bloc in the early 1960s, while economic relations were lagging behind. In relation with the Complex-Program Cuba specialized in sugar production for the other markets of the CMEA, while receiving large-scale support for its domestic development schemes that was boosted by an artificially inflated price the Cuban government received for its sugar exports.[32] This was a peculiar kind of support for developing countries inside the CMEA that didn't apply to countries outside of the CMEA.

The implications of CMEA reforms were first discussed during the session of the PCTA that took place in late May 1969 in the Armenian capital Yerevan. The head of the delegation of the GDR, the minister for foreign trade Sölle, approved a report for internal usage which stated:

> They [the delegations] emphasized that they would take all measures to realize the tasks that result out of the 23rd Council Session for the Permanent Commission of the CMEA for the Coordination of Technical Assistance.
>
> Despite of this, the editorial groups of the delegations of the PRH [Hungary], PRB [Bulgaria], SRR [Romania] and CSSR employed a wait-and-see attitude. Concrete proposals to change the work [of the PCTA], which were brought forward by the delegations of the GDR and PRP [Poland] in particular, didn't enjoy the support of the delegations mentioned previously.[33]

Concerning the discussion of the annual report of the PCTA for 1968 the report of the East German delegation reads:

> Except for the delegation of the GDR only the delegation of the PRH was making some critical remarks on the report. The delegation of the PRH assessed that the coordination on some fields is not sufficient. It stated that the coordination of the FTCs [Foreign Trade Companies] is not satisfactory. Only rarely did a coordination in developing countries occur. . . . Concerning information exchange the delegation of the PRH stated that information exchange didn't allow for concerted positions, since it often gave only a retroactive view. [The delegation of the PRH] suggested to amend the content of the information exchange to enable an alignment of the positions of the CMEA member countries in the most important fields. The critical remarks of the delegations of the GDR and PRH have not been included in the [official] report, since the other country delegations were of the opinion that problems related to an elaboration of the Complex-Program have to be dealt with in a special commission session.[34]

The PCTA thus started its own discussions on improving the cooperation between the Eastern Bloc and the Global South with only a few weeks' delay of the Council. This shows that discussions at the top of the institution were matched by the working organs of the CMEA. However, the report of the GDR delegation indicates that most member states were not too keen on implementing immediate changes in the working procedures of the organs of the CMEA, in particular of the PCTA. The East Germans explicitly mentioned a common front of the GDR and Hungary against the other smaller members in favor of swift acting. The tasks the Council Session had formulated for the PCTA contained, among others, a utilization of the production specialization inside the CMEA for economic cooperation with the Global South, and working out principles for a common set of rules for granting credits. This should be supplemented by multilateral investments and "overcoming the immobility in the work of the organs of the commission."[35]

Nevertheless, the statements of the East German delegation on the stance of its Hungarian counterpart seem to contain some exaggerations. The Hungarian documents on the activities of the PCTA are not as negative as could be assumed by reading only the East German briefings on the behavior of the Hungarian and other delegations.[36] They were rather pragmatic. In their internal documents, the Hungarian trade officials expressed their desire to cooperate primarily with the CSSR and the Soviet Union to increase their share in economic cooperation with the Global South. It is interesting to note that besides these two CMEA countries they already mentioned France, West Germany, and Austria in the mid-1960s for their future plans. This indicates a greater ideological flexibility than was the case with many other CMEA member states when foreign trade was concerned.[37]

However, the mood of the participants seemed to improve the next year. The report of the East German delegation on the 20th session of the PCTA that occurred in November 1970 in Moscow asserted:

> All delegations showed the desire to concentrate on the main tasks as stated in the working plan for 1971 and in the perspective working plan for 1972/1973. Hereby – primarily on the initiative of the delegation of the USSR – concrete country-related resource problems have been included for the first time. It can be stated as another positive fact that the tasks contained in both working plans include more joint and coordinated actions of the member countries. . . . All in all, it can be said that constructive work has been done in the 20th session of the PCTA. It has to be emphasized that on almost all questions, but in particular in principle documents, joint viewpoints could be fixated by the country delegations.[38]

In the same session, the PCTA's participants could also agree on concrete coordination measures like a paper to avoid "unnecessary" competition between the members of the CMEA when they were taking part in the same tenders, e.g., for building factories in the Global South. Such measures could not be in the interest of "developing countries" as they were aiming at increasing the potential profit for the countries of the Eastern Bloc in economic cooperation with the Global South. The price was to be paid by the latter.

However, the discussions surrounding the Complex-Program set a process in motion that occupied a considerable part of the administrative capacity of the Eastern Bloc. This is a clear sign that – independent from the success of the whole endeavor – the respective political elites of the bloc's members showed an interest in the CMEA and put efforts into making it more effective and more suitable for their needs. This meant incurring opportunity costs. The time invested by the government agencies of the bloc and the first tier of highly trained and thus valuable experts could have been employed for other purposes; but it wasn't. In the case of the PCTA other government agencies were closely monitoring its debates. Experts of the East German Planning Commission were writing an extensive memorandum for other state agencies on what they were expecting to change within the PCTA to ensure a better cooperation between East and South in the future. They wrote:

> Where were improvements of the work of the PCTA visible in the year 1970?
>
> In our opinion, the improvements were manifest therein that a bunch of problems has been discussed on the 19th and 20th sessions of the PCTA and during the expert consultations with much more tangible content than hitherto. We want to emphasize the following problems in particular:
>
> 1 The resolution of a long-term program for studying the economies, socioeconomic processes, the trade relations, and perspectives of chosen developing countries with the aim to determine those branches of the[eir] economy which can be used to establish an effective cooperation with the CMEA member countries . . .
> 2 The analysis and compilation of the reasons that are hindering the CMEA member countries from mutual cooperation and the proposals for changing the situation in bilateral respect (e.g., for erecting joint objects in developing countries). . . .
> 3 The start of a working period that will make securing certain deficit resources a core problem of the CMEA member countries.[39]

The authors from the Planning Commission moved on with a section on unresolved problems in their document which was shared with other government agencies, mainly the Ministry for Foreign and inner-German Trade headed by Horst Sölle. They were urging the Secretariat of the CMEA in Moscow to edit the material it received from the member countries on their economic cooperation with the Global South. By handing the material over to the Permanent Representatives without any comments or conclusions they were – in the eyes of the authors of the report – hindering the work of the national agencies. They even used derogatory language to express their anger in the document.[40] Urging the Secretariat in Moscow to edit and filter the documents before they were sent around necessitated a huge amount of trust in this institution.

The commentators from the Planning Commission were thankful for the statistical material shared by the delegations of the PCTA and emphasized that they didn't have a single doubt concerning the validity of the numbers. However, they were complaining that the numbers were shared without further explanations, which made it impossible for the economists to see why a loan had been granted to a country in the Global South and for what kind of project. This was rendering complex intrabloc learning processes impossible. They also gave advice on how the working procedures inside the PCTA should change in the future and put an emphasis on deficit resources. Without stating the term, they advised the trade officials to include opportunity costs inside their consultations by pursuing negotiations with different "developing countries" in parallel. Thereby, it would be possible to assess if a project was not only likely to deliver the desired resources but also if it was economical to do so.[41]

That something was changing indeed due to the process set in motion by another reform program for the CMEA is expressed by an informal exchange of notes between two economic experts that somehow remained in the archival documents. This exchange of handwritten notes occurred between the two East German economic experts, Reinhold and Schönherr, working in the department for foreign trade of the Planning Commission. The notes read:

> The SPK [Planning Commission] is expected to state its opinion on the following questions:
>
> 1 Are we willing to share to <u>all</u> [sic!] CMEA member countries officially via the PCTA all prospective objects 1970–75 (objects= complete plants and ships) sorted after countries in detail?
> 2 Is it suitable to give data for the years 1972–75 to the CMEA member countries, where no perspective plan is in existence?
> 3 Are we willing to make complete statements to the CMEA member countries on sent-out experts, education of cadres for the years up to 1975?
>
> I would opt for an open and detailed display of our projects, if I took the demands of the Complex-Program as starting point, which is orienting itself towards an intensified collaboration with regards to cooperation. Since this is a question of principle, I want to hear your opinion.[42]

The answer was short:

1) compilation yes 2) numbers till 1970 3) no, I am not aware of it[43]

The same Mr. Reinhold wrote in another informal note on the activities of the PCTA in the initial reform process of 1969 and 1970:

> the leader of the GDR-delegation has to disapprove of the work of the commission officially, as its work is not in line with the resolution of the 23rd Session of the Council and the subsequent Session of the ECO [Executive Council]. The material . . . remained totally unsatisfactory. The working style of the commission is outmoded and is increasingly impeding the further development, in particular urgent amendments, of the whole PCTA. The GDR-delegation has to make a firm stance, even if it cannot expect the support of other country delegations.[44]

Such strong opinions are not necessarily representative of the other members of the CMEA. However, they do show that the organization was taken seriously in the third decade of its existence and that the efforts to change it could alter the perceptions of the policy-makers involved as the exchange of notes between Reinhold and Schönherr demonstrates. In their written consultations they were arguing about basic questions of information exchange. They used the term "Complex-Program" in a way that questioned their previous practices of collaboration inside the bloc. In this way, the Complex-Program can be termed a success.

## The Resource-Program II

The Resource-Program to find new sources of supply for so-called deficit resources remained an important issue during the 1970s. The negotiations on the Complex-Program evolved into demands on the PCTA to speed up its work and to yield tangible results. This demand was supported by the national economic planning agencies, as shown previously. Furthermore, it was agreed on already in 1971 that the PCTA should rely on the newly founded International Investment Bank to finance the projects of the Resource-Program multilaterally. For this reason, a special fund should be formed at the IIB.[45]

The PCTA met four times in 1972 alone to discuss the implementation of the demands of the Complex-Program with the first meeting taking place in early January. At the top of the agenda was the Resource-Program.[46] As in the years before, the respective country delegations were headed by the ministers for foreign trade. In between the sessions of the PCTA, several expert consultations and consultations of practitioners like the heads of state combines were taking place under the umbrella of the PCTA. The number of such consultations on East–South economic cooperation was increasing rapidly during the 1970s.[47]

This shows that the fabric of economic cooperation and mutual consultations became denser following the negotiations on the Complex-Program. Even if the character of these cooperation measures remained rudimentary, it signaled a new quality of exchange in the eyes of the persons involved. The report on a meeting of the executive directors of state combines involved in East–South economic cooperation who met in the new headquarters of the CMEA in Moscow reads:

> While some FTOs [Foreign Trade Organizations] deemed it sufficient to merely restate their written information, the majority of the FTOs of the CMEA member countries was discussing the main problems. It was remarkable that the PRP [Polish], USSR-delegation, as well as the GDR-delegation pointed at their commercial problems concerning the cooperation of the FTOs of the CMEA member countries with developing countries for the first time during a meeting of executive directors in their contributions to the discussion.[48]

A gradual shift of attitudes becomes visible in the cited statement. As the previous meetings of the heads of trade organizations and state combines were confined by pointing out what already was inside the written information sent around prior to the meetings, the participants of the consultations were ready to share more information with their colleagues than they had hitherto done. The quality of this information exchange and the learning processes it could initiate was most likely meager compared to similar processes in big multinational Western companies or the European Community during the 1970s but it showed a dynamic that was pointing towards more, not less mutual exchange.

As concerned the Resource-Program, despite four sessions of the PCTA during 1972, the results were modest at best. At the end of the year, all delegations could agree on a common program but the policy paper that came out of the discussions remained very vague. A consensus could be reached on the different kinds of resources that were sought after. These included oil, phosphate, exotic woods, cotton and wool, raw skins and pelts, as well as nonferrous metals. A special working group on phosphates was formed, while the other resources were still talked about in one complex. The special role of phosphate is explained by its importance for modern agriculture. Without significant inputs of phosphate, it would have been impossible for the Eastern Bloc to build up an agrochemical industry. However, four sessions of the PCTA were not sufficient to agree on the responsibilities of the individual member countries of the CMEA, even if the delegation of the Soviet Union stated that it would try to take up the position as leading negotiator for such projects where the smaller countries were still hesitant to do so, thereby taking on the main part of the potential financial risks.[49]

The report on the 27th session of the PCTA, held in mid-November 1973 in Moscow, stated on the issue:

> The demeanor of the delegations was marked by the insight that the international development in the resource sector and the rising demand of the economies of the CMEA-countries in decisive resources necessitates the speeding-up of efforts to realize all measures agreed on in the "Resource-Program."
>
> In relation to this, the delegation of the USSR has pointed out that the available possibilities in securing important resources like phosphate, bauxite, and oil, in developing countries have not been sufficiently used by the CMEA member countries to secure their needs. The delegation of the USSR expressed that a consequent usage of the available possibilities in the Arabic and North African countries would enable [the CMEA member states] to secure their demand in e.g., phosphates from 1980 on.[50]

1973 was the year of the first post-war oil crisis that originated in the Middle East and left its mark on the world economy. This explains the slightly dramatic tone of the document. One could therefore expect the member states of the CMEA to really speed up their efforts to secure claims on important resources in the Global South before other international actors like Western companies would do so. Nevertheless, the spirit described in the document proved short-lived. Three sessions of the PCTA later not much had changed in the report:

> The delegation of the USSR pointed out again that the members of the CMEA should primarily concentrate on realizing such objects that serve satisfying

> the import needs of the members of the CMEA from developing countries in oil, phosphate and bauxite.[51]

Again, three sessions of the PCTA later, the realization of any of the objects encompassed by the Resource-Program hadn't moved an inch:

> It has been stated as a result of the consultation that the current state of realization of the "Resource-Program" is not satisfactory. There are no concrete agreements on cooperation between the members of the CMEA on any of the objects of the Resource-Program.[52]

Since 14 years had passed between the first session that had the Resource-Program on its agenda and the 33rd Session of the PCTA and no tangible results could be reported, some of the projects had already become obsolete with time. This was true for the most advanced of the projects, producing phosphate in the Iraqi desert, near the settlement of Akashat. The project was talked about for so long and the Iraqi side kept in suspense that the Iraqi policy-makers decided to come to a close. They sold the project to a Belgian company in 1975.[53]

## Conclusion

The archival material shows that the reform efforts of the late 1960s and 1970s led to a gradual change in intrabloc procedures. These changes were not limited to the general secretaries of the Communist Parties or the prime ministers of the Eastern Bloc who were involved in the negotiations between 1969 and 1971. They are also discernable on the level of the directors of state combines and economic experts. More information was mutually shared and the different dialogues that took place were more engaged than before. Even if intrabloc cooperation remained rudimentary, this increased level of coordination necessitated higher levels of mutual trust. The fact that the CMEA was gaining in importance despite all its contradictions was recognized by contemporary Western scholars, as well, and led to creative comparisons:

> In many respects, however, CMEA is like the bumble-bee which according to the laws of aeronautical engineering, cannot fly, because its wings are too small for its body; but, never having heard of aeronautical engineering, the bumble-bee flies anyway.[54]

Although the Complex-Program led to the realization of at least two large-scale intrabloc projects in the energy sector, the same cannot be said about the economic cooperation between East and South. This failure in fulfilling grand designs was not due to a lack of ideas. The so-called Resource-Program was envisioned to be such a grand design that would suit both the needs of the Eastern Bloc and of the Global South. It remained on the agenda for the bigger part of the 1970s but was a failure, since none of the projects were realized in the end. Where the

Complex-Program proved successful in the realm of the PCTA was the increased level of information exchange between its members. Despite the failure of the Resource-Program, cooperation schemes between CMEA member states and countries of the Global South were evolving during the 1970s on a smaller scale.

One such scheme to build a cement industry in Syria from scratch will be the main topic of the next chapter. This project between Bulgaria, East Germany, and Syria was regarded as a prime example of cooperation in the spirit of the Complex-Program, because two members of the CMEA were combining their relative strength to deliver tangible results in a chosen "developing country." However, the project was plagued by a wide range of problems that will be analyzed. Concerning the Resource-Program one could think that its failure was attributable to the lack of entrepreneurial spirit on the side of socialist trade representatives and their inability to cooperate with each other on the world market. This view is inaccurate, as will be shown later. Its failure reveals more about intrabloc power relations than about the lack of competence of the trade officials of the Eastern Bloc.

## Notes

1 Pittaway, *Eastern Europe*, 75–8.
2 Brabant, *Economic Integration in Eastern Europe*, 136.
3 Brabant, 136.
4 Zwass, *Der Rat Für Gegenseitige Wirtschaftshilfe*, 83–84; Brabant, *Economic Integration in Eastern Europe*, 79–81.
5 Much more clearly visible is the influence of the events in Czechoslovakia on domestic reform programs like in Hungary where economic reforms were stalled from 1968 on till the mid-1980s.
6 Zwass, *Der Rat Für Gegenseitige Wirtschaftshilfe*, 83–4.
7 Zwass, 83–4.
8 Brabant, *Economic Integration in Eastern Europe*, 85.
9 Brabant, 85–6.
10 Brabant, 86–7.
11 Brabant, 86–7.
12 Zwass, *Der Rat Für Gegenseitige Wirtschaftshilfe*, 86–7.
13 Zwass, 86–7.
14 Zwass, 90.
15 Zwass, 107.
16 Zwass, 108–9.
17 Zwass, 89.
18 Brabant, *Economic Integration in Eastern Europe*, 91.
19 Brabant, 91.
20 One couldn't simply change TR for US dollars or West German marks.
21 Zwass, *Der Rat Für Gegenseitige Wirtschaftshilfe*, 56–60.
22 Zwass, 59.
23 Stone, "CMEA's International Investment Bank," 50.
24 Stone, 58.
25 Stone, 59.
26 Stone, 64.
27 Stone, 61–2.
28 Stone, 60–1.
29 Stone, 48.

30 Stone, 62.
31 Stone, 67–9.
32 Lavigne, "Implications of Reform in Eastern Europe," 165–6.
33 "Bericht über die 16. Tagung der Ständigen Kommission des RGW für die Koordinierung der Technischen Unterstützung, 29.-30. Mai 1969, Jerewan," dated 16 June 1969, Barch Berlin, DE 1/54932.
34 Ibid.
35 Ibid.
36 "A KGST-tagállamok és a fejlődő országok közötti gazdasági- és müszaki együttmüködés általános elvei," dated 06 October 1969, MNL Budapest, XIX-A-90-c 88. doboz; and "Előterjesztés A Müszaki Segitségnyujtási Állondó Kormánybizottság részére," dated 01 November 1969, ibid.
37 "Kapcsolataink A Fejlődő Országokkal," dated 12 October 1965, MNL Budapest, XIX-A-90-c 153. doboz.
38 "Bericht über die 20. Tagung der Ständigen Kommission des RGW für die Koordinierung der Technischen Unterstützung (17.-19.11.1970, Moskau)," dated 25 November 1970, Barch Berlin, DE 1/54932.
39 Annex to the letter "Arbeitsplan der SKTU für 1971 (Punkt 4)," dated 18 February 1971, ibid.
40 In the original: "Als Beispiel dafür dienen die Vorschläge für die Jahresarbeitspläne, die uns ungeordnet, ungesichtet, als Abklatsch [sic!] der Zuarbeiten aller Länderdelegationen zur Stellungnahme übersandt werden."
41 Annex to the letter "Arbeitsplan der SKTU für 1971 (Punkt 4)," dated 18 February 1971, Barch Berlin, DE 1/54932.
42 Pencil written note titled "Betr: RGW-Arbeit," without date, Barch Berlin, DE 1/54932.
43 Ibid.
44 "Delegationsberatung für 19. Tagung der SK-Tech. Unterstützung der EL, die Ende Mai 1970 stattfinden soll," dated 06 May 1970, ibid.
45 "Bericht über die 21. Tagung der Ständigen Kommission für die Koordinierung der Technischen Unterstützung (11.-14. Mai 1971, Moskau)," dated 28 May 1971, ibid.
46 "Bericht über die 22. Tagung der Ständigen Kommission des RGW für die Koordinierung der Technischen Unterstützung (5.-7. Januar 1972, Moskau)," dated 17 January 1972, ibid.
47 See "Tagungen der SKTU (GD-Tagungen – Direktiven, Berichte, Informationen, Tender)," without date, Barch Berlin, DL 2/22846.
48 "Bericht der Außenhandelsbetriebe der DDR über die Tagung der Leiter der AHO der ML/RGW zu Fragen der Erweisung technischer Unterstützung an Entwicklungsländer beim Bau von Industriebetrieben und anderen Objekten in Moskau vom 8. bis 11. April 1975," dated 14 May 1977, ibid.
49 "Bericht über die 25. Tagung der SKTU (31.10.-3.11.72, Moskau)," dated 07 November 1972, Barch Berlin, DE 1/55319.
50 "Bericht über die 27. Tagung der SKTU (14.-16.11.1973, Moskau)," dated 23 November 1973, Barch Berlin, DE 1/55820.
51 "Bericht über die 30. Tagung der Ständigen Kommission des RGW für die Koordinierung der Technischen Unterstützung (4. Bis 5. Juni 1975, Moskau)," dated 12 June 1975, ibid.
52 "Bericht über die 33. Tagung der Ständigen Kommission des RGW für die Koordinierung der Technischen Unterstützung (17.-18.11.1976, Moskau)," dated 30 Novemeber 1976, ibid.
53 "Information über die Haltung des Irak zum RGW bzw. zum Dialog der arabischen Länder mit der EWG," dated 18 September 1975, PA AA, MFAA ZR 2406/82.
54 Smith, "Recent Developments in East-West Economic Relations," 173.

# 4 The allure of the West

## Disintegration in the East?

### Questioning the prevalence of doing business with the West

The Complex-Program had been generally regarded as a failure or even as counterproductive both by contemporaries and by scholars.[1] Many scholars thought of it as the last significant action of the CMEA before its dissolution in 1991.[2] This even led to the question, if the Complex-Program and the CMEA itself did not only hinder but actually destroyed trade.[3] At least from a Western perspective, the 1970s have been overshadowed by détente and rapprochement between East and West. In the period between May 1972 and May 1974 alone, the Soviet Union and the US concluded 41 of 105 treaties the two countries could agree on between 1933 and 1980.[4] The political efforts to improve mutual relations culminated in 1975 with the signing of the Helsinki Accords and lost some of their momentum in the second half of the 1970s.[5]

These diplomatic activities were accompanied by economic initiatives. With tensions reduced, an atmosphere more favorable to inter-bloc trade than before could unfold. East–West trade had already started to increase significantly in the mid-1960s after the Cuban Crisis but this process was accelerated in the early 1970s. The import of capital goods by the CMEA countries from OECD member states increased from 998 million US dollars in 1965 to 9.84 billion US dollars in 1975.[6] This was an almost ten-fold increase over the course of ten years. The actual trade volume, including consumer goods, was much bigger. Exports to OECD countries increased from 6.6 billion US dollars in 1971 to 42.3 billion US dollars in 1980, while imports expanded at roughly the same pace from 7.0 billion US dollars in 1971 to 42.8 billion US dollars in 1980.[7] The Soviet Union in particular used the new opportunities to import also massive amounts of grain every year to increase its meat production. It soon became one of the biggest actors on the international grain market, buying more than 15 % of the grain available.[8] This example illustrates the trade dependencies that emerged between East and West in the 1970s very well.

The almost ten-fold increase of capital goods imports by the CMEA countries followed a new development plan in many of its member states. Importing capital goods often meant importing sophisticated Western technology from the OECD countries that was to be integrated in the production processes of the planned economies. In the view of the socialist decision-makers this strategy promised quick results that could not have been achieved with Soviet technology.[9] The import of Western technology was to be financed on credit. The plan was to pay the money back with increased exports enabled by the new technologies and higher productivity.[10] But at first, this strategy meant rapidly increasing debts. Poland under the leadership of Edward Gierek, one of the strongest advocates of the new strategy, accumulated foreign debts amounting to roughly 20 billion US dollars at the end of the 1970s.[11] The share of the CMEA member states among Polish imports decreased to slightly less than 50 % in the 1970s.[12] The development of most socialist countries of Eastern Europe corresponded to the Polish pattern, be it Romania under Ceausescu's leadership or the GDR of the 1970s.[13]

There is no doubt about the validity of the developments described previously. But the fact that the CMEA countries forged new ties with the West doesn't mean that their socialist neighbors became irrelevant for them or even neglected by them. Even the rather extreme case of Poland shows that the majority of its trade was still conducted within the realms of the CMEA. In scholarship, this fact has been overshadowed by the new quality of East–West exchange in the 1970s. Although the import of sophisticated Western technology probably was a very amazing occurrence for Western observers and socialist planners alike, the bread-and-butter trade took place inside socialist Eastern Europe and thus inside the CMEA. It is thus uncalled-for to label the Council for Mutual Economic Assistance as a near dead institution in the early 1970s as is often done in the literature cited previously.

The socialist planners and decision-makers invested a considerable sum of energy and money during the 1970s in order to increase their trade turnover and economic ties with their neighbors within the bloc and with the countries of the Global South. It is the aim of this chapter to show the connection between the East and the South and the relevance the CMEA had gathered by the early 1970s by looking at a multilateral cooperation attempt between the GDR, the People's Republic of Bulgaria, and Syria. After a short introduction into the evolution of East European–Syrian relations, the focus will be placed on the erection of a cement industry in Syria allowing conclusions to be drawn about the importance of the CMEA, inter-socialist cooperation, and the chances and problems of providing "technical assistance" to a "developing country" like Syria.

## Syria and the Soviet bloc

Trade relations between the CMEA countries and Syria were quite meager up to the mid-1950s. The first Soviet–Syrian trade agreement had been signed in 1955, the same year the first East German and Czechoslovakian treaties had been ratified.[14] In 1956 the share of the CMEA countries in Syria's overall trade stood at just little above 4 %.[15] Economic and technical cooperation started to gain momentum in October 1957 with a joint Soviet–Syrian treaty and credit agreement in which the Soviet Union promised the Syrian government 78.75 million Rubles in credit for the construction of 24 objects, mostly in the field of infrastructure.[16]

This early takeoff of mutual relations was abruptly stopped when Syria entered into a union with Nasser's Egypt forming the United Arab Republic in 1958.[17] Nasser could thereby counter the increasing Soviet influence in Syria despite being himself reliant on Soviet help in the aftermath of the Suez Crisis which illustrates the fact that right from the beginning of mutual relations, Third World leaders didn't necessarily back down in front of any superpower, even if they were dependent on them. The union between Egypt and Syria lasted for three years until a military coup in Syria brought about its dissolution. The coup of 1961 was followed by eight additional ones up to 1966. By that time, it had become clear that the Ba'ath Party had come to dominate Syrian politics.[18]

The relations between the socialist bloc and Syria intensified again in the 1960s with the takeover of the Ba'ath Party in Damascus.[19] After initial skepticism on both sides after the aspiration to power by Hafiz al-Asad in 1970, who became the Syrian Ba'athist strongman, the mutual relations continued to take a steady development.[20] This development was also driven by the worsening of relations between the socialist bloc and post-Nasserite Egypt. Nasser's successor, Sadat, had thrown his Soviet advisers out of Egypt and tried to negotiate a peace agreement with Israel after the Yom Kippur War.[21] Despite certain common interests, the ideological basis between Ba'athists and East European communists was shaky since Ba'athists were neither Marxists nor adherents of scientific socialism.[22]

Already in the 1960s, the socialist countries of Eastern Europe, especially the GDR and the Soviet Union, were sending experts to Syria to train administrative and technical personnel. This was characterized by a certain degree of work sharing. The experts from East Berlin, for example, took the task of strengthening the party apparatus of the Ba'athists and expanding their power base among the populace.[23] The same is true for the state-planning apparatus. East German experts played a prominent role in the – at least superficial – Sovietization of the state institutions. Under their auspices the Syrian Council of Ministers, the State Planning Commission, and the Central Bureau of Statistics were established or severely transformed.[24] These socialist experts thus helped the Ba'ath regime to nationalize important parts of the economy and to build up a planning apparatus that resembled the socialist bloc to a certain degree. While Soviet experts were also active in the civilian sector, their focus was, in contrast to the East Germans, more on the military sector.[25]

This transfer of administrative know-how was accompanied by a transfer of technical know-how and credit flows from the Eastern Bloc to Syria meant to contribute to a fast development of the Syrian economy. The five-year plans Syrian officials started to advocate were heavily influenced by Soviet thinking and put an emphasis on the buildup of heavy industry and infrastructure. The most important project of the late 1960s and early 1970s in this regard was the Euphrates dam between Aleppo and Raqqa, built with money, materials, and technical personnel from the Soviet Union. The construction of the dam was bound to a Soviet credit of approximately 150 million US dollars.[26] The works on the dam project had started in 1968 and involved ca. 850 Soviet specialists along with 10,000 Syrian laborers.[27] Once the dam had been finished in 1973, it became the major source of power generation in Syria providing 95 % of the country's electric power in 1978, thus laying the infrastructural groundwork for industrialization.[28] After having put a focus on developing agriculture in the 1960s, the 1970s were thus meant to promote industrialization in Syria.[29] The second most important task of the five-year plans of the 1970s was the building of a cement industry in Syria from scratch.[30]

## Cement for Syria: proving the merits of CMEA cooperation?

These plans included the construction of eight cement factories with a joint output capacity of several million tons a year by the end of the 1970s.[31] It is not clear from the documents available how the Syrian plans evolved internally. Access to Syrian archival documents is impossible at the moment. It is possible that the Syrian planners made their decisions where and when to build which factory, with only indirect assistance by experts from the Eastern bloc. It is unclear to what extent their decisions were influenced by political motives in the sense of inner-Syrian power asymmetries and to what extent by purely economic thinking. A look at the prospect building destinations shows that the factories were to be erected at the Syrian coast and the Damascus area, both power bases of the Asad regime and the most populous areas of the country. Thus, the chosen destinations are sensible according to a political logic but also according to a more economically inclined thinking, since cement as a building material was needed the most in urban and fast-growing areas.

After the Syrian planning entities had worked out the guidelines for the project, they were published and open for competition. The GDR filed a tender in 1971 which was supposed to be a guiding example for the cooperation between two socialist countries and a former colony striving for economic development. The GDR state combine for heavy machine building[32] (SKET) was to provide the engineering know-how, the equipment, the factory design, and training courses for Syrians, while the Bulgarian state building organization "Tekhnoeksportstroi" (TES) was to assemble the factories at their planned destinations in Syria according to the technical documentation delivered by the GDR experts. This cooperation and division of labor was to prove its worth by building three cement factories with a combined capacity of 1 million tons between 1973 and 1975 in a first stage of the project.[33] The proposal possessed a direct link to the reform program of the CMEA, the discussions of which had started in 1968. The guidelines of the so-called "Complex-Program" were finalized and agreed upon in 1971 and aimed at a further and accelerated development of economic ties between the CMEA member states. But this was not limited to the borders of the CMEA. Members were urged to cooperate also outside the bloc, to promote the aims and working methods of the CMEA, especially in the Southern hemisphere by multilateral cooperation.

This comprised as much a political as an economic logic. By joining forces in the South, the respective socialist countries could hope for economies of scale. They could reduce costs by combining their strengths and improving their overall efficiency by focusing on what they could do best. In this particular example, the

GDR provided engineering know-how and sophisticated technology, while the Bulgarians promised to assemble the factories at high speed and low cost. On paper, the CMEA partners should have increased their competitiveness by such measures and should have improved their relative position against the West by being able to offer better terms and conditions. This, as the socialist decision-makers hoped, would show the countries of the Global South the advantages of the socialist system in a very practical – and by building huge factories also highly touchable sense – and produce political gains as an automatic side effect. For the Bulgarians, this had the additional benefit that the East Germans – who had much closer ties with Damascus – could work as a door opener by taking them as a junior partner.

Of course, all rhetoric aside, the GDR and the People's Republic of Bulgaria at no time intended to build a whole cement industry of several million tons capacity free of charge. The whole tender for eight cement factories was worth 670 million Valutamark[34] which equates to roughly 270 million US dollars.[35] Twenty percent of the sum was reserved for assembling the factories and thus for the Bulgarian partner of the GDR contractor.[36] This leads to the question of the true nature of the arrangement. Officially, the East European experts – and also the Syrian ones – defined the whole project as "technical assistance" which was the most common equivalent for "development aid" in the East. It is worth dissecting the terminology again at this point. Both terms are highly problematic and get easily associated with a certain kind of generosity that is rather alien to the practical meaning of the projects labeled "development aid" or "technical assistance."

The most basic definition of "aid" is that it should contain a certain grant element. This however, is a matter of definition as giving credit to someone who is deemed not creditworthy at all by market consensus could already be defined as a grant. The moral issues attached to this question and the implications of different definitions were neither discussed by the East Germans and Bulgarians, nor by the Syrians. What they considered as an aid element was the transfer of technology from the East to the South, the training of Syrian personnel in running the machines, and the conditions of the tender. Before 1976, the Syrians had to pay the bills partially in hard currency and partially in so called Clearing Dollar. The former was fully convertible and consisted of US dollars that could be transferred out of the country. The latter were neither convertible nor transferable. This meant that they could only be used to buy Syrian goods. Since Syria was mainly exporting cotton and oil, and both raw materials were in high demand in the bloc, payment in Clearing Dollar meant payment in cotton and crude oil. To secure strategic resources was – at least initially – an important part of the whole story. By exporting factories, the GDR not only hoped to receive money but also resources for its domestic industry.[37] This was very much in line with the agreements concluded inside the Permanent Commission for Technical Assistance.

With the beginning of 1976, the payment system was altered and the Syrians as well as the East Germans and other bloc members changed their trade to full convertibility, meaning complete payment in US dollars.[38] Nevertheless, the Syrians had to pay only a fraction of ten to 15 % beforehand in cash, 85 to 90 % of the costs were financed by the East Germans on credit that had to be repaid within the long-term period of up to ten years at a rather low interest rate of 4 %.[39] Thus, the Syrians could watch the factories being built without emptying their pockets for them, at least for the time being.

To be fair, the East Germans made it clear to their Syrian partners that although the project had political implications, economics were the main motive.[40] They had chosen to work together with the Syrians and Bulgarians in building cement factories, not only because of close political ties – though these were important to cement the deal – but because it fit into the export program of the GDR. They utilized economies of scale by applying their designs for a future Cuban cement factory to Syria. This copy and paste approach lowered the costs.[41] The Syrians on the other hand were keen not to pay too high a price and to compare different offers. They put particular effort in securing favorable terms of payment.[42] The main long-term economic goal of the East Germans is well expressed in the following statement on approving the second stage of the project by the Deputy Minister for Foreign Trade Friedmar Clausnitzer, who chaired the "developing countries" section:

> Three cement factories worth 100 million VM will be exported to the SAR by Invest-Export on the basis of the concluded treaty. With your request to approve the planned expansion of the deliveries already agreed on, the GDR will get a monopoly position on the cement sector in the SAR. Under this point of view, your request is in general approved, since, furthermore, we can count on future deliveries of equipment and spare parts by the GDR.[43]

A more detailed reasoning is given in a letter by the East German state combine to the director of the credit department inside the Ministry for Foreign Trade:

1 The intrusion of other suppliers into the Syrian market has to be prevented. . . . If we don't succeed in impeding the invasion of other suppliers, the GDR will lose the Syrian market from 1978 on . . .
2 The repeatability of the expansions wished for by the Syrian side is improving the profitability decisively.
3 By relocating the activities for exporting cement factories to other markets, the advantages will be lost and can't be recovered in the prevailing stiff competition . . .
4 The competition for selling cement factories is intensifying continuously, because the cutback and downturn of investment activity in the construction sector and the crises in the capitalist industrial countries require [them] to utilize the capacities provided during the cement boom for exporting cement factories.
5 Therefore we have to make maximum use of the good conditions prevailing in the SAR[44]

The planners in East Berlin wanted to use the opportunity to acquire a monopoly position. Labeling their deal as "technical assistance" and providing long-term credits accordingly was providing the necessary entry card for them. This had a certain sense of economic imperialism. But it was born not out of strength but out of a perceived and very real weakness. They rightfully feared that with the first oil crisis unfolding in 1973, the good times of the investment boom were over. Western companies which had built up capacities in the years before were facing stagnating or declining demand at home. They thus had to look for new customers abroad at the very time when the CMEA countries were looking for new economic and political partners abroad, as well. The GDR thought to have found a safe haven in Ba'athist Syria that would do business with them and would shield them from the most severe consequences of direct competition with the West.

At first look the whole arrangement shows some asymmetries: the East Germans provided funding, the technology, the building plans, and technical training. The Bulgarians simply lend their hands in doing what the East Germans wanted them to do without contributing any kind of sophisticated machinery or technology themselves. The Syrians mainly stood at the sidelines and watched the others working. So, this setting seems rather to reproduce power asymmetries than to alleviate the situation of neither the Bulgarians who were inferior in their technological level inside the bloc in comparison to the GDR nor of the Syrians. The reality, however, proved to be more complicated and not as clear as the expectations raised by the setting of the project.

## Emerging complications

The East Germans had arranged with their Syrian partner, the state-run General Organization for Executing Industrial Projects (GOEIP), that the Syrians would level the building ground and provide storage capacity beforehand. This was the responsibility of the Syrian state building company Syrabco. Then the East Germans would send the first shipment to Syrian harbors and the Bulgarian builders would travel to Syria.[45] This arrangement already contained too many variables in order to work out properly. The Syrians did not manage to level the ground and provide storage at every future building site in time. The reasons for this were partially due to mismanagement and partially to the outcome of the Yom Kippur War which caused severe economic problems and labor shortages.[46] This alone was not necessarily a fatal problem. The East German ships with the machines and documentations had reached their Syrian harbor without delay, so the first steps in building could have been undertaken. But what aggravated the situation was the fact that despite the shipment having been unloaded, big parts of it didn't make it to the building sites. Five hundred tons of material were still lost two years after they had been unloaded.[47] They had simply disappeared from the Syrian harbors. This, however, made any time plans fully dispensable.

To add insult to injury, the problems didn't stop there. Even though the factories were designed in the GDR and pre-fabricated in Magdeburg, Dessau, and Berlin, they required significant imports from abroad. In this particular case – building cement factories in Syria in the mid-1970s – this meant imports from the CSSR and the Soviet Union. Production cooperation with these two countries caused problems for the project: the combine "Schwermaschinenbau Ernst Thälmann" in Magdeburg had delegated the main responsibility for the execution of the project to its subsidiary "Zementanlagenbau (ZAB) Dessau" which itself had asked the combine "Kombinat Elektroprojekt und Anlagenbau Berlin (KEAB)" to provide the electrical equipment for the factories. Since KEAB could not produce all parts on its own, it cooperated with a Czechoslovak combine and was reliant on its know-how. Unfortunately for the East Germans, the Czechoslovak combine could not deliver the electrical equipment in time causing further delays on the building sites in Syria.[48]

It is clear from the archival documents that even for building rather unsophisticated, non-high-tech cement factories, the East German planners relied on a rather sophisticated and elaborate import system. The GDR had at least three different suppliers of electrical equipment for cement factories in the mid-1970s and also three different kind of customers, at least implicitly differentiated by their technological level: for a project in Bulgaria, they relied on Romanian equipment, for a project in Yugoslavia they used Belgian equipment, and in Syria Czechoslovak equipment.[49] Belgian electrics could most likely not be acquired without paying the full price in convertible currencies like US dollar or West German Mark. The East German experts, while writing to the Ministry of Foreign Trade, made it clear that they didn't regard all of their three suppliers as being on equal footing with each other. They wrote about the prospective cement factory in Bulgaria:

> The electrical equipment is being imported from Romania. A conversion of this production line for export to non-socialist markets [non-CMEA countries] is not possible because of the technological level of the electrics.[50]

This illustrates that socialist planners always had three overlapping but different worlds in mind while doing business. Difficulties arose also with imports from the Soviet Union. The main ovens for the factories were imported from a Soviet combine and directly delivered to Syria. While installing the ovens on the construction site, the workers and engineers noted the poor quality of the welding:

> The quality of the welding conducted in the Soviet Union proved to be a significant problem. . . . The chief engineer of the Soviet producing factory who later arrived in Syria acknowledged that the standards previously agreed on had been neglected but thought it not necessary to repair the already assembled oven.
>
> An agreement between Invest-Export and Mashino-Export is imminent, since, according to the opinion of our experts, 41m of the welding have to be repaired (oven length 60m). Meanwhile, the defects have become known to the Syrian customer. Since we promised him a correction of all defects without delay, no official action has been taken on a higher level, yet.[51]

The problems with the Soviet oven and the delaying tactics of the Soviet authorities caused another postponement of three months.[52] The manifold problems forced the GDR officials to try to renegotiate with their Bulgarian builders. But their efforts were to no avail. The Bulgarians were waiting in Syria and they didn't care much that equipment was lost in Syrian harbors, that Czechoslovak and Soviet suppliers didn't deliver in time, or that the Syrian partners didn't keep up with their promises. This does, of course, not mean that the GDR planners and engineers were without any responsibility for the complicated situation. They at least partially acknowledged their own mistakes, like handing over the design plans too late.[53] But they could point out, especially to the Bulgarian builders, that the majority of the problems were beyond their control. The fact that there was nothing to do for the TES workers was not hindering them from filing bills which they presented to the GDR officials demanding payment. The Bulgarian company also demanded an extra compensation for the delays which led to an unplanned payment of one million US dollars.[54] Since the Syrians didn't raise the budget for the project, the money dented the revenues of the GDR. There was no space for intrabloc solidarity.

This put the East Germans under pressure and made the issue a top priority, alerting the Foreign Trade Minister, Sölle, to take action.[55] Although they didn't like it, they had to pay the Bulgarians and calm the Syrian officials who wanted to see progress. When the work could finally get started on most building sites, the East Germans wanted the Bulgarians to use their time reserves, so that the plan could still be fulfilled. But they refused and even had less personnel on the building sites than had been promised originally.[56] They even threatened to withdraw all their workers and in one case unilaterally did so.[57] On top of that, some of the buildings already erected were of such bad quality that East German and Syrian experts demanded them torn down and built anew.[58] When the Bulgarians started to agitate the Syrians claiming the delays and quality problems were the fault of the East Germans, tensions started to boil.[59] Luckily for the East Germans, the Syrians didn't believe the story and hired Indian consultants who blamed the Bulgarians and convinced the Syrians to demand from the East Germans to get rid of the Bulgarian subcontractor:

> The danger is immanent that the Syrian side will accuse us of the delays. There are even voices in the Syrian public which talk of a failure of the GDR's industry. . . . Our Syrian partners and their Indian consultants have recommended us repeatedly to appoint a more flexible subcontractor [than Tekhnoeksportstroi] for the construction.[60]

## Sidelining the comrades

This provided an interesting situation: A "Third World" country was being advised by another one, in this case Indian experts, in a project that was meant to be a "First World" affair and a unilateral transfer of technology by a benevolent developed country. Power relations on the ground proved not to be equivalent to the expectations derived from a macro-perspective. The Syrians relied on their Indo-Syrian cooperation and didn't trust the East Europeans unanimously. Evidence from the Indian Archives shows that, in general, the trade volume between Syria and India was close to zero. Nevertheless, Indian engineers and planners proved to be a significant factor. In a report on the visit of the Indian Minister of Industry, George Fernandes, to Syria, Iraq, Kuwait, and Jordan in October 1977, the report states:

> India's trade with Syria specially since 1968–69 is practically one-sided. India's imports from Syria are negligible. In 1975–76, the value of India's exports to Syria was about Rs 2 crores [ca. 3 mil US $] and imports were practically nil. The exports mainly consist of jute manufactures, spices and engineering goods, such as, bicycle parts and diesel engines. Our participation in projects is mainly confined to the consultancy field. Development Consultants Pvt. Ltd., Calcutta, have undertaken a consultancy contract for the design of 7 cement plants and have also been awarded contract for supervising the erection and operation of these plants.[61]

This statement is misleading, since the plants were designed by East German engineers. The annual reports by the Indian embassy in Damascus also show that the engineering consultancy company from Calcutta had on average not more than 15 engineers stationed in Syria. The company had started its work in Damascus in 1970.[62] The number of Indian consultants was by no means sufficient to supervise the whole process of erecting a cement industry in Syria nor of monitoring all building sites. Nevertheless, the Indian documents show that the influence of the Indian experts seemed to have been deeper than what was clear to the East Germans who rarely mentioned them. The documents also show that despite tendencies of Sovietization in Ba'athist Syria and despite the fact that trade relations between India and Syria were minimal, a handful of engineers from a country not admired for its technological achievements at that time, could exert a decisive influence and have meaningful leverage. They obviously belonged to a system of checks and balances envisioned by the Syrians.

For the GDR officials this meant a dilemma: if they followed the advice of the Indian consultants, they would risk angering their Bulgarian partners with whom they still had to work together inside the bloc after this project. The political benefit of two socialist countries helping a former colony hand in hand would have vanished. On the other hand, doing nothing meant angering the Syrians and potentially taking the full blame for the impending failure of the project. This could result in all contracts being suspended and lost to a competitor, in the worst case a competitor from the capitalist West.

This danger was real since the Asad regime was contemplating an economic opening to the West from time to time. Despite Syria's anti-Israeli policies and prominent role in the Six Days War and the Yom Kippur War, US president Richard Nixon visited the country from 15–16 June 1974. Following his visit diplomatic relations – which had been broken by the Syrians in 1967 – were taken up again between the US and Asad's Syria. Nixon also had promised Asad significant amounts of economic aid. But as the regime realized that they weren't high up on the priority list of US economic aid, they severed the ties again. Unnecessary to say, that the whole episode had alarmed the socialist countries, foremost the Soviet Union.[63] A rapprochement between Syria and the West would have also had severe repercussions for the position of the minor socialist countries in Syria like the GDR or Bulgaria. This provided the political background for the East German fears expressed in the archival documents.

Threats were thus lurking everywhere. They were coming from the West in the form of big companies like Krupp or Klöckner from West Germany, but also from eastern competitors such as Romania. When East Berlin didn't reply for six months to a request by the Syrian government to build – despite the difficulties – even more cement factories in the late 1970s, than had been agreed on, the Romanian government offered to fill the gap and to provide cheap credit. This alarmed East German officials. They used their influence in Syria to delay the project.[64] As is evident in the letters from the East German embassy in Damascus, there was another particular problem with the Romanians that gave their efforts a certain sense of treason:

> In accordance with SKET [Schwermaschinenbaukombinat Ernst Thälmann] all efforts should be made to prevent the [cement] factory currently erected by the GDR in Musulmiye to be expanded by the SRR [Socialist Republic of Romania], because they are bound by cooperation agreements to the FRG [Federal Republic of Germany].[65]

If the East German officials feared one competitor the most, it was the West Germans, even if they came disguised in the form of Romanian state companies. Since they regarded Syria as their home turf, they wanted to shut the West Germans out of Ba'athist Syria as best as possible. This very multi-layered fear of certain competitors becomes clear from another example. In 1975, the East German planners realized that they could not design and pre-fabricate all the factories demanded by the Syrians all by themselves. They finally had to hand over a contract for the expansion of one factory already built to a competitor. This affected the same factory the Romanians wanted to get their hands on some months earlier. They decided to plan the following:

> The company VÖEST-ALPINE Linz/Austria as licensee of SKET/ZAB Dessau is proposing the Syrian side the offer to deliver the expansion project Musulmiye 2 x 1600 t/24h utilizing GDR know-how, thereby accepting the Syrian demand to ensure full operational capability by the year 1980, VÖEST-ALPINE tries to calculate a minimal price. With this variant, if Invest-Export is not able to conclude a direct export treaty with the Syrian partner, we achieve the following:
>
> The delivery of the cement factory Musulmiye is not done by a competitor like Schneider-Creusot/France or Polysius/Krupp/FRG. These companies,

> knowing the fact that they would be expanding a factory by the GDR, would try to discriminate against the GDR cement industry. Furthermore, "these companies would get detailed insights into GDR cement factories." This means the threat of a know-how drain.[66]

VÖEST, which meant United Austrian Iron and Steel Works, was itself a state company. If they couldn't fulfill the Syrian demands themselves, the second-best option of choice for the East Germans was a state company of a non-aligned country. For reasons not explained further in the files, they thought that a company like VÖEST would not betray them, would use the imprint "designed in GDR," would not discriminate against them, and would not steal their precious know-how. However objectively real the danger was that Krupp could steal engineering know-how from the GDR in Syria, the main reason why the East Germans didn't want to cooperate with a member of the bloc, at least in this particular case of socialist Romania, were their close ties to a Western company. This seems paradoxical, since the GDR itself was importing heavily from West Germany in the 1970s.

To solve the most imminent problem of the Syrian adventure, the East German Minister for Foreign Trade wrote a letter to his colleague in Sofia. In his letter he summoned the great importance of the project for the CMEA and demanded greater efforts:

> This cooperation of two socialist countries on third markets – an example for the realization of the Complex-Program of the Council for Mutual Economic Assistance – should determine both sides to raise the quality of the mutual implementation of the contract to a level that exceeds the mere abidance by the conditions of the contract . . .
>
> The current period for the realization of the assembly is in no way on par with the economic potential of neither the GDR nor the PR Bulgaria.[67]

The results of his letter seemed meager. Inside the Ministry of Foreign Trade in East Berlin, the arguments for and against an ongoing cooperation with their Bulgarian partner were weighed in. A report on the current situation written by a representative of the main East German company for exporting capital goods "Invest-Export" for the Ministry for Foreign Trade read as follows:

> The main problem of our work with the cement objects in the SAR [Syrian Arab Republic] is the acceleration of building and assembling with the aim of the earliest possible date of full operational capability. We are sustaining delays and losses, because the efforts for realizing our goals are ever increasing. Losses are also sustained by our Syrian partner, too, since he has to import cement for a longer time period at steadily increasing prices. Syrabco and TES get all their charges paid as long as they didn't cause the problems themselves. They lack the need to tap all of their reserves.

> Contract-wise we can't enforce more vis-à-vis TES, because, unfortunately, we are always behind some conditions of the contract, like with the delivery of projects and equipment. In these cases, we have to make compromises, which do not push our goals forward but cost us a lot of money that we can't get back.[68]

The situation thus looked rather grim. The East Germans took the blame but couldn't do anything to share the responsibility or improve the situation since negotiating with TES was fruitless, because they got paid anyway. Interestingly, the writer of the report didn't associate the GDR with Bulgaria but emotionally the bond seems to have been stronger with the Syrians as he is talking of East Germans and Syrians mainly taking losses together and sharing the same fate, while the Bulgarian company TES and Syrabco profit. This seems a bit awkward since Syrabco was also a Syrian state company and it was mainly the Syrian side that was rightfully pressuring the East Europeans to stick to their timetables. The sections of the report which were meant to be positive, didn't sound quite enthusiastic either:

> Within the SAR we further try, by forceful but comradely cooperation with our Bulgarian comrades, to unlock their reserves. By doing so, we should make as few compromises as possible. How well the cooperation has already developed can be seen by the fact that TES has for a long time not issued any threats to cease working and to withdraw all their workers.[69]

The fact that missing threats by their Bulgarian partners to shut the whole building site down were seen as a sign of improvement probably illustrates the real situation quite well and demonstrates how untenable the cooperation had become. The final decision rested with the Minister for Foreign Trade, Sölle. He demanded detailed reports by his Deputy Minister, Clausnitzer, who was responsible for the "developing countries" section and a report by the country section responsible for Bulgaria. From an economic angle the situation was quite clear: the Bulgarian organization TES was not cooperative, refused responsibility, and was more interested in short-term gains than in the success of the whole project which was meant to be a showcase for socialist cooperation and solidarity. On the other hand, from a political point of view, there were good reasons for muddling through together with the Bulgarians and simply hoping for better days to come. Angering the Bulgarians could have had political repercussions throughout the bloc.

The report by the country section for Bulgaria was touching upon these sensible political issues:

> Concerning the political aspect of the behavior of socialist countries on third markets the basic principles developed at the 28th Session of the CMEA are generally referred to, striving for an ever closer cooperation. It is possible that in this context discussions could arise from time to time at meetings of

> the GDR/PR Bulgaria committee. We explicitly point out that this should not be made a big political issue, because doing so could damage the relations with the PRB. The remark has been made that the PRB showed little political understanding for problems immediately after the war broke out when they welcomed the unilateral action by the construction collective that left the building site without any regards to prior agreements.
>
> We recommend in preparation for possible discussions with the Bulgarian side to order Invest-Export to make a compilation of negative examples of the construction process in chronological order . . . the demanded change of the construction company could be used to agree on more favorable terms for cooperation on third markets with the Bulgarian side in the future.[70]

The country section for Bulgaria therefore recommended to change the construction company but to keep low profile about it. The East Germans should not raise the issue themselves before the Council for Mutual Economic Assistance, in order not to further alienate the Bulgarians, but they should nevertheless be prepared, if the Bulgarians took action. On top of detailed accusations that were to be prepared by Invest-Export the report also mentions the possibility of a general accusation of cowardice and general lack of political understanding. They are obviously referring to the conduct of the Bulgarian collective during the Yom Kippur War. Of particular interest is the suggestion to use this opportunity to cut ties with the Bulgarians for some time to pressure them to accept terms more beneficial for the East Germans in the future, since this was exactly what the decision-makers in East Berlin would try to do.

## The Lebanese liaison

The GDR officials finally decided to get rid of "Tekhnoeksportstroi," at least for the moment.[71] Finding a replacement for the Bulgarians in a short time span and under pressure by their Syrian customer proved to be no easy task. They started to search for a new partner inside the bloc at first but their efforts proved to be almost fruitless. The only interested contractor they could find came from Yugoslavia.[72] Since there are no further archival documents on negotiations between the Yugoslavian and East German side, most likely one of them did not take the offer seriously and the negotiations broke off quickly. Thus, the experts in East Berlin had to look for partners outside the bloc which they finally located in close proximity to their Syrian customer.

They were flirting with two Lebanese companies for the most urgent building sites, located in Adra – an industrial suburb of Damascus – and Hama. Their decision for prospective Lebanese partners was motivated foremost by economic considerations. They were negotiating with the two companies "Lahoud" and "Contracting and Trading Co. (C.A.T.)." Negotiations had already started in 1974.[73] The former company guaranteed the full operational capability of the plant after the assembly, which they promised to accomplish in time, but possessed the disadvantage that they wanted to be paid half in freely convertible US dollars and half in Syrian Pounds. Since US dollars were scarce, their offer thus contained drawbacks.[74]

Even more so than Lahoud, the representatives of the construction company C.A.T. offered more professionalism and entrepreneurial thinking. They agreed to share the responsibility for the whole project, even if calamities should happen that were not entirely their fault. They also accepted to start working before all machines and equipment had been delivered to the building site. The Bulgarians on the other hand had refused to do so, even if the missing equipment was needed only for the final stages of assembling. C.A.T. also promised to increase its on short notice workforce, if necessary, and to reduce the workforce, if there was no work to be done because of lack of supplies. The Bulgarian company TES had never offered such flexibility. C.A.T. agreed to be paid if certain progress on the building site had been achieved and not simply if certain pre-fixed dates had passed by – a concept rather alien to the Bulgarian company – and accepted exclusive payment in Syrian and Lebanese Pounds, so, the GDR wouldn't have to use its US dollar reserves. TES in comparison wanted 27 % of the full amount to be paid in US dollars.[75]

The Lebanese firms thus offered better terms and flexibility. They even showed greater technical expertise than the Bulgarians which meant that the GDR had to send only half of their own engineers to the building sites than were needed for the Bulgarian subcontractor. How bad things were going and how bad the experts in East Berlin regarded the quality of work of their Bulgarian partners is best illustrated by the following statement:

> The number of GDR-consultants can be reduced, if C.A.T. takes over the assembly, from 30 to 15. The experience with our cement factories currently assembled by TES in the SAR shows that – despite the promise of a complete assembly – a high contingent of GDR-consultants is required.[76]

Nevertheless, politics still played a role. At least one of the two Lebanese companies, C.A.T., possessed another advantage:

> This company [C.A.T.] was recommended to us by the Communist Party of Lebanon on the occasion of the visit of the delegation of the CP of Lebanon in the GDR. This recommendation is supported by the responsible department inside the Central Committee of the Socialist Unity Party of Germany [SED].
>
> We could hereby set a precedent on how to boost developing countries in their development by awarding such contracts.[77]

The available documents indicate that the GDR awarded each of the two Lebanese companies one contract. It is interesting that while decisions were mainly driven by economic considerations, politics always remained a strong undercurrent. The decision to hire Lebanese companies and to get rid of their Bulgarian partner had to be justified also in political terms leading to the consideration of presenting the change of partners as a virtue, as can be seen in the statement previously. The benefits of socialism were also visible by cooperating with locals. The fact that C.A.T. was recommended to East Berlin by the Lebanese CP was of great advantage and probably calmed down the conscience of East German decision-makers who had abandoned their Bulgarian comrades. Communist allegiance could also advance the necessary trust to seal a deal.

To ease the tensions between Berlin and Sofia, the talks with the Bulgarian company were continued and they were picked again as subcontractor for cement factories in Syria that were to be built in the late 1970s and early 1980s.[78] This proved a difficult situation in the meantime and the GDR officials were expecting severe criticism by the Bulgarians at the official CMEA meetings. Bulgarian representatives had already complained bilaterally to the Council of Ministers of the GDR in 1975.[79] Fortunately for the East Germans, no public disputes arose out of the issue. Inside the CMEA's Permanent Commission for Technical Assistance, both blamed the Syrians for all problems by claiming that the Syrians neither provided enough building materials, nor prepared the building sites, nor supplied adequate machinery.[80] The last point in particular is very astonishing, since it was never the task of the Syrians to provide any sophisticated machinery for the building process. This behavior clearly expresses the desire by the GDR and Bulgarian representatives to avoid an open debate about what went wrong and what could be done to improve the situation for the benefit of the whole bloc in the future. Instead, they chose the more comfortable and short-term solution of blaming the outsiders who were not sitting at the CMEA negotiating table.

As far as the Lebanese companies are concerned, there is no further mention of them in the files of the late 1970s. So, their fate remains unclear. Considering the outbreak of the civil war in Lebanon in the mid-1970s, it is quite possible that the cooperation had to be discontinued because of the devastations caused by the conflict. This made the shift back to the former Bulgarian partner look as being forced by the circumstances and not taken out of free will. But since the most imminent problems had been solved by employing the Lebanese companies, renewing cooperation with the Bulgarians promised to ease political tensions looming inside the CMEA, while having no immediate negative side effects like angering the Syrian partners.

This does not mean that everything was fine in the long run. Since the Bulgarians and East Germans refused to solve the immediate causes for their cooperation complications, there was no assurance that these problems would not resurface to haunt them again. And indeed, problems arose again in 1979 and 1980. The coordination between the East German state combines and the Bulgarian building company TES hadn't improved in the meantime. Delays occurred that demanded extra payments by the East German authorities. The East German chief engineers in Syria even tried to speed up the work of their Bulgarian builders by promising them a premium of more than 160,000 US dollars, if they managed to complete the assembly in time. The plan failed utterly. Not only did the Bulgarians demand extra payment, although they hadn't achieved the targets set, the East German export organization "Invest-Export" and the State Planning Commission refused responsibility, since neither a chief engineer nor the corresponding state combine were allowed to distribute bonuses in their view.[81]

## A success story?

Nevertheless, the factories were built and fully operational in the end. Some of them even exceeded their planned production capacity by up to 15 %.[82] So the whole project could be called a success. Syria contained no cement industry worthy of that name at the start of the 1970s. At the end of the decade it could produce more than four million tons annually.[83] This was development in a basic sense. The reasoning behind it was to produce Syrian cement for Syrian buildings, abolishing the need for imports. At the beginning of the first stage of the project, the SAR had to import almost 4 million tons of cement annually at a price of 60 US dollars per ton.[84] Substituting all imports of cement thus meant saving more than 200 million dollars of imports every year. This was an effect the planners already had in mind beforehand.[85] Producing Syrian cement also meant more jobs for a rapidly growing population.[86] It seems evident that providing jobs for young people is urgent in a society that is expanding fast and threatened by unrest resulting from high unemployment among young people. However, this argument is hard to find in the sources of the CMEA countries. That the creation of a sizable number of jobs in the field of industry indeed played a big role for Syrian and other decision-makers from "developing countries" is confirmed by former negotiators of the CMEA member states.[87]

On a more abstract level, the whole project can be defined as industrialization by import substitution. Recurring to chapter two, this was no development method invented by Soviet economists as it was very popular throughout the 20th century in many different countries.[88] Economically, it can be defined as a simple Solow-model. It was based on the assumption that developing countries needed to build up a capital stock fast in order to close the economic gap. To achieve this aim, they were in need of external help. This assumption was also very popular in the West and guided Western development experts and economists to a significant degree, at least up to the early 1980s.[89] A question not asked in the documents but of economic importance concerns the opportunity costs: were the cement factories worth the price? The calculation includes not only the 270 million US dollars in credit but also the potential costs and benefits of projects rejected instead of the cement plan. To answer this question, access to Syrian documents would be needed.

From a political perspective, the project was not the success story originally intended. The multilateral cooperation between two countries of the socialist bloc – one of them considered severely backward at least up to the Second World War – and a former colony proved to be a near-failure. It didn't lead to catastrophe but the cooperation had to be suspended for some time and the GDR officials had to choose another partner from outside the bloc. The problems could not be hidden from the Syrians. The project thus couldn't provide substantial propaganda gains for the CMEA in the South, even if the factories were built eventually.

Concerning the relationship triangle between the GDR, Bulgaria, and Syria, the economically most advanced of the three countries was not the one always in charge of the situation. When the project had started, the GDR officials were often pressured by others, be it their Bulgarian partners from inside the bloc, their

Syrian customers, or the outside consultants from India who had a decisive influence in a critical phase of the project. The East Germans managed to survive but they were nervous that they could lose. They feared competition from both the West – especially West Germany – and from the East. At times, they suspected the Romanians of sabotaging their plans and offering better conditions to the Syrians. This shows that solidarity inside the bloc and between the bloc and the emerging nation states was more than merely an empty promise, as can be seen in the careful communication between Berlin and Sofia. However, it stood on very shaky grounds. Solidarity was affordable, as long as the "economics" of solidarity proved to be beneficial for recipient and donor.

Problems arose also from the complexity of the whole project. Building a cement industry in Syria demanded not only close cooperation between the Bulgarian and East German partners. It also demanded sophisticated planning beforehand, much of it being the responsibility of the planners in the East German state combines. The cement factories had to be designed and pre-fabricated, complex logistics had to be envisioned and organized, engineers and experts had to be summoned who were able to work under different conditions in Syria and to provide understanding for the particular problems of their Syrian customers, including difficult negotiations. A certain Sovietization of the Syrian administration by the socialist bloc countries probably had eased cultural differences and differences in working attitudes between East German and Syrian state planners, but they didn't cease to exist.

Concerning the Syrian side, it is clear that despite a certain ideological affinity to the Eastern bloc and socialist-trained bureaucrats, the decision-makers at no time followed the Eastern experts blindly. They retained their autonomy and controlled the Eastern experts by seeking expertise and advice from multiple sources. The fact that a big part of the project was financed on credit, provided them with a certain leverage. They could pressure their Eastern partners and delay payments, if they wished, without having to fear severe consequences.

Further archival material suggests that the Syrian case was less of an anomaly but rather representative for the technical assistance of the GDR. Similar problems occurred in neighboring Iraq when at the same time during the late 1970s East German engineers tried to build a modern slaughterhouse in Bagdad. This was another multimillion-dollar project that the East Germans had acquired not because of their superior technology compared to their West German competitors but because of their good relations to the Ba'ath Party of Iraq. It was also meant to be a guiding example of socialist cooperation envisioned on CMEA principles. The only difference was that they cooperated not with TES but took the Romanian construction company Arcom as a partner.[90]

## Conclusion

The aim of this chapter was to thwart a popular narrative of the socialist countries going borrowing in the West in the 1970s and concentrating all their efforts on capitalizing on the new opportunities caused by détente. Although it is true that the socialist countries did try to use the economic and political benefits arising in the West in the 1970s, this didn't stop them from cooperating with the Global South and with each other. On the contrary, the 1970s proved to be the time of an unprecedented close cooperation between the CMEA countries and between the East and the South. This more often than not is forgotten or hardly mentioned in contemporary research.

The whole episode described in this chapter showed several characteristics of a Shakespearean drama. A well-thought plan was becoming obsolete and haunted by bad luck almost immediately after it had been put to practice. The two partners – Bulgaria and the GDR – who wanted to show the merits of socialist cooperation, got into quarrels soon. They almost broke apart about the issues that had arisen among them. When the third party, the Syrians, got to know the full scale of the problems, they asked their Indian consultants, whose involvement was not obvious to the East Europeans, for advice. The East Germans were forced to make a decision and decided to part from their Bulgarian brethren to get the work done. But their separation didn't last long and they were reconciled again in the late 1970s. This could be described as a happy end. But as is true for any Elizabethan drama, the worst times were yet to come.

Nevertheless, it is clear that the administrative personnel and political elite of the socialist bloc invested a lot of its energy into forging not only political but also economic ties with the Global South. The Syrian example could be interpreted as a failure. But on the other hand, the problems described in this chapter also show the complexity of economic and political relations that had been achieved inside the CMEA – illustrated by the sophisticated supply chains and the East German-Bulgarian division of labor – and between CMEA countries and the Global South. The CMEA as an entity was something the socialist decision-makers had increasingly in mind as the cooperation between Bulgarian and East German state companies was an affair that exceeded the mere national and bilateral level. The potential repercussions of their steps taken in Syria for CMEA negotiations thus played a role in influencing decisions in Sofia and East Berlin. None of these close ties had been present 20 years before.

## Notes

1 See Zwass, *Der Rat Für Gegenseitige Wirtschaftshilfe*, 116–7.
2 Müller, "Der RGW Als Schlüssel," 43–5.
3 Dangerfield, "Sozialistische Ökonomische Integration," 361.
4 Boden, "Soviet World Policy," 186.
5 Zubok, "The Soviet Union and Détente," 433.
6 Dangerfield, "Sozialistische Ökonomische Integration," 363–4.
7 Zwass, *Der Rat Für Gegenseitige Wirtschaftshilfe*, 91.
8 Gaidar, *Collapse of an Empire*, 95.
9 Stone, *Satellites and Commissars*, 186–7.
10 Kotkin, "The Kiss of Debt," 80.
11 Kotkin, 85.
12 Jajesniak-Quast, "Polen, Die CSSR Und Die Europäische Wirtschaftsgemeinschaft," 381.
13 Steiner, *Von Plan Zu Plan*, 219–20.

14 Ramet, *The Soviet-Syrian Relationship*, 219.
15 Gasztold-Sen, "Cooperation by Ideology?" 6.
16 "Sovetsko-siriiskoe ekonomicheskoe i tehnicheskoe sotrudnichestgo," dated 1967, RGAE, Fond 561, op. 53, d. 27, ll. 18–20.
17 Ramet, *The Soviet-Syrian Relationship*, 25–6.
18 Gôlan, *Soviet Policies in the Middle East*, 140–3.
19 Gôlan, 142–3.
20 Karsh, *The Soviet Union and Syria*, 4–9.
21 Gôlan, *Soviet Policies in the Middle East*, 13.
22 Gôlan, 162–3.
23 Trentin, "Between Solidarity and Convenience," 50–1.
24 Trentin, 49.
25 Karsh, *The Soviet Union and Syria*, 8–9.
26 Ramet, *The Soviet-Syrian Relationship*, 39–40.
27 Ramet, 220.
28 Ramet, 222–3.
29 Owen and Pamuk, *A History of the Middle East Economies*, 157.
30 "Information über Zementanlagen SAR," dated 11 September 1974, Barch Berlin, DL 2/16445.
31 "Berichterstattung zur Objektrealisierung," dated 25 June 1976, ibid.
32 "Schwermaschinenbaukombinat Ernst Thälmann" in Magdeburg. Responsible for the execution of the project was its subsidiary "Zementanlagenbau (ZAB)" in Dessau.
33 "Informationen über Zementanlagen SAR," dated 11 September 1974, Barch Berlin, DL 2/16445.
34 1 Valutamark (VM) was the equivalent of 1 West German Mark (DM).
35 "Berichterstattung zur Objektrealisierung," dated 25 June 1976, Barch Berlin, DL 2/16445.
36 "Antrag auf Geschäftsgenehmigung für die Realisierung weiterer Zementanlagenobjekte in der SAR 1976–1978," dated 07 February 1975, ibid.
37 "Vermerk über eine am 29.3.1974 beim Stellvertreter des Ministers, Gen. Clausnitzer durchgeführte Beratung," dated 04 April 1974, ibid.
38 "Antrag auf Geschäftsgenehmigung für die Realisierung weiterer Zementanlagenobjekte in der SAR 1976–1978," dated 07 February 1975, ibid.
39 "Unser Antrag auf Genehmigung eines langfristigen Zielgeschäftes für den Abschluß einer Globalvereinbarung über die Lieferung von Zementanlagen in die Syrische Arabische Republik vom 15.03.1973," dated 20 March 1973, ibid.
40 "Vermerk über eine am 29.3.1974 beim Stellvertreter des Ministers, Gen. Clausnitzer durchgeführte Beratung," dated 04 April 1974, ibid.
41 Ibid.
42 "Antrag auf Geschäftsgenehmigung für die Realisierung weiterer Zementanlagenobjekte in der SAR 1976/1978," dated 30 June 1975, ibid.
43 "Stellungnahme zum Antrag des AHB Invest-Export auf Genehmigung eines langfristigen Zielgeschäftes für den Export von 2 Zementanlagen – 4. und 5. Linie – in die SAR," dated 10 March 1973, ibid.
44 "Anlage 1 zum Schreiben an das MAH Gen. Dr. Fenske," dated 07 February 1975, ibid.
45 "Informationen über Zementanlagen SAR," dated 11 September 1974, ibid.
46 "Bericht über die in der Zeit vom 30.3.74 bis 18.5.74 geführten Verhandlungen in der SAR zum Vertragsabschluß Zementwerk Adra sowie zur Realisierungssituation Zementanlagen Syrien," dated 06 June 1974, ibid.
47 "Bericht über Stand Realisierung Zementanlagen Syrien," dated 15 October 1974, ibid.
48 Ibid.

49 "Darlegung des Standpunktes des AHB Invest-Export zur Steigerung des Exportes von Zementanlagen des VEB ZAB Dessau – Betrieb des VEB SKET sowie gegenwärtig Konzeption des Exportes von Zementanlagen im Zeitraum 1974–80," dated 15 March 1974, ibid.
50 Ibid.
51 "Information über Zementanlagen SAR," dated 11 September 1974, ibid.
52 "Bericht über Stand Realisierung Zementanlagen Syrien," dated 15 October 1974, ibid.
53 "Information über Zementanlagen SAR," dated 11 September 1974, ibid.
54 "Vorlage für Genossen Minister Sölle – Beabsichtigter Wechsel der Montagefirma für die Errichtung von Zementfabriken in der SAR," dated 06 September 1974, ibid.
55 Ibid.
56 "Bericht über Stand Realisierung Zementanlagen Syrien," dated 15 October 1974, and "Information über Zementanlagen SAR," dated 11 September 1974, ibid.
57 "Vorlage für Genossen Minister Sölle – Beabsichtigter Wechsel der Montagefirma für die Errichtung von Zementfabriken in der SAR," dated 06 September 1974, ibid.
58 This affected not only buildings erected by the Bulgarians but also auxiliary buildings like storage facilities erected by Syrabco, "Information über Zementanlagen SAR," dated 11 September 1974, ibid.
59 "Information über Zementanlagen SAR," dated 11 September 1974, ibid.
60 Ibid.
61 "Report on the Visit of Shri George Fernandes, Union Minister of Industry to Kuwait, Jordan, Syria, and Iraq (15th October to 25th October 1977)," without date, NAI, List No. 193, S. No. 1602, 37/528/1977-PMS.
62 "Annual Consular Report for the Year 1974," dated 07 August 1975, NAI, List No. 217 S. No. 547, HI/1011 (42)/75.
63 Karsh, *The Soviet Union and Syria*, 19–20.
64 "Information über Zementanlagen SAR," dated 11 September 1974, Barch Berlin, DL 2/16445, and "Antrag auf Geschäftsgenehmigung für die Realisierung weiterer Zementanlagenobjekte in der SAR 1976–1978," dated 07 February 1975, Barch Berlin, DL 2/16445.
65 "Mitteilung des Handelsrates Genossen Schönherr zum abgeschlossenen Kreditabkommen SAR/SR Rumänien," dated 07 May 1974, ibid.
66 "Situation Zementanlagenexporte in die Syrische Arabische Republik," dated 11 June 1976, ibid.
67 "Entwurf Aide Memoire," without date (most likely early September 1974), ibid. There is only a draft of the letter left in the file. Taking into consideration the other documents of the file leads to the assumption that this draft was sent with minor corrections.
68 "Information über Zementanlagen SAR," dated 11 September 1974, ibid.
69 Ibid.
70 "Standpunkt der Ländersektion VR Bulgarien zum Antrag des AHB Invest-Export auf Veränderung der Montagefirma für den Aufbau der Zementfabrik Adra," dated 01 August 1974, ibid.
71 "Bericht über Stand Realisierung Zementanlagen Syrien," dated 15 October 1974, ibid.
72 Ibid.
73 "Montage Zementwerke Hama und Adra SAR, Vorlage zur Durchsprache und Entscheidung über Währungsfragen, Zahlungsbedingungen und andere in diesem Zusammenhang stehende Fragen," dated 31 January 1975, ibid.
74 Ibid.
75 "Montageausführung des Zementwerkes 'Adra' – SAR," dated 21 June 1974, ibid.
76 Ibid.
77 "Montageausführung des Zementwerks 'Adra' – SAR," dated 14 May 1974, ibid.

78 "Information über Effektivitätsprobleme beim Export von Zementanlagen nach Syrien," dated 11 January 1980, Barch Berlin, DN 1/20698.
79 Letter by the department for economic policy at the East German embassy in Sofia to the Deputy Head of the Council of Ministers, Dr. Weiz, dated 27 March 1975, Barch Berlin, DL 2/16445.
80 "Informatsiia k soveshchaniiu predstavitelei VTO stran-chlenov SEV po voprosam okazaniia tekhnicheskogo sodeistviia razvivaiushchimsia stranam v stroitel'stve predpriiatii stroitel'noi promyshlennosti, kotoroe sostoitsia v noiabre 1979 g. v g. Varshave," dated 12 October 1979, RGAE, Fond 561, op. 53, d. 101, ll. 251–4.
81 "Information über Effektivitätsprobleme beim Export von Zementanlagen nach Syrien," dated 11 January 1980, Barch Berlin, DN 1/20698.
82 "Bericht über die am 30.4.1976 geführte Beratung mit dem Stellvertreter des Generaldirektors des AHB Invest-Export, Genossen Nolte," dated 04 May 1976, Barch Berlin, DL 2/16445.
83 According to the planned daily capacity of the cement factories built in the 1970s, multiplied by 330, the yearly operational time span assumed by the East German designers.
84 "Information über Zementanlagen SAR," dated 11 September 1974, Barch Berlin, DL 2/16445.
85 Ibid.
86 The population of Syria had expanded from 325 million in 1950 to 63 million in 1970. By 1990 it exceeded 12 million.
87 Interview with Dr. Erich Klober, Berlin, dated 08 January 2016.
88 Arndt, *Economic Development*, 72–3.
89 Arndt, 54–5.
90 "Ökonomische Gesamtrechnung des Anlagenexportvorhabens ‚Modernes Schlachthaus Bagdad'," dated 20 August1979, Barch Berlin, DN 1/20698.

# 5 Power and dissent

## Empire, what empire?

In February 1974, a report from the embassy in Prague was cabled to New Delhi containing the following lines:

> The principle, "Who holds Bohemia holds Europe," is a truism: it determines the condition of Czechoslovakia. There is no burking the issue that Czechoslovakia is and will continue to be, so long as the Soviet Union is a Super Power, under Russian hegemony. It would be a mistake however incontinently to consign Czechoslovakia to the status of a helot. The degree of freedom which the Soviet Union allows the countries immediately beyond its Western marches is, when all is said and done, considerably greater than any other Great Power would give in similar economic, geographic and strategic circumstances. Had Western Europe not been separated from the United States by the Atlantic moat, American hegemony could not have differed from the Russian.[1]

The statement from the Indian ambassador to Czechoslovakia, Venkata Siddharthacharry, certainly represents a rather radical point of view. Nevertheless, the ambassador himself could hardly be called a communist. He was educated at Cambridge and Oxford in the interwar period and proud of his Brahminic heritage. He was a diplomat of considerable experience having met Ho Chi Minh, Julius Nyerere, and other high-ranking politicians in his career before being appointed Indian ambassador to the CSSR.[2] He could claim for himself to have an outside view on the bloc from a non-aligned country. So, the question underpinning his statement and prominent in this chapter is the question of the true nature of the Soviets' grip on Central Eastern Europe. Did it constitute an empire or was the relationship between the Soviets of a different, "gentler" nature? This question will be discussed from the angle of CMEA material on East–East and East–South relations and negotiations, in particular on the discussions inside the Permanent Commission for Technical Assistance.

To answer this question, it is important to define the characteristics of an empire. The Soviet Union had been called an empire uncounted times during the

Cold War and after with the "evil empire" being one of the most important political slogans of the 1980s. However, during the Cold War, empire was a concept often ignored by scholars with the exception of those on the political far-right and far-left.[3] This changed with the demise of the Soviet Union. Its dissolution evoked huge scholarly interest. Thereby, for parts of academia, the Soviet Union became an empire in the moment of its downfall with scholarly attention focused not only on intrabloc relations but more prominently on the interrelationship of the union republics and different ethnicities inside the Soviet Union.[4]

With regard to economic control and exploitation inside the Eastern Bloc and the CMEA, scholars have repeatedly argued back and forth already during the Cold War, if the Soviet Union actually subsidized the smaller CMEA member states by delivering oil and gas at special rates or exploited them by tying them to their inferior economic realm, extracting reparations in the immediate post-war years, and forcing them to stick to the Soviet model of command economy.[5] The fact that the Soviet Union supplied the smaller members of the bloc with vital resources and that it had stationed a considerable part of its army in most states of the bloc – which the Soviet leadership had used to crush revolts in the GDR in 1953, in Hungary in 1956, and precautionarily in the CSSR in 1968 – seems to be enough to take the notion of the Soviet Union as an empire for granted. Nevertheless, there is more to say about this topic, as everyday life inside the bloc consisted of more than military interventions.

To understand what constitutes an empire and to subsequently analyze the intrabloc relationship, the structural theory presented by Alexander J. Motyl and laid out in his book "Imperial Ends" will be used.[6] In his book, Motyl also applies his theory to several political entities and asks, if and what kind of empire the Habsburg, the Romanov, and the Soviet empires, among others, constituted. His view is the view of a historically informed political scientist. Thus, his judgements on the political entities suspected to have constituted empires are only indirectly based on archival research conducted by researchers at the end of the 1990s. Therefore, his judgements are not always in line with newest research. Furthermore, he uses concepts, like the concept of totalitarianism, rather uncritically from a historian's point of view.[7] Nevertheless, the undisputed value of his book lies in the compact, dense, and analytically rich theory of empire presented by him.

## The pillars of empire

According to Motyl, an empire is a hierarchically organized political system with a hub-like structure. He compares an empire to a rimless wheel. The elites of the imperial core hereby control the flow of resources and information from the periphery to the core and back to the periphery. The peripheral elites cannot communicate with each other directly; they are always in need of the core elites to serve as intermediaries for them. Hence, the "imperial wheel" has no rim, because peripheral elites are not allowed to communicate with each other without the full consent and knowledge of the imperial center.[8] The absence of a rim that connects the different spokes is the important point here. The moment the imperial wheel is expanded by a rim, it stops to be imperial; this equates the moment peripheries start to significantly communicate with each other or with non-imperial polities in the wider world by themselves.[9]

Empires can be continuous or discontinuous with the former implicating a territorially tightly massed empire and the latter involving overseas territories or a stretched territorial layout of the different imperial possessions. If imperial possessions are stretched out, the spokes of the imperial wheel are rather long, while the spokes of a continuous empire controlling a comparably small number of peripheries are short.[10] Imperial rule of the core elites over the peripheral elites can be either formal or informal.[11] However, the differentiation between formal and informal rule is not a distinctive feature of empire but of all possible kinds of rule. The structure of imperial rule, the wheel without a rim, is of far greater importance for Motyl than are formal or informal rule.[12]

An imperial relationship must always be marked by one society controlling another, non-native, society.[13] Since the relationship between one center and one periphery does not allow to clearly differentiate between intra-state relations and an imperial system of control, an empire, according to Motyl, always needs at least two peripheries to be able to form an imperial system and thus an imperial wheel.[14] This means that Communist Czechoslovakia never constituted an empire, because it controlled only one periphery, namely Slovakia. Neither can Tito's Yugoslavia be called an empire due to the significant exchange among its different republics without the core elites necessarily being involved; thus the Yugoslavian wheel enjoyed a sizeable rim.[15]

Core elites control foreign and defense policy including overseeing borders, regulating the economy, controlling the flow of information, maintaining order, enacting legislation, and extracting resources.[16] Within their structurally centralized imperial system the core elites control and direct the flow of resources and information. An imperial center and its core elites allowing or even urging its peripheries to interact significantly with each other would withdraw from empire themselves.[17] For Motyl, empire ends "not because the core ceases to dominate the peripheries but when or because the peripheries implicated in such domination begin to interact with one another significantly."[18] This also includes the relationship between peripheries and non-imperial polities.

However, empires are not necessarily exploitative only but also contain pull-factors that can make it attractive for the peripheries to cooperate with the center. The imperial center can use its power and resource advantage to provide security and stability for the peripheral societies in general and the peripheral elites in particular. The core elites are also able to promote the development of more remote or poorer regions within their area of control by transferring resources and investment from richer to poorer regions. This system can be very stable not because it is confrontational but actually cooperative. It perpetuates the role of the peripheral elites in their societies, while ensuring that the peripheral elites compete with each other for the patronage of the core elites. Their goodwill in return would strengthen the position of the peripheral elites again in their respective societies and vis-à-vis competing peripheral elites in other parts of the empire.[19]

The efficient flow of resources is thus of extraordinary importance for the stability of empires.[20] However, administering the flow of resources efficiently calls for a bureaucratic apparatus able to obtain all the necessary information on every spoke of the imperial wheel. The sophisticated state apparatus in the core has to be matched by sufficient administrative capacity in the peripheries able to assist the core and to execute its commands. Since the demands on the core tend to increase with time to guarantee stability and satisfy the peripheral elites and since the information-gathering process is never producing sufficiently accurate results, this bureaucratic apparatus in the core has to become constantly bigger, thereby consuming more and more resources. Therefore, by becoming more complex and having to satisfy more and more demands, empires become increasingly untenable, finally starting to unfold.[21]

Motyl calls this process imperial decay which means a loosening of center-periphery relations due to the increasing difficulty of maintaining imperial relations encountered by the core elites. Decay can be slowed down or even halted by some factors like an extraordinarily centralized core state or internally generated "easy money" like the discovery of rich deposits of natural resources enabling the core elites to step up their levels of imperial expenditure, although their economy would otherwise not be able to generate enough funds anymore.[22] Decay is followed by attrition, the actual loss of imperial territory.[23] The more peripheries an empire contains, the larger the demands on its bureaucratic apparatus to gather information and allocate resources, leading to accelerated decay in comparison to smaller empires with fewer peripheries. The same mechanism applies to discontinuous as well as informal empires which tend to wither away faster than continuous and formal ones, according to Motyl's theory.[24]

To come back to the initial statement of the Indian ambassador to the CSSR, Venkata Siddharthacharry: what he meant by talking about the "Atlantic moat" barring the US from exerting the same level of control over Western Europe, as the Soviet Union did over Central Eastern Europe, was the different length of the "spokes" of the wheel in Motyl's theory. While any American empire spanning over the Atlantic Ocean must have been discontinuous – if there ever was one transatlantic American empire – its Soviet equivalent must have been continuous, thereby allowing for a far greater level of imperial control and imperial interference in the day-to-day affairs of the peripheral elites.

## The CMEA as an instrument of imperial control?

How does the CMEA fit into such a system based on Motyl's theory? In fact, the CMEA was dominated by the Soviet Union. The headquarters of the CMEA were based in Moscow, for the most part of the time in a high-rise located at the former Kalinin Prospekt which is today's New Arbat Avenue. The Secretariat of the CMEA was headed by a Soviet official during the entire time of its existence. The same is true for most, but not all, permanent commissions inside the CMEA and the different sub-organizations of the CMEA. The PCTA in particular was chaired by Semën A. Skachkov right from its foundation till the 1980s. Skachkov had served as first deputy of the minister for transport machine building of the USSR in the mid-1950s before becoming head of the state committee for foreign economic relations of the Council of Ministers of the USSR in 1958. He retained this post till he became a pensioner in 1983, having been elevated to the rank of minister in 1978.[25]

Skachkov was thus not solely a representative of the CMEA but served in two functions, one in the CMEA and one inside the Soviet Union. But he was no exception, since all delegations to the PCTA were headed by high-ranking foreign trade officials, in general by the ministers for foreign trade. This also applies to other organs of the CMEA. The number of people who worked solely for the CMEA was very limited. Even the permanent representatives in the Executive Council were also high-ranking politicians in their home countries, as they were obliged to be deputy heads of government. This was done on purpose and meant that the bureaucracy of the CMEA could hardly develop a life of its own. The majority of the meetings of the PCTA took place in Moscow but some also occurred at other locations in the different union republics or the capitals of the smaller members of the CMEA. The picture is more mixed for conferences of economic experts or general directors of state combines under the umbrella of the PCTA. These conferences took place in different state capitals inside the CMEA without a clear preference for one place.

Besides the places where the meetings of the CMEA and its commissions took place and the origin of the people who headed these commissions, the CMEA was an organization made up of unequal members. The Soviet Union was by far the most powerful country among all of the CMEA member states. It could employ the largest army, was the only country in the CMEA to possess atomic weapons and its military technology was sophisticated enough to be a challenge to the US military. The Soviet Union had a population by far exceeding the ones of all other members of the CMEA combined, even including Cuba and Vietnam. Its economic output, taken at gross value, could hardly be challenged by any other of the member states. Furthermore, it was the biggest country on earth with huge amounts of natural resources and the "motherland of the revolution" which meant that some kind of moral authority emanated from Soviet leaders.

However, the fact that the military might the Soviet leadership could wield was frightening and that the Soviet Union was far more populous and bigger than the other members of the CMEA doesn't necessarily make for an empire. This tells something about power imbalances, not necessarily about imperial structures being at work. This can be made clear by a thought experiment. Such power imbalances as experienced in the CMEA would also be in place in an economic union consisting of Germany, Belgium, and Luxemburg only. Germany would in a certain sense inevitably dominate such a community due to its sufficiently larger population and military as well as economic power.

These power imbalances would be in place regardless of this hypothetical union forming an empire with Germany at its core or not. If the secretariat of this organization were seated in the Belgian capital of Brussels or in Berlin wouldn't alter the picture significantly, as this would be a decision of cosmetic or propagandistic character only. It is no coincidence that current European leaders like the Hungarian prime minister Viktor Orbán criticize the European Union for forming an empire dominated either by Brussels or by Germany. However, empire in this sense is reduced to power imbalances, as the countries on the European periphery, for example Poland and Hungary, are free to cooperate with each other and to form a common front against the perceived core.[26]

Furthermore, first cracks in the façade of a domineering Soviet Union forming the core of an empire appear when one looks at the different technological levels inside the CMEA. In general, the economies on its Western peripheries were far more advanced than the Soviet one. It was in fact part of the deal of the "Imperial Scavenger," as described by Jersild, to extract know-how and technology from the Western peripheries of the conquered territories as fast as possible to the Soviet Union to level the difference. This strategy proved unsuccessful in the sense that the same technological imbalances were still in place 20 or even 40 years later. By the late 1980s, the GDR provided a significant part of the machines employed in factories all over the Eastern Bloc.

This meant that many branches of the economy of the CMEA member states were dependent on developments in East German machine building.[27] The dependency of the Soviet core on East German inventions and machines was aggravated by production specialization agreements inside the CMEA.[28] However, this is no sufficiently strong criterion for determining the existence or absence of an empire, either. The core territories of the Habsburg, Ottoman, or Persian Empire, to make a case in point, never formed the economic and technological powerhouses of their respective empires.[29] Still, the imperial core controlled the peripheries.

The American scholar Randall W. Stone argued in his influential book "Satellites and Commissars" published in 1996 that the internal cohesion of the Eastern Bloc was actually very weak, much weaker than scholars had hitherto assumed.[30] His study is based to a large part on interviews with high-ranking officials from all over the bloc, but his focus lies on economic relations and economic exchange inside the bloc. He claimed that the representatives of the Soviet Union were bad negotiators who could not put the theoretic power of the Soviet Union to practical use.[31] The totalitarian system and the strong centralized hierarchy inside the Soviet Union didn't make the Soviet bureaucracy more assertive, but actually weaker and exposed to its socialist negotiating partners inside the bloc weaknesses that could be exploited by them.[32] According to Stone, the Soviet Union was the main motor of reform inside the CMEA, its attempts at reform being sabotaged and delayed by the smaller member states or "satellites."[33]

However, there is no convincing evidence to assume the Soviet negotiators were far worse and more incapable than their counterparts from the smaller member countries of the CMEA. Any insufficiencies due to the nature of the Soviet system would have applied more or less to them, too. Since the members of the Eastern Bloc never ceased being planned economies, all trade officials were bound more or less to their respective five-year plans. Quite on the contrary, Stone's argument is rather counterintuitive, as a centralized bureaucracy, as Motyl has argued, can delay imperial decay and doesn't feed it, at least in the medium term. Furthermore, its sophisticated intelligence apparatus provided the Soviet elite with much more information than the ones of the smaller members of the bloc. If there were effects that were crippling the elites of the Soviet empire due to its vast extension, there were also effects that were empowering them vis-à-vis the smaller member states of the bloc. Neither is archival material hinting at a comparatively high volatility in Soviet cadre politics in the Cold War era.

As concerns Stone's claim that the Soviet Union was the epicenter of reform programs inside the CMEA and was sabotaged by the smaller countries, there is some support to this thesis at first. The reform programs initiated under the auspices of the Khrushchev administration as well as those that started in 1969 experienced severe setbacks by rather limited support from the smaller socialist countries. This was true in particular for the far-reaching reform programs of the Khrushchev period which involved the introduction of supranational planning. However, this is a rather superficial view on the CMEA and leaves aside the fact that the discussions of reforms were taking place on a continuous level and not only during the Council Sessions, as the material of the PCTA, among others, shows. Furthermore, it can be justifiably claimed that the Soviet leadership was rather conservative on reforming economic mechanisms and was by itself hindering reform attempts which often also originated from Polish or Hungarian representatives.[34] The reason most likely is not that the Soviet bureaucracy was less competent that other bureaucracies inside the bloc or overburdened. The reason for the failure of the reform programs is to be found in the nature of an organization like the CMEA.

The basic point is that an organization like the CMEA is inappropriate to entertain for any kind of empire. Empires thrive on directing the flows of information and resources within their imperial system without the peripheral elites being in significant direct contact with their peers. The imperial wheel remains imperial as long as it doesn't have a rim. The moment peripheral elites start to communicate with each other, the wheel ceases being imperial. The CMEA is by definition an international organization, where all its members were commonly discussing important issues on a multilateral basis. The fact that the Soviet leadership, or the core elites in Motyl's words, sat at one table at the same time with most of the peripheral elites of the Eastern Bloc was per se dangerous, as the peripheral elites could cooperate with each other to undermine the core elites.

Thus, the CMEA was the rim to the wheel. It is not important, whether the CMEA was "successful," as this is a very relative statement depending on differing sets of assumptions, or whether the CMEA member states were still conducting the bulk of their trade on a bilateral basis. The important issue is that they were discussing significant topics on a multilateral basis and didn't just assemble in Moscow to receive the newest orders of the supreme leader one by one, thereby competing for his or her goodwill. That the topics the delegates to the different meetings and sessions of the CMEA were discussing proved significant indeed, is obvious. They were dealing with nothing less than the Eastern Bloc's economic future and paths of development. Since none of the member states could survive on its own, probably not even the Soviet Union, cooperation was essential for survival.

However, the different members of the CMEA had differing opinions on what this future should look like. The failure of reform is therefore not due to the fact that the Soviet bureaucracy was inept but that it couldn't command the others. The voice of the Soviet leadership was important but it was not the only voice in the bloc. By embarking on a path of cooperation in the late 1950s and thereafter, by allowing the wheel to get a rim, the Soviet empire ceased to exist and became a different kind of political entity. The power imbalances remained but the system underpinning the relations inside the bloc was not imperial in a structural sense anymore, as defined by Motyl.

This gets even clearer by looking at the dynamics inside the Eastern Bloc and the fortunes of the CMEA in the early phase of its existence. The CMEA was founded in 1949 to create a counterweight to Western institution-building and was most likely meant to develop a long-term strategy for integrating the newly conquered territories. Nevertheless, the CMEA as an institution was sacked almost immediately after its establishment. It met a few times till Stalin's death but its actions were not significant. Out of an imperial logic, sacking the CMEA was the only right thing to do. Wherever peripheral elites met for mutual discussions, the empire was in danger.[35]

Instead, during the late Stalin years, the Soviet leadership relied on its embassy system. The peripheral elites were thereby taking orders from Soviet representatives without much room for discussions or negotiations. These demands of the core elites were handed over to the peripheral elites individually. The peripheral elites remained in isolation, they were competing for the benevolence of the core elites, mostly personified by Stalin, but they were not acting multilaterally or in close contact with each other. The structure of this system of communication was imperial indeed: the core elites controlled the flow of information and resources, as they were the only ones in possession of information on any of the spokes of their imperial system. There was no rim connecting the spokes worthy of that name.

This makes the changes under the Khrushchev administration and the forces that supported his leadership the more meaningful. By reviving the CMEA, he empowered and encouraged the peripheral elites to communicate with each other. The core elites lost their information monopoly and it became harder for them to play the peripheral elites off against each other. This was not only true for intra-CMEA relations but also for intrabloc relations and relations with non-imperial polities. The former is exemplified by the increasing contacts between the smaller CMEA countries and the People's Republic of China without Moscow serving as omnipresent intermediary anymore, and the latter is shown by increasing contacts with the West, in particular during the 1960s but also with the former colonies which became independent countries. When Khrushchev tried to transform the CMEA into a supranational planning authority for all member states, the peripheral elites feared a backlash of the Stalin years. They didn't need to.

If the post-1953 Soviet elites had liked to push through supranational planning, directly controlling every single move of the peripheral economies, there would have been no need for them to turn to the CMEA. They could have utilized the old embassy system for that purpose, too, presenting the peripheral elites with a draft version from a Moscow planning agency on an individual basis. This would have hindered the peripheral elites from plotting collectively against the core elites undermining their grand designs. But something had changed inside the Soviet leadership. The fact that the Khrushchev administration used the CMEA to introduce a system of supranational planning showed its unwillingness or lacking means to rely on the old system of imperial rule. The new system was far more cooperative and not imperial anymore. When the peripheral elites mostly rejected the Soviet plans to introduce supranational planning in the early 1960s as well as in the 1970s, the Soviet elites accepted this decision.

Nevertheless, a closer look will be taken at different forms and agents of dissent inside the CMEA to show that the Soviet leadership was hardly in any position to command the smaller members of the organization and to underpin the statement and thoughts on the CMEA as an "anti-imperial" institution in the sense that it formed a rim to the spokes of the wheel. The examples are taken out of the context of the PCTA but they are not limited to this commission, as the topics for discussion were also on the agenda of the national planning entities and governments as well as on the agenda of the Executive Committee and the Council Sessions.

## Dissent: the Cuban case

Cuba had joined the CMEA only after the Complex-Program had been negotiated. Therefore, more than a decade had passed between the successful revolution led by Fidel Castro and the accession of Cuba to the CMEA. Cuba could hardly contribute much economically to the CMEA but its membership could be expected to boost the prestige of the Eastern Bloc in the Global South. In an economic sense the membership of Cuba was an experiment due to the large gap between the state of its economy and of the Western periphery of the CMEA. Although Cuba remained firm inside the bloc, its representatives made their voices heard occasionally; not always in a way the older members of the CMEA appreciated. The report of the East German delegation on the events of the 28th session of the PCTA in Moscow in July 1974 reads:

> The delegation of the Republic of Cuba recognized the support of the CMEA member states for the developing countries also. Nevertheless, the leader of the Cuban delegation emphasized in this context that the support hitherto given is not sufficient according to the view of Cuba [sentence underlined]. The policy of the CMEA member states towards the developing countries should be scrutinized. He [the leader of the Cuban delegation] pointed to Latin America in particular. The inclusion of such a point into the resolution of the 28th session on topic one was rejected by the other delegations. In order to come to terms with the Cuban delegation, who was advancing its view obstinately [sub clause underlined], merely a remark had been included into the preamble of the resolution that the economic policy towards the developing country needs further refinement.[36]

The report continues as follows on the conduct of the Cuban delegations and the lessons learned:

> The conduct of the Cuban delegation allows to draw the conclusion that they will set such questions up on the agenda for discussion forcefully. (In view of this and "to give the other country delegations enough time to come up with a position of their own on this demand", the head of the department for Technical Assistance inside the Secretariat of the CMEA has crossed out the thematic complex "main direction of the collaboration of the CMEA member countries for granting economic and technical assistance to developing countries in the years 1976–1980" of the preliminary agenda for the 29th session in October this year).[37]

This passage is particularly interesting, since it shows that the European members of the CMEA were not too fond of being directly confronted with the voices of the Global South. When the Cuban delegation tried to formulate some kind of critique the other members of the CMEA were quite shocked. Nevertheless, the Cuban delegation had just reacted as could be expected from a "developing country" demanding more action and more support not only by granting development aid and technical assistance but also by giving preferential treatment for country-specific products like sugar in the Cuban case. It seems that the European delegations had simply expected their Cuban counterpart to follow their lead and not try to act independently.

It was not enough for the European members of the commission to simply reject the claims and demands of the Cuban delegation. They were evidently fearing a general discussion of development aid, as this could have revealed some painful truths about its effectiveness and value for the recipients, despite the official rhetoric of ever mutually beneficial relations. The European delegations actually conspired against their Cuban counterpart. They falsified the protocol with the assistance of the Secretariat of the CMEA. By crossing the Cuban issue out of the agenda, they were using a formal trick to prevent the issue from being raised again, since conference meetings have to stick to their preliminary agenda which cannot simply be expanded spontaneously. However, the Cuban delegation was sensible enough to back down in the next meeting.[38]

In the end, Cuba itself had too much to lose by angering the European CMEA countries which were expanding the Cuban economy by granting credits and building up different kinds of industry in Cuba. The Cuban delegation to the PCTA remained almost completely quiet during the rest of the 1970s. This was connected to the topics discussed by the PCTA, for Cuba could not participate in industrializing other "developing countries." The Cuban delegation showed great interest in general pricing mechanisms inside the CMEA, as the price for sugar was of vital importance for its economy.[39] Nevertheless, the example shows that the inclusion of a "developing country" in an economic organization like the CMEA didn't necessarily lead to dialogue, in this particular case it resulted in a clear front line between Cuba and the Europeans. It is interesting to note that the

Mongolian delegation played no role in this incident. The Mongolian delegation played in general a very minor role in the PCTA, a fact which can be explained by its rather low international standing compared with the People's Republic of China or Cuba in the "Third World" and it's very limited economic capacity.

## Dissent: the Romanian case

The Romanian case shows a much more profound history of dissent. Actually, the origins of this behavior date back to the opposition to supranational planning in the early 1960s. But Romanian obstructionism was not limited to the main Council Sessions. It was manifest in the PCTA in the mid-1960s, and thus in the early meetings of the PCTA, too. The report of the East German delegation on the 6th meeting of the PCTA that took place in Moscow in May 1964 states:

> The commission could not finish its work in the proposed timeframe (25.-27.5.64). This was due to the conduct of the delegation of the RPR [Romanian People's Republic] in the editorial groups.
>
> All delegations – with the exception of the RPR – were anxious to further improve and deepen the coordination of the activities of the member countries of the CMEA in granting economic aid and technical assistance to developing countries . . . But the delegation of the RPR led protracted discussions in the editorial groups to prevent the formulation of resolutions, if possible.[40]

The same picture emerged out of the 7th meeting of the PCTA six months later:

> The delegation of the RPR also often based [its arguments] on the aforementioned resolutions [of the Executive Council and the Council Sessions], but only in cases, where it could reach a certain limitation of the tasks to be executed, like limiting them to information exchange or an exchange of opinions.[41]

The two reports hint at a very undiplomatic attitude of the Romanian delegation which seemed to be needlessly confrontational. According to the documents cited previously, there was no clear policy aim on the part of the Romanian delegation besides delaying all possible integration measures inside the CMEA. Thus, the opposition of the Romanian leadership was not only limited to grand designs inside the CMEA, it was also evident in day-to-day business. The meetings of the PCTA rather constituted expert meetings than highly ideologized debates on main principles, even if the delegations were led in general by the ministers for foreign trade of the respective member country. Still, the attitude presented by the Romanian representatives remained similar to the one manifest during the large-scale reform attempts of the CMEA in the early 1960s.

While the discussions of the Complex-Program were still being shaped by the negotiations in the Council Sessions, the Romanian delegation to the PCTA tried to influence their practical meaning by curbing the influence of the ongoing negotiations on the PCTA. This was evident at the 17th meeting in July 1969 in Moscow:

> The delegation of the RPR tried in both commissions [the PCTA and the one on foreign trade which were holding their meetings directly after one another, often with the same delegates] skillfully and persistently to force through with reference to the XXIII. Council Session and the 41st Session of the ECO [Executive Council] that the Complex-Program aims at information exchange and the studying of problems in most fields. The delegation of the RPR was eager to limit demands for a coordinated conduct to a minimum.[42]

This kind of behavior in the organs of the CMEA didn't change with the adoption of the Complex-Program but proceeded in the 1970s. Even after the Council Session of the CMEA had accepted the reform proposals, did the Romanian delegation to the PCTA try to scale back what had already been achieved as in the case of the 22nd meeting of the PCTA in January 1972:

> There were several disagreements on principle between the delegation of the RPR and all other country delegations as concerned the specification of the recommendation on mutual exchange of information from 1963. Whereas the expert meeting to prepare new recommendations in October 1971 had been marked by a consensus to exchange concrete, current and foremost relevant information, the Romanian delegation tried to reverse all these improvements under the disguise of simplification [of exchange]. The [Romanian] proposal aimed at exchanging less and more general information than in the recommendation already adopted in 1963.
>
> The position of the delegation of the RPR has not been supported by any other delegation. It can be assumed that the clear stance of the Soviet comrades, who said that the delegation of the RPR would not receive any kind of information under these circumstances or the recommendation adopted in 1963 would remain in place, was responsible for the delegation of the RPR withdrawing its proposal.[43]

There is no hint in the non-Romanian files, why the Romanian delegation acted like it did. However, its behavior must have made an awkward impression, since it was not very sensible to try to turn the clock back, the more so because high-ranking Romanian officials had been present during the negotiations of the Complex-Program in general and the negotiations of the expert meeting mentioned in the statement previously in particular. So, either the Romanian representatives in the CMEA simply wanted to tease their peers or acted like sore losers. This poses the question why they participated at all in the meetings of the CMEA. The passage cited previously gives a hint. First, the remark in the East German report that the Soviet delegation saved the day is a bit misleading. It seems more appropriate to say that the Soviet delegation simply stated the obvious in this situation.

But when threatened that the Romanian government would not receive any information at all from the collected materials of the CMEA, they backed down.

This and other archival documents indicate that the Romanian leadership was eager to receive as much information from the other delegations as possible without submitting meaningful material of its own and – most important – without having to commit to binding policy programs. This provided the Romanian leadership with the advantage of getting to know about potentially attractive economic partners in the Global South and profiting from the knowledge of the more developed and economically more capable members of the CMEA who were sharing some of their "business secrets" with the other member states. Since this attitude was against the spirit of economic cooperation and too obviously centered on a narrow definition of national interests, the other members of the CMEA were often more suspicious of the moves of the Romanian representatives than of the ones of all other member states.

On the 24th session of the PCTA, discussions were planned to center around common rules for granting credits to countries of the Global South, in particular governmental credits which often came at beneficial rates for the debtor.

> The delegation of the RPR turns against the agreement that governmental credits should be granted to developing countries, the governments of which pursue politics of friendship towards the donor country and all other CMEA member countries [underlined in the document following the word country]. [The delegation of the RPR] proposes to cross out "and all other CMEA member countries" . . . The delegation of the RPR turns against the agreement to credit primarily such objects the production of which is interesting for the CMEA member countries. [The delegation of the RPR] proposes the formulation . . . "for the creditor."[44]

This was again a very blunt attempt to cripple the CMEA or at least to delay its actions with demands that were directly or indirectly questioning the existence of such an international organization like the CMEA that was meant to foster economic cooperation. The Romanian leadership also didn't make friends when they started to claim that Romania was actually a developing country, too. The report on the 31st meeting of the PCTA in Tbilisi in November 1975 reads:

> The delegation of the RPR stated repeatedly that the RPR in general doesn't take part in the coordination of a common conduct of the CMEA member countries. This stance was justified with the position of the RPR as a "developing country" and its low development level in comparison to other developing countries [sic!]. These differences would eliminate any practicality and necessity for a coordination with other CMEA member countries.
>
> . . .This position of the delegation of the RPR was not approved by any other country delegation in the commission. However, this could not hinder the delegation of the RPR to formulate its separate point of view.[45]

It is very interesting to note that the Romanian delegation described their country not only as a "developing country" but also as "underdeveloped" in comparison to other "developing countries." Since the European socialist countries of the CMEA based their economic assistance on the assumption they could give something unique to the Global South and were thus somewhat more developed, this statement was potentially damaging for the prestige of the CMEA and self-destructive for Romania. In the end the Romanian delegation formulated its separate point of view in the official protocol of the meeting. This move as such did not have any direct practical consequences. Nevertheless, the other members of the CMEA felt so annoyed by this move of the Romanian delegation that they wanted to prevent it from happening.

The exchange of words between the Romanian and other delegations could also be very rough in tone occasionally. This happened during the 40th meeting of the Permanent Commission for Foreign Trade that in most cases saw the same make-up of the delegations as in the PCTA which often started the day after the commission on foreign trade had ended its session. According to the East German report on the meeting, the following had occurred in Moscow in May 1974:

> [The Romanian delegation] was eager to avoid the term "socialist community of states." The discussions of the communique triggered hard quarrels when the leader of the Romanian delegation
>
> - argued against [the agreement] that the main tasks of the foreign trade relations of the CMEA member countries are solved by their mutual trade . . .
>
> Due to the forceful appearance of the other delegation leaders, the communique remained unchanged . . .
>
> The leader of the delegation of the RPR talked about trade difficulties between the RPR and the other CMEA member countries, because the other partner countries – allegedly – are not able to satisfy its demand for machines, resources, and semi-finished products. . . . The RPR is concerned that a positive balance of ca. 180 million rubles is evolving in its trade with the CMEA member states.[46]

This was again a very rude behavior of the Romanian representatives by simply hijacking the meeting to demand their money back. According to the report the Romanian delegation dropped the issue after the Soviet delegation had countered the accusations by mentioning they actually had to scrap an important Romanian delivery. That the Romanian delegation was complaining about the bad quality of the deliveries of the other members of the CMEA and about being exploited by them, makes for an awkward impression, as Romania's industrialization was fueled by distributing effects from the Western periphery to the South East in the CMEA during the 1950s and 1960s in particular.

Cases can be found in the archival documents which make the Romanians appear to be some kind of boogeyman inside the CMEA. The reputation of the

Romanian leadership was such that others didn't want to get associated with them at times regardless of the policy contents. One such example is represented by an exchange of letters between the East German Minister for Foreign Trade, Sölle, and the head of the East German planning commission, Schürer. The content of the letter was related to discussions inside the PCTA to formulate a common recommendation for granting governmental credits, an issue on which the leadership of the GDR had stated some reservations together with the Romanians. The letter was related to the dynamic unraveled by the start of negotiations on the Complex-Program. After having stated that the commission showed positive developments recently, the foreign trade minister proceeded:

> We have to commence our considerations from the fact that the delegations of the PRB [Bulgaria], HPR [Hungary], PRP [Poland], USSR and CSSR on the one hand will hardly be able to understand our point of view on the mentioned recommendations, while the delegation of the RPR on the other hand will try to exploit the argumentation of the GDR for its own benefit. It is in this case alarming that the delegation of the GDR is arguing together with the delegation of the RPR against the opinion of all the other country delegations. This could lead to a false assessment of the role of the GDR in the Permanent Commission of the CMEA for the Coordination of Technical Assistance. The other country delegations could get the impression that the GDR is not utilizing all common possibilities for granting economic aid and technical assistance to developing countries.
>
> If the GDR spoke out in favor of the application of the stated recommendations between the interested member countries of the CMEA, this would without doubt contribute to the promotion of certain positive developments in the work of the commission.[47]

This exemplifies a very interesting kind of dynamic. Since the GDR didn't want to be associated too closely with the position of the Romanian delegation to the PCTA, it was changing its position out of principle. However, this dynamic was taking place between the peripheries of the CMEA and not with the center as intermediary. Therefore, it could also easily work against the Soviet Union. As gets evident in particular from the Romanian examples, the Soviet leadership proved unable or unwilling to interfere strongly. The Soviet delegation could use its authority due to the CMEA being a community of unequals but it could neither control communication and exchange among the peripheries nor could it silence dissent. When the Romanian delegates to the CMEA remained alone in their obstructionism, they proved a thorn on the side of the others, but the work could proceed with their discussions anyhow, as long as they formed a common front.

Nevertheless, the behavior of the Romanian leadership inside the CMEA created a precedent, others could refer back to. Since the Soviet leadership didn't punish their Romanian counterpart the way they did with Tito in the late Stalin years, others didn't need to fear grave consequences. The fact that the Romanian delegation could formulate its – often not very convincing and selfish – viewpoints inevitably shaped the expectations of all other members of the CMEA. This became important when the Romanian leadership opposed supranational planning and was joined by many other members of the CMEA thereby stopping the project entirely. Opposition didn't have to be built up from scratch in such cases, since there already was an opposition present. Even if there was no sympathy involved in the relationship, power makes for strange bedfellows.

The Romanian and Cuban delegations were not the only ones to dissent from time to time. It could also be the East German or Polish one.[48] It is interesting to note that at least in the East German files the Soviet delegation is often presented as being conciliatory and ready to compromise on many issues.[49] This seems logical and is not simply or not only a sign of ideological devotion to the "big brother," since the Soviet leadership could hardly afford to alienate the other members of the CMEA. Due to its potential power it was expected to lead and to show initiative by making proposals that were acceptable for a majority at least. The delegations and leadership of the smaller member states had no incentive to do so. This was also a factor enabling the Romanian leadership to act like it did, because they were in the comfortable position to be able to formulate radical positions without considering the interests of the whole bloc. This was not an imperial but simply an institutional logic being at work.

## The Resource-Program III

Maintaining an empire is, according to Motyl, about the core elites controlling the flow of resources and information between center and periphery. Therefore, nothing would be more suitable than to take a closer look at the Resource-Program discussed in the PCTA, since it dealt with the flow of resources in the most literal sense possible. It also constituted the most defining issue of the discussions inside the PCTA during the 1960s and 1970s. It is clear from the archival evidence that the Resource-Program was foremost a program that the Soviet side wanted to push through which makes it particularly worthwhile to analyze with the question in mind what the discussions say about a structural imperial system in place in the Eastern Bloc.

One of the occasions where the Soviet delegation demanded progress was the 23rd session of the CMEA in March 1972 in Moscow:

> Further discussions on the necessity and the preconditions for securing the resource supply of the CMEA member countries from developing countries took center stage during the meeting . . . The demeanor of the Soviet comrades allows for the conclusion that the Soviet Union is decisively urging the CMEA member countries to carry out joint effective measures in the near term by erecting objects in developing countries to secure the resource needs of the CMEA member countries in the long-term from developing countries.[50]

The Soviet delegation continued to press the issue forward. The report on the 24th meeting of the PCTA in mid-1972 states:

> The rising importance of the developing countries for securing the resource needs of the CMEA member countries became evident again in the consultations. With particular vigor did the delegation of the USSR urge the CMEA member countries to conduct common, effective measures to secure their long-term resource needs increasingly by deliveries from developing countries.[51]

During the 29th session of the PCTA the delegation of the Soviet Union proposed to utilize special funds of the International Investment Bank to finance the projects of the Resource-Program. By using these funds, the multilateral building of factories and other objects in the Global South was to be credited. The debtors were then to repay the loan with resources.[52] The prospective volume of this fund was to amount to one billion Transferable Rubles. Between 5 and 10 % of this sum were to be paid in convertible currency. The first payments had to be made in 1974. The protocols show that the negotiations to create these funds were driven by the Soviet representatives, while the other delegations were very reluctant to agree on a concrete sum, in particular when this sum contained payments in convertible currency.[53] The fact that the delegations of the smaller member states were simply presented with a Soviet proposal that wasn't revised by all member states led to resistance inside the Council of the IIB.[54] In the end, all members agreed to form a special funds.[55] But the smaller countries which were not content with the demeanor of the Soviets found another way to show their disagreement: they never paid the bills. Actually, the money was never transferred to the IIB or not more than a tiny fraction of it. By late 1976, only 25 million Transferable Rubles had been transferred.[56] Thus, there were no funds to be utilized.

The Soviet policy goal clearly postulated in the PCTA, the Council Session of the CMEA, and the Executive Committee was for the other members of the CMEA to import central resources like phosphates, bauxite, and oil to a large extent from developing countries by 1980.[57] The smaller CMEA member states hardly showed any initiatives by themselves to advance the Resource-Program aggressively. As is shown previously, the Resource-Program remained largely unsuccessful during the 1970s. In 1977, the Soviet Union took the lead in 27 out of 29 remaining objects of the Resource-Program.[58] However, it didn't result in any advances in fulfilling the targets set. This move shows how reluctant the smaller member countries of the CMEA were when it came to build factories in the Global South to import resources. However, in the statistical material sent around by the Secretariat of the CMEA the respective representatives could point out some successes in their trade statistics, even though the coordination attempts by the Soviet Union had failed.

The imports of raw materials were increasing during the 1970s. As concerns oil, the CMEA countries increased their imports from the countries of the Global

South from 4.6 million tons in 1970, to 5.6 million tons in 1971, 10.7 in 1972, and 22.7 in 1973. These numbers were supposed to rise as high as 51.5 million tons by 1980. Of this, 35.5 million tons should be imported from Iraq, where the CMEA countries were developing the huge oil field of North Rumeila with an expected annual production of up to 50 million tons.[59] Furthermore, the CMEA countries were building oil pipelines in Iraq between Bagdad and Basra and a huge oil refinery in the city of Mosul.[60] As concerned cotton, another vital import position of the European CMEA countries, they paid 330 million Transferable Rubles in 1972 to buy up 42.7 % of the Egyptian, 40 % of the Syrian, and 7.5 % of the Turkish cotton exports.[61]

So, one could argue that the Soviet Union had pushed through its agenda successfully at least concerning the bloc's imports of cotton and oil. However, a closer look at the numbers shatters this viewpoint completely. The fact that the smaller CMEA countries were investing 330 million Transferable Rubles to import cotton doesn't indicate they were not reliant on the Soviet Union as their main supplier of cotton anymore. With the exception of the CSSR and Romania, all other smaller CMEA member states were still importing more than half of their cotton from the Soviet Union in 1972.[62] Even the numbers stated for oil imports don't look as impressive anymore, if one takes into account that over half of the amount was actually imported by the Soviet Union. Out of 22.7 million tons of oil imported by the CMEA countries from the Global South in 1973, 13.2 million tons, or 58.2 %, constituted the share of the Soviet Union. The share of Romania was the second highest with 3.5 million tons, while Bulgaria imported 2.1 million tons from the Global South in 1973, the GDR 2.0, the CSSR and Hungary 0.8 each, and Poland 0.3 million tons.[63]

This wasn't meant to be this way. The Soviet share in oil imports was planned to peak at an average of 10.2 million tons during the latter half of the 1970s, while the Romanians were supposed to import between 10 and 12 million tons annually, the Polish side between 8 and 12, the East Germans 5.5, the CSSR 4.3, the Hungarians between 4 and 4.5, and the Bulgarians 3 million tons.[64] Thus, in 1973 the Soviets had already far exceeded their projected share, while all the others, possibly with the exception of Bulgaria, were lagging behind their plans. There is also reason to believe that the increase in oil imports in the early 1970s was mostly limited to the Soviet Union, as the smaller CMEA member states had already imported minor quantities prior to the 1970s. Although imports from Iraq increased to slightly more than 20 million tons by the late 1970s, the bulk of the deliveries were still absorbed by the Soviet Union and even 20 million tons was far behind the target number.[65]

The GDR, to make a case in point, had started to import oil from Egypt already back in 1965 and had made its first oil deals with Syria in the 1960s, too. In 1970, the GDR was already importing more than 1 million tons of oil combined from these two countries alone.[66] These numbers put the change indicated in the CMEA documents into perspective. The GDR still imported more than 19 million tons of oil annually during the 1970s from the Soviet Union.[67] So, when the East

German delegation to the PCTA submitted its import statistics to the Secretariat of the CMEA, one could hardly call these numbers a success from the angle of the aims of the Resource-Program. One should also keep in mind that the chemical composition of oil is not the same in all regions of the world. Thus, the CMEA member countries inevitably had to import a certain amount of non-Soviet oil for their industry, even if the Soviet Union hadn't urged them to do so.

## Reasons for the failure

The smaller members of the CMEA brought forward several arguments to explain the failure of the Resource-Program. The arguments employed by them related to a mix of the economics and politics of the projects included in the Resource-Program. One of these projects was mining copper in Zambia. East German geologists together with Czechoslovak ones played an important role in assessing the project and had therefore traveled to Zambia themselves to file a report for the PCTA. They were joined in their fieldwork by Hungarian, Bulgarian, and Soviet colleagues.[68] One problem encountered by the East Germans in particular was a deterioration of their relations with Zambia which made it uncertain if the Zambian government would accept a further involvement of the East Germans since it had closed down the East German embassy.[69]

Another important point was that the project demanded high initial investments. The geologists estimated the costs per ton mined in this particular Zambian project to be twice the price of what they would have to pay for a ton of copper on the world market. This would therefore counterbalance the fact that the exchange with Zambia didn't demand using convertible currency. Furthermore, the excavation side would not yield sufficient amounts of copper per year to satisfy the demands of all CMEA countries interested in the project. The annual share of the GDR would have amounted to 2,000 tons, while its industry needed 25,000 tons each year.[70]

A similar project was being evaluated in Chile under the auspices of East German experts. Like in Zambia, the aim was to mine copper for the Eastern Bloc in exchange for building infrastructure and factories.[71] This project was discussed and assessed in the early 1970s which were also the years of the democratically elected Marxist Allende government in Chile. After the military coup by Augusto Pinochet in 1973, the idea to mine copper in Chile came to a halt due to the extreme ideological differences between the Eastern Bloc that tried to establish closer ties with socialist Chile and the right-wing military dictatorship that had bloodily replaced it. The CMEA countries were thus confronted with the volatile political situation that was often prevalent in many countries of the Global South. It proved difficult to establish stable long-term relationships. While big multinational companies could often balance these problems out by relying on different suppliers, the CMEA countries didn't possess the means to diversify their investments in such a way.

The smaller CMEA countries complained repeatedly that the Resource-Program was putting severe strains on their economies and put them on the brink of economic overstretch. The report on the 24th meeting of the PCTA in mid-1972 reads:

> The consultations showed more clearly than before that the countries, although they can make the high investment expenditures only to a limited extent, are investigating the material consequences of securing resources in developing countries and are considering them to a certain extent in their national plans . . . The CSSR and PRB [Bulgaria] will double their support for the developing countries in this time [1971–1975]. The Soviet Union plans to grant support to the developing countries worth 2.4 billion rubles and plans to build 350 objects. [The Soviet Union] aims at a complete utilization of the available capacities in the developing countries and at an increased cooperation of the CMEA member countries.[72]

On the 32nd session of the PCTA in May 1976 in Moscow other arguments were presented for the meager progress:

> There is no object of the Resource-Program that is currently being realized together by the interested CMEA member countries.
>
> The preliminary works on the majority of the multilateral objects envisioned in the Resource-Program are impeded by complicated technical and commercial negotiations with the respective developing country. The works are furthermore partially hindered by unresolved problems in the cooperation between the CMEA member states or by an insufficient readiness to cooperate.[73]

Thus, one problem – according to the documents – was that the smaller CMEA member countries feared to be unable to possess the necessary investment funds to fulfill the targets set by the Resource-Program. Another problem was constituted by the difficulties in negotiations with governments in the Global South and the other countries of the Eastern Bloc at the same time. The latter pointed at insufficient managerial rather than industrial capacities in the Eastern Bloc. By the late 1970s the smaller CMEA member states seemed to be rather annoyed by the Soviets putting the Resource-Program on the agenda again and again. This gets evident in the report on the 34th session that took place in 1977:

> The specification of the Resource-Program adopted by the 25th meeting of the commission (1972), the formulation of proposals for including chosen objects of the Resource-Program into the "target program energy, fuels, and resources," the relations between the CMEA, Columbia, and Guyana, and the request of the SRV [Vietnam] to support them in the field of cadres' education, took center stage at the consultations.
>
> It had been repeatedly emphasized during the discussions of this problem that the CMEA member states are already granting extensive economic and technical assistance to the developing countries. The possibilities of the

> CMEA member states are not unlimited, so that satisfying all wishes of the developing countries is not an option.[74]

The smaller member countries of the CMEA were not too fond of building factories in exchange for resources. They rather wanted to build factories to generate foreign exchange earnings that they could spend more freely. The manuscript for the statements the East German foreign trade minister was to give during the 32nd meeting of the PCTA contains the following passage on the Resource-Program:

> Securing the resources the CMEA member countries need in developing countries poses obstacles for the export power of our countries. It is about creating the preconditions for financing these imports. Hereby, the export of complete objects as well as plants and equipment to the developing countries is gaining in importance. . . . Thereby, it is out of economic and other reasons not in every case appropriate and necessary to tie the supply of such objects and plants to payments with certain resources like oil.
>
> For the reasons stated above, the delegation of the GDR considers it appropriate to create more possibilities for common actions – in excess of objects agreed upon in the Resource-Program – to grant technical assistance, in particular in the field of erecting complete objects in developing countries, which are only indirectly connected to securing certain resources and serve the purpose to create financial preconditions and certain securities for the supply with resources.[75]

One has to keep in mind that the CMEA member countries with the exception of the Soviet Union had no strong incentive to participate in the Resource-Program. Diversifying their sources for importing raw materials meant for the smaller countries a worsening of their economic prospects, because the main source of supply had hitherto been the Soviet Union which was paid at rather favorable conditions from the viewpoint of the smaller countries. Thus, their opportunity costs for actively participating in the Resource-Program were far higher than any possible benefits. They had a very strong interest in preserving the status quo. The only country to benefit was the Soviet Union which could save exports to the smaller members of the bloc in order to sell them on the world market for convertible currency instead.

The smaller countries of the CMEA had an interest in increasing their exports to the Global South only insofar as they could bolster their disposable income. If they increased their exports but actually received close to nothing in return, they would have concluded a rather bad deal. The arguments they brought forward for the stalling of the Resource-Program don't stand a critical examination. It is implausible that the smaller countries, in particular the GDR and CSSR, were unable to build more factories in the Global South. They certainly had the necessary investment funds and production capacity but they rather wanted to spend them in a different way and not in the way the Soviet leadership wanted them to. They also had quite high expectations concerning prospective resource objects like in Zambia. They seemed to be ready to participate in actually developing the objects only if the deposits were of premium quality and could be processed at below average costs. The question never asked in the documents is why any country should offer the CMEA sites for development with first-grade raw material deposits in exchange for their plants and equipment, if they could sell the same deposits to Western multinational companies that would pay them in US dollars which they could in return spend on whatever they wanted.

It is also clear from the documents that already in the 1960s the Soviet leadership had lost its information monopoly on the potential riches of the Global South. The smaller countries were cooperating with each other and exchanging information. This development becomes evident from a report filed in 1964:

> On the basis of previous experiences, the CSSR is conducting thorough studies prior to any initiation of business talks. In particular, the experiences in African countries have demonstrated that the capitalist mother countries of the former colonies have developed productive and favorably located resource deposits during their reign, so that in most cases newly explored or new prospective deposits demand high investment expenditures and are not yielding high investment returns.[76]

This material was obtained by the East German embassy in Prague and it shows that the imperial wheel already had a rim by that time. The Soviet leadership could hardly lure the peripheries into following its lead without them scrutinizing the proposals of the Soviets. The Soviet leadership was not able to urge the peripheries to follow in negotiations on a one on one basis. It is furthermore important to scrutinize the meaning of the Resource-Program. The Soviet Union was pushing the smaller member countries to diversify their import sources and thus to become less dependent on the Soviet Union. This strongly defies any imperial logic. It also puts the participation of the smaller states in the expansion of the Soviet pipeline system in the late 1970s into perspective. The same is due for the reform of the pricing mechanism inside the CMEA which tied the price for the export of oil and gas from the Soviet Union to the other CMEA countries to the average world market price of the five preceding years.[77]

It also shows that the old view, according to which the Soviet Union constantly tried to bind its periphery ever closer to its own economy, is not adequate.[78] The Soviet leadership had preferred the smaller European members of the bloc to be able to care for themselves. Binding them to Soviet resource exports was only the second-best choice for the Soviet Union, yet the first choice for the other members of the bloc. Thus, the peripheral elites could more or less impose their own will on the Soviet leadership. In return, they had to accept price increases and a participation in the Soviet investment efforts to develop the Siberian oil and gas fields. By the early 1980s, they also had to accept cuts in their supplies from the Soviet Union which the Soviet leadership redirected to the world market instead.[79]

The question is: what kind of an empire is it that can't control the most basic elements of resource and information flows within its own realm? The answer is: none at all. It seems that the Indian ambassador was quite right in his assessment. What remains unresolved is how to define the Eastern Bloc, the relationship among its members, and its power imbalances. Alexander Motyl provides another category in his book, which he terms "hegemonic non-imperial relationship."[80] Such a relationship is, according to Motyl, marked by a very limited influence of the hegemon on the peripheries. Nevertheless, the hegemon is able to determine the external policy agenda and to influence external policies.[81] This would be appropriate to describe the post-Stalin relationship in the bloc and is evident in the files.

As concerns the Resource-Program the smaller members of the bloc never openly defied Soviet demands. They brought up arguments to explain the delays but never openly put the Resource-Program as such into question. The cautious statements that factories should not necessarily be built in the Global South came the closest to opposition as it could get. However, they didn't need to oppose the Soviet proposals openly. Delaying tactics proved successful enough, as many of the projects became obsolete with time anyway. It is also interesting to note that none of the smaller CMEA member countries ever tried to change the agenda. They accepted that the Soviet delegation could determine the agenda for the discussions. The practical results proved a different matter. The Soviet leadership had only a very limited control over them.

In his description, Motyl states the relationship between the US and Latin America as an example for a hegemonic relationship.[82] The US–Latin American relationship during the Cold War is an appropriate model for describing the relationship inside the Eastern Bloc after Stalin's death. According to this interpretation of the essence of the Eastern Bloc, the events in Hungary in 1956, in the CSSR in 1968, and in Poland in 1980 do not speak in favor of a strong empire tightening its grip or in the case of Poland projecting its power by the mere possibility of intervention. The bloc as such was rather a transnational community.[83] It wasn't an empire. By intervening in the Hungarian and Czechoslovak case, the Soviet leadership saved foremost the peripheral elites, not so much the Soviet Union. One could claim that the fall of Poland or Hungary could have doomed the Soviet Union, too. But this was the same reasoning that made several US governments try to intervene in Guatemala, Cuba, Chile, and Grenada in Latin America.

One should also not forget that although the final decision lay with Moscow, the other members of the bloc exerted considerable influence on the decisions taken by the Soviet leadership. In the cases of the Soviet intervention in the CSSR in 1968, as well as in 1980, the ones pushing most strongly for a Soviet intervention were not the Soviets but rather the peripheral elites like the East German one.[84] It is also an ongoing matter of debate to what extent the Chinese leadership influenced the Soviet decision to intervene in Hungary, an issue on which Khrushchev and his inner circle were split for a long time.[85] An intervention in Western Europe by the US never occurred. However, it is unclear if this was due rather to the high living conditions prevailing in Western Europe which made an intervention unnecessary or due to the character of American–West European relations during the Cold War. Events like the ones surrounding the first elections in Italy, in advance of which the Communist Party was severely discriminated against, cast doubts on the latter view. The American leadership also mingled in European colonial affairs after the Second World War when it more or less blackmailed the Dutch government by forcing them to either grant independence to Indonesia or to be left outside of NATO and without Marshal Fund aid. Whatever one thinks about the morals of colonialism, this was a direct interference in internal Dutch affairs.[86]

## Conclusion

Scrutinizing intrabloc relations from the angle of the CMEA makes it clear that the reinvigoration of this organization proved a clear sign for a significant departure from the Stalin years which were marked by Soviet core elites dealing with the peripheral elites on an individual basis via the Soviet embassy system. The CMEA as an organization was an "anti-imperial" one, because it allowed for the peripheral elites of the Eastern Bloc to communicate with each other on important issues for the future of the bloc without the Soviet leadership as an intermediary. In the words of Alexander Motyl's structural theory of empire, the CMEA was the rim to the imperial wheel which thereby destroyed its hub-like imperial structure.

There were several examples of dissent expressed in the CMEA and in its suborganizations with the behavior of the Romanian representatives often being the most extreme. Nevertheless, the CMEA was marked by severe power imbalances between its members. However, these power imbalances didn't constitute an imperial system of domination they can be better analyzed as a hegemonic relationship with a limited influence of the Soviet elites on the peripheries of the Eastern Bloc. The Soviet elites could set the agenda for discussion, they could in no way trust their power to set the policies of the peripheries. The peripheral elites, with the exception of the Romanian one, hardly openly defied Soviet demands and policy proposals. They employed delaying tactics instead, which often led to the same results as pure obstructionism.

## Notes

1 "Annual Political Apercu for 1973," dated 08 February 1974, NAI, List No. 217 S. No. 427, HI/1011 (25)/74.
2 See on his biography, Siddharthacharry, *Brahmanic Vignettes*.
3 Motyl, *Imperial Ends*, 2.
4 Motyl, 3.
5 See Brabant, *Economic Integration in Eastern Europe*, 357–68; Zwass, *Der Rat Für Gegenseitige Wirtschaftshilfe*, 103, 110–1.
6 Motyl, *Imperial Ends*.
7 To be fair, Motyl himself states repeatedly that his theory and in particular his practical applications thereof are far from perfect. Motyl, 5, 67–8.
8 Motyl, 4–5.
9 Motyl, 16.
10 Motyl, 18–9.
11 Motyl, 4–5.
12 Motyl, 20.

13 Motyl, 13.
14 Motyl, 15–6.
15 Motyl, 16–7.
16 Motyl, 15.
17 Motyl, 21.
18 Motyl, 21.
19 Motyl, 23–4.
20 Motyl, 48.
21 Motyl, 48–9.
22 Motyl, 73.
23 Motyl, 52–4.
24 Motyl, 65.
25 Ivkin, "Skachkov, Semën Andreevich."
26 See e.g., Orbán's speech on Kossuth tér on 15 March 2012, the national holiday celebrating the revolution of 1848 and the "freedom fighters." In his speech, Orbán said that the revolutionaries of 1848 didn't want Hungary to stay on being someone else's colony ("nem leszünk gyarmat"). Orbán moved on by saying that we were the heirs of 1848 and that today our aim was the same as in 1848, that Hungary stops being someone else's colony. This statement was clearly directed against the EU and Germany and there are several similar statements he made since his election in 2010.
27 Brabant, "1992, the Revolutions in Eastern Europe and East-South-North Relations," footnote 4, 232.
28 Zwass, *Der Rat Für Gegenseitige Wirtschaftshilfe*, 83–4; Steiner, "The Council of Mutual Economic Assistance," 244–6.
29 These roles were rather taken up by Bohemia in the Habsburg case, its European possessions for the Ottoman empire, and Mesopotamia for the Persian empire.
30 Stone, *Satellites and Commissars*, 3.
31 Stone, 3–4.
32 Stone, 4, 12, 17–8.
33 Stone, 8.
34 Zwass, *Der Rat Für Gegenseitige Wirtschaftshilfe*, 31–41.
35 One could claim that events like Stalin's birthday celebrations in 1949 were dangerous for the empire, too. However, there is a trade-off to be calculated. A one-time only event taking place in Moscow with Soviet elites forming the majority of participants, could be better controlled than regular, numerous consultations among officials on all levels. An event like Stalin's birthday was organized not according to principles of multilateral consultation, it was an event which showed the power of the empire's leader meant to increase the prestige of the imperial core over its peripheries.
36 Report of the East German delegation on the 28th session of the PCTA from 03.-05 July 1974 in Moscow, Barch Berlin, DE 1/55820.
37 Ibid.
38 The Cuban delegation didn't try to raise the issue again in the 30th session of the PCTA which would have been the next possible occurrence to do so.
39 "Bericht über die 40. Tagung der Ständigen Kommission für Außenhandel, 2.-5.7.74 in Moskau," Barch Berlin, DL 2/6287.
40 "Bericht über die 6. Tagung der Ständigen Kommission des RGW für die Koordinierung der Technischen Unterstützung 25. bis 29. Mai 1964 – Moskau," Barch Berlin, DL 2/22815.
41 "Bericht über die 7. Tagung der Ständigen Kommission des RGW für die Koordinierung der Technischen Unterstützung 19.-21 November 1964, Moskau," dated 25 November 1964, ibid.
42 Report on the 17th meeting of the PCTA in Moscow from 09-10 July 1969, Barch Berlin, DL 2/22859.
43 Report on the 22nd meeting of the PCTA in Moscow from 05.-07 January 1972, Barch Berlin, DL 2/6267.

44 Trade directive for the 24th meeting of the PCTA, Barch Berlin, DL 2/6273.
45 Report on the 31st meeting of the PCTA in Tbilisi from 12.-13 November 1975, Barch Berlin, DL 2/22840.
46 Report on the 40th meeting of the Permanent Commission for Foreign Trade in Moscow from 02.-05 July 1974, Barch Berlin, DL 2/6287.
47 Letter of the Minister for Foreign Trade, Sölle, to the head of the Governmental Planning Commission (SPK), Schürer, dated 09 May 1969, Barch Berlin, DE 1/54932.
48 See e.g., Directive for the 17th meeting of the PCTA, Barch Berlin, DL 2/22859.
49 See e.g., "Bericht über die 22. Tagung der Ständigen Kommission des RGW für die Koordinierung der Technischen Unterstützung (5.-7. January 1972, Moskau)," Barch Berlin, DE 1/54932; "Bericht über die 17. (außerordentliche) Kommissionstagung 9.-10 July 1969 – Moskau," ibid.
50 Report on the 23rd meeting of the PCTA from 01-02 March 1972 in Moscow, Barch Berlin, DE 1/55319.
51 Report on the 24th meeting of the PCTA from 31 May-01 June 1972, ibid.
52 "Direktive für das Auftreten der DDR-Delegation auf der 29. Tagung der SKTU vom 13.-15 November 1974 in Moskau," Barch Berlin, DL 2/6302.
53 "Vermerk über eine Besprechung der Delegationsleiter zur Bildung von Sonderfonds," dated 25 March 1972, KfW Company Archives, Staba 239; Material for the 7th session of the IIB titled "Bildung von Sonderfonds," KfW Company Archives, Staba 241.
54 Letter to Dr. Wittkowski, dated 31 December 1972, ibid.
55 "Abkommen über die Bildung eines Sonderfonds bei der Internationalen Investitionsbank zur Kreditierung von Maßnahmen für die wirtschaftliche und technische Unterstützung von Entwicklungsländern," KfW Company Archives, Staba 242.
56 "Vorschläge zur Ordnung und zu den Formen der Lösung der Valuta-, Finanz- und Kreditfrage bei der Koordinierung der ökonomischen und wissenschaftlich-technischen Hilfe und Unterstützung auf zwei- und mehrseitiger Grundlage für die SRV, Angola und Laos durch die interessierten Mitgliedsländer des RGW, dabei vor allem Vorschläge zur aktiveren Nutzung des in der IIB geschaffenen Sonderfonds zur Kreditierung von Maßnahmen der wirtschaftlichen und technischen Unterstützung von Entwicklungsländern," dated 1976, KfW Company Archives, Staba 2832.
57 "Bericht über den Verlauf der 27. Tagung der SKTU (14.-16.11.1973, Moskau)," dated 23 November 1973, Barch Berlin, DE 1/55820.
58 Report on the 34th meeting of the PCTA from 18-20 May 1977, Barch Berlin, DL 2/6453.
59 "Svodnyi Doklad o sotrudnichestve zainteresovanykh stran-chlenov SEV v oblasti okazaniia ekonomicheskogo i tekhnicheskogo sodeistviia razvivaiushchimsia stranam v vyiavlenii i osvoenii vazhneishikh vidov prirodnykh resorsov," dated 1974, RGAE, Fond 561 op. 26s/pp d. 52 ll. 43–4.
60 Ibid.
61 Ibid., l. 56.
62 Ibid.
63 Ibid., l. 43.
64 Ibid.
65 "Geologie und mineralische Rohstoffe der Republik Irak," dated 15 January 1982, Barch Berlin, DL 2/4933.
66 "Vorlage für den Wissenschaftlichen Rat am 2 June1972," dated 10 May 1972, Barch Berlin, DE 1/55319.
67 Zatlin, *The Currency of Socialism*, 108.
68 "Direktive für das Auftreten der Delegation der DDR auf der 21. Tagung der Ständigen Kommission für Technische Unterstützung des RGW 11-14 May 1971, Moskau," Barch Berlin, DL 2/22859.
69 Report on the 24th meeting of the PCTA from 31 May -01 June 1972, Barch Berlin, DL 2/6273.

70 Draft of the speech of the East German foreign trade minister on the Zambia project in the PCTA, Barch Berlin, DL 2/20056; directive for the 22nd meeting of the PCTA, Barch Berlin, DL 2/6265a.
71 Directive for and report on the 22nd meeting of the PCTA from 05-07 January 1972 in Moscow, Barch Berlin, DL 2/20056.
72 Report on the 24th meeting of the PCTA from 31 May-01 June 1972, Barch Berlin, DE 1/55319.
73 "Bericht über die 32. Tagung der Ständigen Kommission des RGW für die Koordinierung der Technischen Unterstützung (26.-28.5.76, Moskau)," dated 08 June 1976, Barch Berlin, DE 1/55820.
74 Report on the 34th meeting of the PCTA from 18-20 May 1977, Barch Berlin, DL 2/6453.
75 Manuscript for the talk of foreign trade minister Sölle on the 32nd meeting of the PCTA, Barch Berlin, DL 2/22840.
76 "Information über die Haltung der CSSR zur Sicherung ihrer wichtigen Importe aus den Entwicklungsländern," dated 24 July 1964, Barch Berlin, DE 1/49433.
77 Zwass, *Der Rat Für Gegenseitige Wirtschaftshilfe*, 103–4.
78 See on this old view Zwass, 116–8.
79 Zatlin, *The Currency of Socialism*, 108.
80 Motyl, *Imperial Ends*, 19–20.
81 Motyl, 19–20.
82 Motyl, 19–20.
83 Jersild, *The Sino-Soviet Alliance*, 21.
84 Pittaway, *Eastern Europe*, 84; Plaggenborg, *Experiment Moderne*, 279–87.
85 Jersild, *The Sino-Soviet Alliance*, 109–20.
86 Westad, *The Global Cold War*, 114.

# Part III

# Red globalization

# 6 Expansion of the CMEA

## The golden 1970s?

The 1970s seemed promising for the prospects of world revolution. Despite the setback in Egypt for the Eastern Bloc after Anwar el-Sadat had taken power, the Soviet Union and its allies remained a force to be reckoned with in the Middle East. Furthermore, the developments in Egypt were more than counterbalanced by the "successes" in Vietnam. During the latter half of the decade, Sub-Saharan Africa increasingly became a hotspot of the Cold War. While some of the socialist regimes that had emerged in Sub-Saharan Africa in the 1960s like Patrice Lumumba in the Congo could never really establish themselves, others like Kwame Nkrumah's regime in Ghana didn't survive the 1960s either. Thus, socialism in the region seemed to be on the retreat. However, by 1980 several African states were ruled by socialist regimes, many of which were in close contact with the Eastern Bloc and the CMEA.[1]

These political changes were not initiated by the Soviets or Central Eastern Europeans but the new regimes were embraced by the Eastern Bloc after they had come into being. While many of the socialist-minded African leaders of the 1960s had preferred non-alignment and a comparatively soft version of and transition to socialism, the new generation of leaders that came to power in the 1970s actively sought the support of the Eastern Bloc and often pushed for radically altering their respective societies, even if their Soviet advisers had opted for less radical and more conciliatory policies. These new African socialist leaders of the 1970s were adherents of Marxism-Leninism and their revolutionary fervor was often to the liking of the established rulers in the Eastern Bloc.[2]

The political turmoil in Sub-Saharan Africa was to a large degree related to the decay and finally attrition of the last European empire still present in the area. The one European state not directly affected by decolonization in the immediate postwar years was the Portuguese Empire. Portugal, itself a member of NATO, fought African nationalists in its colonial possessions with American support during the 1960s.[3] The Marxist People's Movement for the Liberation of Angola (MPLA) found an early supporter in Fidel Castro's Cuba who decided to help the revolutionary movement before Moscow had jumped onto the bandwagon. The support from Cuba – together with Soviet weapons deliveries later on – was decisive for the success of the MPLA.[4]

After they had won the battle, the Angolan leadership emphasized its independence again and together with the support of the Cuban government and Cuban advisers restrained Soviet demands.[5] Thus, in Angola the Soviets had to accept that they were only one power factor among others. Although, their deliveries of weapons were a precondition for victory, Cuban advisers exerted a greater influence on the Angolan Marxists.[6] This provides an interesting example for intrabloc relations: although the Soviets were the most powerful in the bloc and guaranteeing the security of the Cuban as well as the Angolan regime, they could not prevent the Angolan and Cuban leadership from acting independently from the Soviet core. Developments in Mozambique, where the Marxists of the Mozambique Liberation Front (FRELIMO) had taken power in 1975, followed a similar trajectory.

Another African country turned Marxist-Leninist in the 1970s was Ethiopia. Ethiopia was a particular prestigious country to get associated with, because it was the only country that had successfully repelled European colonizers, namely the Italians.[7] The Ethiopian leader Mengistu Haile Mariam relied heavily on support from the Eastern Bloc which was not only confined to military supplies. The aim was to push the country forcefully and rapidly into "modernity."[8] The events in Ethiopia, Mozambique, and Angola were connected with each other in as much as the Soviet leadership and the leaders of the smaller members of the bloc were emboldened by the military successes in Angola, which made them believe that socialism was advancing, thus increasing their willingness to invest in the countries concerned.[9] By the end of the 1970s, the number of civil and military advisers from the Eastern Bloc in Ethiopia alone surpassed 7,000.[10] The socialist revolutions in Sub-Saharan Africa subsequently set a process in motion that became a great experiment in Eastern developmentalism. Ethiopia, Mozambique, and Angola became important issues at the top of the agenda of the CMEA when it came to the Global South for the remaining time of its existence.

The CMEA expanded its membership in the Global South to Cuba and Vietnam during the 1970s. The countries that turned socialist or Marxist-Leninist during the second half of the decade played an important part in the CMEA. Although they never became full members of the CMEA till the dissolution of the CMEA, their membership was a long-term option, with some kind of association with the CMEA being discussed and implemented. The CMEA became a subject of international trade affairs already before by concluding cooperation treaties with Mexico and Iraq in the 1970s. These treaties will be examined in this chapter and followed by analyzing the discussions inside the CMEA on expanding the organization by including more countries from the Global South in the early- and mid-1980s. At the end of the 1970s, not only the Middle East and Sub-Saharan Africa were important regions for the CMEA member countries but also the issues of what to do with Afghanistan and Nicaragua had to be dealt with.

## Relations with Iraq

One country that took center stage in particular during the first half of the 1970s in the CMEA negotiations was Iraq. The relationship between the Soviet Union and Iraq had started in 1958 after a successful Ba'athist coup. The Iraqi Ba'athist Party was on the surface similar to its Syrian counterpart, but was often at odds with its sibling in Damascus. The Iraqi Ba'athists were further away from "scientific socialism" than their Syrian counterparts rejecting class struggle and calling for national unity. Nevertheless, the party's program from 1968 called for friendship between the Eastern Bloc and Iraq based on anti-Western sentiments and "anti-Imperialism."[11] In 1972, the Iraqi government signed a treaty of friendship and cooperation with the Soviet Union which gave the Iraqi side the necessary backing to nationalize the oil industry. This didn't coincide with a closer ideological alignment, as the new Iraqi strongman, Saddam Hussein, didn't sympathize with the Soviet version of communism. Nevertheless, the CP of Iraq was legalized again in 1973 and a national front was formed, measures which had merely symbolical value.[12]

Relations cooled down again in the mid-1970s when the sprawling oil trade enabled the Iraqi leadership to diversify its economic and political partners and drew it closer to the West again. The Ba'ath regime had reached a final settlement with the former private oil companies in 1973 which allowed the Iraqi side to market its own oil.[13] The nationalization of the oil industry came at the right time to profit from the price increases of the 1970s. The Iraqi leadership could afford to import Western as well as Eastern civil and military goods on an unprecedented scale. In 1978, Saddam Hussein, fearing a Communist plot under Soviet guidance, ordered Iraqi Communists tracked down once more.[14] Mutual relations recovered again but this shows that the relations between the Eastern Bloc and Iraq constituted no patron–client relationship, as the Iraqi side could exercise a considerable amount of leverage.

It is interesting to follow the ascendance in importance of Iraq for the CMEA member countries. While the prospects of Iraq were judged as being rather doubtful during the 1960s, this changed rapidly after the nationalization of the oil industry and the sharp increases in commodity prices following the first oil shock. Iraq increasingly became an issue for discussion inside the CMEA and the PCTA in the late 1960s. The CMEA member states were approving the fact that their share in Iraq's foreign trade had increased from 12.9 % in 1964 to 22.9 % in 1968. They furthermore approved of the foreign policy actions of the Iraqi government which stated its opposition towards the West and employed a positive attitude towards the East.[15]

However, trade in the late 1960s, although increasing, remained rather marginal. Hungary, to make a case in point, rarely imported goods worth more than 0.2 million US dollars during the 1960s from Iraq, while its exports equaled four million US dollars.[16] The import numbers for the Polish economy were similar, while exports were slightly higher.[17] In the case of East Germany trade with Iraq remained marginal during the entire decade. This only began to change when the East German government granted a credit worth roughly 100 million US dollars.[18] The reason for the low value of mutual exchange was that most of the smaller CMEA member states didn't import Iraqi oil during the 1960s. Their imports concentrated on traditional Iraqi products, mainly dried fruits. Since the oil industry wasn't yet nationalized and the first oil shock lay still ahead, the Iraqi government could employ only very modest resources to finance any industrialization and development schemes. A Soviet report on the financial situation of Iraq written before the nationalization of the oil industry and shared via the PCTA reads as follows:

> The economy of Iraq has developed pretty sluggish in the last years which is testified by the low growth of industrial and agricultural production, the low level of investment, the slow and erratic growth of imports. . . . The financial situation of Iraq has been tenuous over the last years. The need to grant more money for military purposes has significantly grown in relation with the aggressive acts of Israel [sic!] and the Kurdish conflict which is a huge liability for the national finances and limits the investment program.[19]

This had changed by the late 1970s. An East German report on the financial and economic situation of Iraq filed in 1977 judged the financial situation of Iraq as excellent due to the high revenues from oil exports. In spite of many export revenues from oil being invested in the buildup of a national industry, the efficiency and rentability of it was considered low by the East German experts. This didn't need to bother them, since the Iraqi government was investing 8 billion US dollars in 1977 alone, while the government pledged to invest 49 billion US dollars between 1976–80.[20] This was positive news as the investments necessitated imports of capital goods which constituted a relative advantage of the export economies of the CMEA member countries. However, by the late 1970s, the mood among the Central Eastern Europeans had somewhat faded, since the Iraqi government was trying to tone down its spending spree and Western competitors were increasing their activities on the Iraqi market:

> Increasing economic disproportions prompted the Iraqi government to focus more on questions of necessity while planning new projects than had hitherto been the case. The "generosity" of the last years when it came to approving new projects and imports has been significantly curtailed.[21]

Documents of the early 1980s show that the honeymoon period was finally over. The repressions against Iraqi Communists and the increasingly independent and aggressive foreign policy style of Saddam Hussein became obstacles that provided for a mixed picture in the early 1980s.[22] These documents hint at the high volatility of relations with the Global South, as the political stability of many countries was often in grave jeopardy. When the Iraqi government felt weak and insecure close alignment with the Eastern Bloc seemed advisable. The moment it could choose among Western and Eastern partners alike, a political line navigating in between the two blocs was sought after. Despite the criticism against Saddam Hussein's regime most evidently expressed in the documents of the early 1980s, Iraq remained a close, if unpredictable, partner for the Eastern Bloc. The countries of the Eastern Bloc couldn't control the Iraqi leadership but they could more often than not count on practical support. As with the example briefly mentioned in chapter 4 when East German and Romanian companies erected a modern slaughterhouse in Bagdad, political sympathy could tip the balance in favor of the Eastern Bloc and to the detriment of Western competitors.[23]

## The CMEA's treaty with Iraq

Despite the problems emerging at the end of the decade, the prospects of economic cooperation with Iraq seemed promising in the early 1970s. The same year the Iraqi government signed a treaty of friendship and cooperation with the Soviet Union, negotiations were taken up to conclude the first treaty between the CMEA and an Arab country. The protocol of a meeting between the Secretary of the CMEA, Faddeev, and the Iraqi ambassador to the Soviet Union, Salih Mehdi Amash, in the building of the CMEA in November 1972 reads as follows:

> N.V. Faddeev referred to the note of the embassy . . . and informed the ambassador that all CMEA member countries have received the wish of the government of his country for cooperation with the Council with satisfaction and have given their consent in principle.
>
> Furthermore, N.V. Faddeev mentioned the readiness of the Secretariat of the Council to discuss on a preliminary basis with the responsible representative of Iraq the areas and questions of cooperation of interest for the Iraqi side as well as the possible forms and conditions of the cooperation of Iraq with the CMEA, and proposed to conduct these discussions in the CMEA building in November/December this year. He [Faddeev] made the remark that it would be suitable for the Iraqi side to take primarily the Complex-Program, which marks a broad circle of areas and problems of cooperation of the CMEA member countries, into consideration for preparing for the discussions of a cooperation of Iraq with the Council.[24]

The discussion between the Iraqi ambassador and the Secretary of the CMEA continued:

> N.[V.] Faddeev emphasized the democratic character of the CMEA, the voluntariness of cooperation inside the Council, the absence of supranational organs in the Council and as a consequence of this the vitality of the recommendations adopted by the Council, whereupon he proved this by the example of the oil pipeline "Friendship" [druzhba], the energy system "Peace" [mir], and others. . . .
>
> The ambassador thanked the Secretary of the Council . . . and referred to the uniformity of the views of Iraq and the CMEA member countries with regards to the negative role of capitalist groups, in particular of the "Common Market" [European Community].
>
> He stated furthermore that the cooperation of Iraq within the bounds of the CMEA expands the "geography" of the Council, contributes to a change in the balance of power between East and West in oil production to the advantage

> of the CMEA member countries, and [stated] that – most importantly – this will be an example for the other Arab countries in the sense of fostering their friendship and cooperation with the CMEA member countries.[25]

The protocol of this meeting is not only interesting, because it marked the beginning of negotiations between the CMEA and the government of Iraq but also because of the specific tone. The Secretary of the CMEA emphasized the "democratic" character of the CMEA with which he meant the non-binding character of most of its resolutions which enabled members to cherry-pick to a certain extent. He denied that the CMEA contained any supranational elements in spite of ongoing discussions inside the CMEA to transform the CMEA in such a direction, which was also favored by the Soviet leadership, one of the proponents of supranational, binding planning. The Iraqi ambassador associated himself with the Eastern Bloc in the way that a treaty between the CMEA and Iraq would strengthen the bloc to the detriment of the West. He thus emphasized the geopolitical implications of such a treaty and implied that the Iraqi oil reserves could serve the Eastern Bloc's interests. This discussion has to be seen within the context of the Resource-Program.

A Cooperation Agreement between the CMEA and Iraq was signed on 4 July 1975.[26] It was the first agreement between the CMEA and a country of the Global South without the respective country becoming a full member. Its aim was to foster economic and scientific-technical cooperation on a multilateral basis.[27] The CMEA member countries could profit in two ways from their treaty with Iraq and the nationalization of its oil industry. Their experts estimated Iraqi oil reserves to amount to 4.2 billion tons with an annual production of more than 80 million tons in 1971.[28] They could therefore either build factories and deliver equipment in exchange for oil or profit from Iraqi export revenues by being paid with convertible currencies for their deliveries. Both methods were employed by the CMEA member states.[29]

The close alignment of Iraq to the Eastern Bloc didn't materialize, even if it seemed possible in 1972–73. Neither could the CMEA member countries command the Iraqi oil reserves. It remains an open question, if Iraq was proposed to join the CMEA as a full member in the mid- or long-term. However, the balance of power had indeed shifted as the Iraqi ambassador had predicted. But these shifts were rather in favor of the Iraqi regime than the Eastern Bloc, as the oil revenues enabled the Iraqi leadership to transform their country into an aggressive regional power that seemed in no need of a strong protector. In the early 1970s the Iraqi ambassador to the Soviet Union had furthermore promised the Secretary of the CMEA that the oil production of his country would roughly triple between 1972 and 1980 to 250 million tons annually by 1980.[30] This plan proved too ambitious. The oil production of Iraq, while amounting to only 7.1 million tons in 1950 and 47.5 million tons in 1960, advanced to 168.6 million tons in 1979. Due to the outbreak of hostilities between Iraq and Iran, the production declined sharply and reached only 138 million tons in 1980.[31] For 1981 the experts of the CMEA expected the Iraqi oil production to slump to the levels of the late 1950s and early 1960s.[32]

Nevertheless, trade between the CMEA countries and Iraq increased significantly during the 1970s, in particular in comparison to the meager economic relations that prevailed during the preceding decade. In comparison to the average of the 1960s, East German exports, to make a case in point, exceeded the former value by more than 20 times in the late 1970s. East German exports varied during the 1970s between 200 and 400 million Valutamark with imports much more volatile than exports. The 400 million VM equated to roughly 160 million US dollars in the mid-1970s. While the GDR had accumulated huge trade surpluses during the early 1970s, these were counterbalanced by oil imports of up to 1.2 million tons annually in the late 1970s. This made Iraq the biggest non-CMEA oil supplier of the GDR. However, the GDR began to accumulate extremely high trade surpluses again after the outbreak of the First Gulf War in 1980, because the Iraqi government proved unable or unwilling to export any more oil to the CMEA countries.[33] This again proved the high volatility of relations with the Global South.

The situation was similar in the other CMEA member states. Polish exports to Iraq exceeded 100 million US dollars annually during the second half of the 1970s which was more than 16 times the value of the late 1960s. In contrast to the GDR, the Polish leadership started to import significant amounts of oil from Iraq only in 1978. The Polish government had to pay 200 million US dollars for importing 2.2 million tons of Iraqi oil in 1979.[34] But as was the case in the GDR, these imports proved unsustainable after the outbreak of the war between Iraq and Iran. This made any of the import quotas planned for in the Resource-Program obsolete.

## Negotiations with Mexico

Similar negotiations like the ones between Iraq and the CMEA simultaneously took place between the CMEA and Mexico. On 13 April 1973, N. Faddeev and the Permanent Representative of the Soviet Union to the CMEA, M.A. Lesechko, met with the Mexican Deputy Minister for Industry and Trade, Elisso Mendoza Berrueto, in Moscow. In their conversation, Berrueto asked the Secretary of the CMEA what advantages his organization could offer for its members and what possibilities to cooperate exist for non-member states. In his answer, Faddeev referred to the special funds of the International Investment Bank for "developing countries," the growing importance of the Transferable Ruble, and the development successes of the CMEA member states. Having the situation of 1973 in mind, he mentioned the already existing cooperation between the CMEA, Yugoslavia, and Finland. He proposed to the Mexican minister that the CMEA could establish joint ventures in Mexico and build factories to develop the Mexican economy. Mr. Berrueto was cautious to refer to all the possibilities for cooperation mentioned by Faddeev. Nevertheless, he showed distinct interest in using the funds of the International Investment Bank for developing Mexican industries. At the end of their talk, he emphasized the interest of his government to establish formal links with the CMEA not only in the area of trade but also when it came to investment projects. Their discussion lasted almost two hours.[35]

The mutual discussions became more concrete in the following months. In October 1973, the Secretary of the CMEA talked with the Mexican ambassador to the Soviet Union about sending a Mexican expert delegation to the CMEA to discuss joint economic projects and a treaty between the CMEA and Mexico.[36] In the end of October the following year, a Mexican delegation encompassing 14 persons and led by Mr. Berrueto met an expert delegation of the CMEA in the Secretariat of the CMEA in Moscow headed by N. Faddeev. The delegation of the CMEA included 20 persons. During the four days of the conference, the Mexicans were intensively briefed on the activities of the CMEA, its aims, and methods. The CMEA experts emphasized the importance of the Complex-Program and the aims of Socialist Economic Integration.[37] Their remarks were convincing enough for the Mexican delegation. Deputy Minister Berrueto stated the willingness of his country to conclude a treaty with the CMEA but mentioned that his government had to act cautiously and negotiations to be conducted off-the-record at first.[38]

It is interesting to see that the Secretary of the CMEA emphasized the Complex-Program and the International Investment Bank in his discussions with the Mexican representatives. The last point in particular is surprising, since the special funds of the IIB for countries of the Global South never really took off due to the reluctance of the smaller members of the CMEA to pay their share into the funds. The same was true for the Transferable Ruble which was well established in the early 1970s, but still lacked essential features for a successful currency such as full convertibility. He was also cautious to speak of the CMEA as a community of equals and regarded himself in his talks with Mexican officials not as a Soviet but as a CMEA representative. By June 1975, the treaty was already negotiated but not yet signed and ratified, as is clear from the protocol of a meeting between the Secretary of the CMEA and the Mexican ambassador who was urging the Secretary for a quick ratification of the treaty.[39]

In a meeting on 23 June 1976, Faddeev was told by the Mexican ambassador that large parts of Mexican society approve of a closer cooperation between the CMEA and Mexico and attach high expectations to such endeavors. However, he mentioned the unstable political situation in his country, as a new government could easily repeal any steps already taken.[40] The treaty between Mexico and the CMEA was signed in August 1975 and finally approved by the 30th Council Session in July 1976 which took place in East Berlin.[41] The first meeting of the Joint Commission CMEA-Mexico occurred between 19–20 October 1976. In his speech, the Mexican delegation leader appealed to the spirit of the revolution of 1910 when a popular revolt had ended the dictatorship of Porfirio Díaz. He emphasized that the foreign policy of Mexico since then was guided by two principles: the defense of Mexico's sovereignty and the development of its economy, politics, and culture. Both principles he saw embodied in the treaty between his country and the CMEA.[42] Faddeev, who was also present on the occasion, seconded the head of the Mexican delegation. He talked mainly about the values of friendship and sovereignty after which the work of the CMEA was modeled. He mentioned socialism only in the last quarter of his speech. He talked about "socialist help" that enabled the CMEA member countries to reach a higher development level. The aim of the CMEA was to disseminate the benefits of "socialist help" internationally.[43]

In its first session, the two delegations decided to form three different working groups. One should focus on scientific-technical cooperation, one on the fishing industry, and the third on increasing mutual trade in general with a particular emphasis on projects in the consumer and capital goods sectors. The first group was headed by a Soviet foreign trade official, the second by a Polish, and the third by a Hungarian one. Energy production, machine building, geological prospecting, and delivering complete objects for the health and education system were regarded as promising to increase trade with Mexico. These subgroups were headed by experts whose countries enjoyed an intrabloc comparative advantage in the respective area. East German experts were responsible for finding opportunities in machine building, Czechoslovak ones for energy generation, and Polish experts for prospecting coal, to make a case in point.[44] Some of the meetings of the subgroups, like the one on the fishing industry, also took place in Cuba.[45]

Mutual trade between the CMEA member countries and Mexico increased in the late 1970s. Trade between the CSSR and Mexico stagnated in the early 1970s at roughly 6 million US dollars annually. In the late 1970s, the value of Czechoslovak-Mexican trade reached 20 million US dollars.[46] In 1981 the value peaked at 46 million US dollars.[47] The Czechoslovak side achieved an export surplus in every single year. While the CSSR imported mainly agrarian goods from Mexico like coffee, tobacco, and cocoa, they exported metal goods, machines, and tractors.[48] The same applied to the GDR, the trade of which with Mexico reached its high point in 1981 at 70 million US dollars.[49] Polish trade with Mexico reached 12 million US dollars in 1976 and was projected to increase to 52 million US dollars by 1980.[50] All in all, trade between the CMEA area and Mexico had increased from 12.9 million US dollars in 1970 to 113.3 million US dollars in 1976 and continued to rise till 1981.[51] Although these increases in trade turnover were impressive in relation to the numbers prevailing in the early 1970s, they show that Mexico remained a rather insignificant trading partner, at least for the European CMEA countries. It may be surprising at first glance that Cuba was the biggest Mexican trading partner among the CMEA countries in the mid-1970s and also the one with the biggest increase from 0 US dollars in 1970 to 31.7 million US dollars in 1976.[52]

Mexican officials didn't stop to lobby the Secretary of the CMEA after the treaty had come into effect. They wanted to profit from the technological lead of the European members of the CMEA in comparison to the Mexican level of technological development. The Mexican side wanted to acquire knowledge in fields ranging from agriculture in arid areas to building and operating nuclear power plants and mining uranium.[53] The trade numbers show that the Soviet side didn't profit much from the CMEA-Mexico treaty. The profiteers were Cuba and the smaller European members of the CMEA. While the former could import much needed goods from Mexico, the latter could export their machines and received foreign exchange and small amounts of coffee and other tropical goods in return. The Joint Commission was furthermore not under strict control of Soviet officials.

At least during the 1980s, its work was coordinated in the Secretariat by an East German, Helmut Gallitz.[54] The Joint Commission itself was headed by another East German, Deputy Minister for Foreign Trade Dr. Eduard Schwierz.[55]

## Afghanistan, Ethiopia, and Nicaragua

Relations between Afghanistan and the Soviet Union predated its relations with the smaller countries of Central Eastern Europe. Soviet-Afghan relations started with the signing of a treaty of friendship in 1921. Till their expulsion in 1936 a small number of up to 120 Soviet experts worked in Kabul.[56] For a short period after the end of the Second World War the US was the biggest donor for Afghanistan and tried to build huge dams and irrigation schemes in Helmand modeled after the Tennessee Valley Authority with disastrous consequences.[57] After Stalin's death, relations improved again and the Soviets stepped up their economic aid to Afghanistan which was considered more beneficial than the American one. For the Soviets this had the advantage that they could secure their Southern flank by aligning or at least neutralizing Afghanistan as a political factor.[58]

Although the smaller countries of the CMEA were conducting economic projects in Afghanistan in the 1960s, like the CSSR erecting a canning factory in 1962, economic aid to Afghanistan remained a Soviet affair.[59] Due to the proximity of the two countries, the Soviets were the biggest Afghan trading partner and the only country able to buy the most important export good, gas.[60] After the Soviet leadership had decided to intervene in Afghanistan, the Afghan Communist leaders could often exercise much greater leverage over their Soviet allies than the other way around. The reason was that the Soviet leadership, while opting for a slow implementation of socialism, could not simply withdraw from the country in order to restrain the Afghan Communists without losing face.[61]

Economic cooperation with Afghanistan became an issue in the PCTA in the mid-1970s. An information exchange between the CMEA member states was scheduled for the 29th meeting of the PCTA in mid-November 1974.[62] These talks were continued in 1975 and thus preceded the Communist takeover in Afghanistan. The aim was to elaborate on a multilateral cooperation scheme for Afghanistan, although some countries, like the GDR, had no economic relations with Afghanistan up to that date.[63] Most CMEA member states had concluded their first formal trade treaties with Afghanistan in the late 1960s like Bulgaria or the early 1970s as in the case of Hungary. Their main import positions from Afghanistan consisted of very basic items like animal skins or sesame seeds.[64] Some kind of industrial base should be developed in Afghanistan in exchange for a share of Afghanistan's mineral resources which still had to be prospected to a large extent.[65] However, no formal agreement between the CMEA and Afghanistan was signed till 1986 as is clear from the protocol of a meeting between the Secretary of the CMEA and Afghan representatives in December 1986.[66] The first meeting of the Joint Commission CMEA-Afghanistan took place from 28–29 March 1987.[67]

Although a treaty between the CMEA and Afghanistan would probably have never occurred were it not for the Soviets intervening in Afghanistan to stabilize Communist rule, it took quite long for such a treaty to materialize. The main reason for this is that Afghanistan was economically not interesting for the smaller members of the CMEA. Resources that still had to be prospected in an area increasingly destabilized by civil war are far less attractive than mining them in areas that are already prospected and politically more stable than Afghanistan.

In contrast to Afghanistan, the smaller CMEA member states showed a greater interest in forging economic ties with Nicaragua. Up to the takeover of the Sandinistas in Nicaragua in Summer 1979, Nicaragua had never been placed prominently, if at all, on the agenda of the CMEA or the PCTA. Because of its highly ideologized new leadership and the support of counterinsurgencies by the Reagan administration, it became an issue during the 1980s. Subsequently, a treaty between the CMEA and Nicaragua came into being faster than with Afghanistan. The first session of the Joint Commission CMEA-Nicaragua took place in the Bulgarian town of Plovdiv from 4th to 6th September 1984.[68]

Due to the poverty of Nicaragua, the ongoing war, and the small population base of the country, trade relations, while expanding, remained rather insignificant during the 1980s and consisted to a larger than usual degree of grants.[69] Although Nicaraguan external trade amounted to more than one billion US dollars annually in the mid-1980s, Nicaragua imported much more than it exported. While overall exports fluctuated between 300 and 429 million US dollars, imports often exceeded 800 million US dollars. These numbers include trade with European and Latin American countries and show the modest economic importance of Nicaragua for the Eastern Bloc in comparison to a country like Iraq.[70] Nevertheless, the CMEA member states accomplished a sizable number of multilateral development projects in Nicaragua, building up infrastructure and industrial complexes. These endeavors encompassed – among others – East German and Czechoslovak joint projects to build textile and cement factories, and East German-Bulgarian development schemes for a harbor on the coast and fostering cocoa production in Nicaragua.[71]

The first talks between Ethiopian representatives and the Secretary of the CMEA occurred in spring 1978. N.V. Faddeev praised the courage of the Ethiopian revolutionaries in the first of these meetings and promised that the CMEA member countries would do more than merely providing morale support. The members of the CMEA would be able to elaborate on huge development schemes and build up the capital stock of Ethiopia. In order to do so, the Ethiopian side would have to meet certain preliminary conditions like establishing plan coordination with the CMEA member states.[72] Despite his promises, working out a treaty between the CMEA and Ethiopia took several years. The Ethiopian government was urging the Secretariat of the CMEA to finalize the treaty in a letter from 16th February 1986:

> During the visit to the USSR, in November, of Comrade Mengistu Haile Mariam . . . the desire of Socialist Ethiopia to conclude with the Council for Mutual Economic Assistance the Agreement on Economic, Scientific and

> Technical Co-operation and establish a Joint Ethio-CMEA-Commission was expressed.
>
> This letter is, therefore, a confirmation of the desire of the Ethiopian Government to conclude the above General Agreement on Co-operation with CMEA and to establish the Ethio-CMEA Joint Commission. The Ethiopian side would like to propose that delegations of CMEA and Socialist Ethiopia meet in appropriate time to negotiate the contents of the Agreement.[73]

The treaty was finally approved on 13th October 1986.[74] Trade between the CMEA member countries and Ethiopia had expanded from ca. 100 million rubles in 1978 to 274 million rubles in 1984, while the Ethiopian government was promised economic development projects worth 872 million rubles.[75]

## New members?

The elephant in the room was whether the CMEA member states were willing and able to take up new full members from the Global South after the accession of Cuba and Vietnam in the 1970s. In the end no full member was taken up after the accession of Vietnam in 1978. The government of Mozambique unsuccessfully tried to gain full membership for their country on the 37th Council Session in October 1983 in East Berlin.[76] This Session was also the last headed by N.V. Fadeev who was succeeded by the Soviet V.V. Sychev. The reasons for this failed attempt cited in the textbook literature are speculative, since they are not based on archival material but official protocols and newspaper articles. Scholars in the 1980s often concluded that in particular the smaller CMEA member states were unwilling to take up another "developing country" next to Mongolia, Cuba, and Vietnam, because they were unable and unwilling to finance the necessary development aid and that these countries could offer nothing in return.[77]

This view is inaccurate. There is no hard-archival evidence that the European CMEA member states were entirely opposed to new members from the Global South. In a letter to Secretary Faddeev from 22 October 1980, the Permanent Representative of Bulgaria, Andrei Lukanov, was arguing that the CMEA should pursue a more aggressive path to attract attention in the Global South, increase mutual cooperation, and to emphasize the meaning of the CMEA as an alternative model to the Western model of development and economic cooperation:

> We think that with this view on the strategic aims of cooperation of the CMEA with developing countries our propagandistic work has to become more effective and deliberate, has to touch vital problems of these countries, has to open possibilities and alternatives for their decisions on the basis of our own experiences.
>
> It is known that a significant part of the countries of the Third World has not finally decided on their own social-economic orientation. Furthermore, the inner economic, technical and cadre potential of these countries is not sufficient for decisions on these problems, in connection with the development

> of their domestic economies. This forces them to actively seek the decision in international cooperation. . . . Due to a lack of experience, they are often copying the capitalist integration model. . . . As practice shows, the utilization of this model under specific conditions has not delivered the desired results. As a consequence, symptoms of disappointment already appeared in the Third World in the 1960s and in the present time developing countries and their group show an extraordinary affection for international cooperation, in particular in the field of industry. The CMEA is presiding over rich experiences and practical results namely in this field. From this point of view the increased interest of the developing countries in the CMEA is completely explicable. This includes not only the countries which chose the non-capitalist path of development but also those other countries which show interest in industrial cooperation.[78]

He moved on with concrete policy proposals:

> We therefore think that the main task of the propaganda activity of the CMEA in the Third World has to be the popularization of our integration model and the socio-economic results of its thirty years of existence.
>
> Special attention has to be given to popularizing our system of cooperation in the fields of planning and foreign trade and their coordination with industrial cooperation. In a word: Broad propaganda on the mechanism of Socialist Integration is needed.
>
> We have to use forms of indirect contacts far more actively, such as: sending experts or groups for studying specified fields in the name of the CMEA (and not of single countries); organizing seminars, conferences, and other measures with the aim of studying technical problems of industrial cooperation; educating specialists from developing countries in issues of the Socialist International Division of Labor; expanding connections with regional organizations with the purpose to utilize their actions or organization for joint activities.
>
> You understand, the activation of propagandistic activities has to coincide with the practical actions of the CMEA, foremost in the field of industrial cooperation.[79]

The Permanent Representative of Bulgaria conveys the impression that the turn of the 1970s to the 1980s would prove decisive for the success of Soviet-style socialism in the Global South. He also paints the countries of the Global South as being in need of a guiding hand, which would require the CMEA to act proactively and be ready to help. His letter shows that the frontlines within the CMEA were not as clear as could be thought from the outside. While some remarks were highly hypocritical, it shows the connectedness between politics and economics. The smaller European members of the CMEA could opt for maximizing their own economic benefit like they did during the negotiations of the Resource-Program, but they could also push forward a common socialist agenda in the Global South.

It is furthermore interesting to note that the Soviets reacted quite reservedly on the Bulgarian letter, while the Permanent Representatives of the CSSR and Hungary were embracing the Bulgarian proposals.[80] This also indicates that the Eastern Bloc post-Stalin is better understood as a transnational community than as an imperial construct. There was no clear fault line between center and periphery, Soviet Union, smaller European members of the CMEA, and non-European members from the Global South.

To stir further confusion, it could also be "developing countries" themselves within the CMEA opposing a quick integration and take up of other countries from the Global South. One year before the coup against the left-leaning Prime Minister of Grenada, Maurice Bishop, and the subsequent US intervention, his Minister of Agriculture, George Louison, wrote a letter to the Deputy Secretary of the CMEA elaborating on a cooperation between his country and the CMEA:

> Esteemed Cde Libit,
>
> On behalf of the Grenada delegation and myself I wish to thank you and your staff for having provided the time to meet with us during our visit to the U.S.S.R. It was certainly very informative and interesting to receive a first-hand presentation and detailed documentation of the work of the Council and to learn of its achievements in energy, trade, transport, agriculture, and planning.
>
> It is our desire to strengthen areas of cooperation between the Council and Grenada through the many opportunities available to developing countries. In this connection I wish to reiterate the desire of the Revolutionary Government of Grenada to commence these activities by inviting the Council to send a mission of technicians to visit Grenada in the final quarter of this year or early in 1983. It is proposed that this mission would familiarise itself with our economy, assess our economic plans and programmes, and identify areas of future cooperation between Grenada and the Council.[81]

Soviet experts took a very cautious approach towards the prospects of economic cooperation with Grenada and noted that the leadership of Grenada was just starting to expand their relations with the CMEA member countries. They were therefore recommending to urge the Grenadian leadership to develop relations on a bilateral basis first before multilateral cooperation schemes could be envisioned. Furthermore, they were expressing doubts that the Grenadians had understood the working mechanisms of the CMEA completely, since they were urging the CMEA to send experts without specifying, if they were calling for experts from the Secretariat of the CMEA or for a team of experts assembled by the CMEA member states.[82] The Permanent Representative of Cuba, Carlos Rafael Rodriges, was far more blunt in his answer to the Grenadian letter and used the opportunity to cast doubts on the motives and prospects of other countries from the Global South that expressed their desire to conclude treaties of cooperation with the CMEA:

> In relation to the invitation which we have received from the Minister of Agriculture of Grenada, Comrade Luison, for the visit of specialists from the

> CMEA to Grenada and the determination of fields of cooperation, it seems necessary for me to emphasize that we – before making a decision on our participation – have to discuss, if there are any real possibilities to satisfy the wishes of Grenada to any degree.
>
> I am deeply concerned by the fact that a growing number of developing countries is understanding the CMEA as a possibility to solve grave problems that are caused by the weak development of their countries. They are deluding themselves and subsequently will be disappointed by the weak results of their cooperation with the CMEA.
>
> I am not opposed to a visit [to Grenada] but I think it necessary to analyze the possibilities of this visit beforehand in relating to the issues stated above which I will present to the other Representatives of the member countries for examination.[83]

The Permanent Representative of the same country that had played a leading role for the success of the revolution in Angola was thus urging its allies to be very skeptical and cautious about the prospects of the Global South. This is surprising, although his view was probably very realistic. Concluding treaties with the CMEA before solving internal problems was no road to salvation. Mozambique, one of the countries falling into this category, was living through economic hardship during the 1980s caused by internal conflicts and a lack of economic reforms. Its exports decreased from 285 million US dollars in 1981 to 80 million US dollars in 1986, while the country's debts were increasing in the same time to three billion US dollars.[84] Angola could export raw materials like oil and was exporting goods worth roughly two billion US dollars in the early 1980s but Angola marketed most of these resources in the West and conducted only a small amount of its trade with the CMEA member countries. Its biggest trading partners were Portugal and France.[85] As long as this trade hierarchy remained in place, it was not advisable to include a country like Angola as a full member of the CMEA. The same was true for Mozambique that was conducting three-fourths of its trade with non-CMEA countries at the time that its leadership allegedly considered becoming a full member of the CMEA. Economic experts from Mozambique themselves mentioned in a discussion with the Secretary of the CMEA that this dependence on trade with the West was curtailing their freedom of action.[86]

## Conclusion

The aim of this chapter was to show that the CMEA was actively expanding its reach in the 1970s. This expansion didn't take place by some cooperation schemes between two or more member countries or the accession of Cuba and Vietnam as full members alone. The CMEA developed new forms of cooperation that allowed countries from the Global South to profit from multilateral cooperation without becoming full members themselves. This allowed closer ties to be forged with countries that were not known as aligning to the Eastern Bloc before. In connection with the reform program of the CMEA in the early 1970s, this drew the attention of countries as different as Iraq and Mexico. The cooperation treaties with these countries allowed mutual trade to expand rapidly, at least on a relative level.

The 1970s were also a decade that seemed to brighten up the prospects for state socialism in particular in Sub-Saharan Africa. Countries like Angola, Mozambique, and Ethiopia were actively seeking close ties with the Eastern Bloc without becoming client states of the Soviet Union or the smaller socialist states of Central Eastern Europe. The archival evidence shows that the members of the CMEA were not necessarily opposed to take up new members from the Global South. Skeptical remarks can rather be found in countries like Cuba that would not have had to pay for new members from the Global South but could have actually increased their own bargaining power vis-à-vis the European countries with new allies inside the organization. However, the CMEA member states didn't succeed in forging economic ties strong enough to offer a realistic path to full membership for the new Marxist-Leninist regimes in the mid-term.

## Notes

1 Ottaway, *Afrocommunism*, 1–5.
2 Ottaway, 7–9; Westad, *The Global Cold War*, 251–3, 287.
3 Westad, 207–10.
4 Westad, 212–3.
5 Westad, 240–1.
6 Westad, 240–1.
7 Westad, 251.
8 Westad, 252–3.
9 Westad, 252–3.
10 Westad, 279.
11 Gôlan, *Soviet Policies in the Middle East*, 162–3.
12 Gôlan, 166–7.
13 Owen and Pamuk, *A History of the Middle East Economies*, 166–7.
14 Gôlan, *Soviet Policies in the Middle East*, 170–2.
15 "Informatsiia o polozhenii i perpsktivakh razvitiia sviazei stran-chlenov SEV," dated 11 July 1969, RGAE, Fond 561 op. 53 d. 39 ll. 49–54.
16 Ibid.
17 "Informatsiia o torgovom obmene mezhdu Pol'shei i Irakom, a takzhe o perspektivakh ego razvitiia," ibid. ll. 88–92.
18 "Ländermappe Irak," dated January 1982, Barch Berlin, DL 2/4933.
19 "Die Valuta- und Finanzlage des Irak," dated 1970, Barch Berlin, DL 2/22808.
20 Report on the economic and financial situation of Iraq, dated 20 May 1977, Barch Berlin, DL 2/6453.
21 Ibid.
22 "Ländermappe Irak," dated January 1982, Barch Berlin, DL 2/4933.
23 "Ökonomische Gesamtrechnung des Anlagenexportvorhabens 'Modernes Schlachthaus Bagdad'," dated 20 August 1979, Barch Berlin, DN 1/20698.
24 "Niederschrift des Gesprächs des Sekretärs des RGW, N. Faddejew, mit dem Botschafter der Republik Irak in der UdSSR, Salih Mehdi Amasch, im RGW-Sekretariat am 2 November 1972," PA AA, C 825/77.
25 Ibid.
26 Treaty CMEA-Iraq in Arabic and Russian, dated 04 July 1975, RGAE, Fond 302 op. 2 d. 1417 ll. 10–27.

27 "Information über die Haltung des Irak zum RGW bzw. zum Dialog der arabischen Länder mit der EWG," dated 18 September 1975, PA AA, ZR 2406/82.
28 "O vozmozhnykh sovmestnykh deistviiakh zainteresovannykh stran-chlenov SEV po okazaniiu tekhnicheskogo sodeistviia v razvitii neftianoi promyshlennosti Iraka, ARE, Irana, Sirii, Anzhira i drugikh stran v tselyakh razvitiia importa nefti iz etikh stran," RGAE, Fond 561 op. 26s/pp d. 43 ll. 28–35.
29 "O vozmozhnykh sovmestnykh desistviiakh stran po stroitel'stvu predpriiarii dlia drugikh ostraslei promyshlennosti v stranakh-eksporterakh nefti, postavkam oborudovaniia i tovarov, okazaniiu uslug i drugikh vidov ekonomicheskogo sodeistviia," ibid. ll. 36–43.
30 "Niederschrift des Gesprächs des Sekretärs des RGW, N. Faddejew, mit dem Botschafter der Republik Irak in der UdSSR, Dalih Mehdi Amasch, im RGW-Sekretariat am 2 November 1972," PA AA, C 825/77.
31 "Geologie und mineralische Rohstoffe der Republik Irak," dated 15 January 1982, Barch Berlin, DL 2/4933.
32 "Information über den Stand und die Perspektiven der Entwicklung der Zusammenarbeit der ML/RGW mit Irak," dated 14 October 1981, Barch Berlin, DL 2/16952.
33 "Ländermappe Irak," dated January 1982, Barch Berlin, DL 2/4933.
34 "Informatsiia o razvitii torgovykh otnoshenenii mezhdu PNR i Irakskoi Respublikoi v period 1978–1979 gg.," dated 21 November 1979, RGAE, Fond 561 op. 53 d. 96 ll. 195–8.
35 "Zapis' besedy postoiannovo predstavitelia SSSR v SEV, zamestitelem ministra promyshlennosti i torgovli Meksikanskikh Soedinennykh Shtatov Elisso Mendosa Berrueto i direktorom izdatelstva "fond ekonomicheskoi kultury" Meksikanskikh Soediennykh Shtatov Fransisko Chavierom Alekho, sosstoiavsheisia 13 aprelia 1973 g.," RGAE, Fond 302 op. 2 d. 954 ll. 54–7.
36 "Zapis' besedy sekretaria s poslom Meksiki v SSSR R. Gonsalesom Salasarom, sostoiavsheisia 9 oktiabria 1973 g.," ibid. ll. 178–9.
37 "Pamiatnaia Zapiska o vstrechakh Meksikanskoi Ekonomicheskoi delegatsii s Sekretarem SEV N. V. Faddeevem," RGAE, Fond 302 op. 2 d. 1276 ll. 42–4.
38 "Informatsiia o besedakh v Sekretariate SEV s meksikanskoi ekonomicheskoi delegatsici, sostoiavshikhsia 21–25 oktiabria 1974 g.," ibid. ll. 45–51.
39 "Zapis' besedy Sekretaria SEV Faddeeva N. V. s Chrezvychainym i Polnomochnym Poslom Meksiki v SSSR V. Flores Olea, sostoiavsheisia v Sekretariate SEV 16 Iiunia 1975 g.," RGAE, Fond 302 op. 2 d. 1303 ll. 67–8.
40 "Zapis' besedy Sekretaria Soveta N. Faddeeva s Poslom Meksiki v SSSR V. Floresa Olea, sostoiavsheisia 23 iiunia s.g.," RGAE, Fond 302 op. 2 d. 1517 ll. 9–11.
41 "Prilozhenie 4 k pamiatnoi zapiske," ibid. ll. 1–6, 37–42.
42 "Rech' glavy Meksikanskoi delegatsii Ektora Ernandesa na pervom sasedanii Smeshannoi Komissii Meksika – Sovet Ekonomicheskoi Vzaimopomoshchi," ibid. ll. 43–6.
43 Speech of the Secretary of the CMEA N. V. Faddeev on the occasion of the first meeting of the Joint Committee CMEA-Mexico, ibid. ll. 47–50.
44 "Pamiatnaia Zapiska o resul'tatakh soveshaniia predstavitelei stran-chlenov SEV v Smeshannoi komissii po sotrudnichestvu Soveta Ekonomicheskoi Vzaimopomoshchi i Meksikanskikh Soedinennykh Shtatov, kotoroe sostoialos' 18 Oktiabria 1976 g.," ibid. ll. 26–8; "Oblasti vozmozhnogo sotrudnichestva stran-chlenov SEV s Meksikoi," ibid. l. 29.
45 Information on the first meeting of the sub-group on the fishing industry 16-17 June 1977 in Havana, RGAE, Fond 561 op. 53 d. 80 l. 155.
46 "Izkhodnyi material dlia sasedaniia gruppy ekspertov po vneshnei torgovle stran-chlenov SEV v ramkakh Smeshannoi Komisii SEV-Meksika, kotoroe dolzhno sostoiat'sia v Budapeshte s 21 po 25 Marta 1977 g.," ibid. ll. 34–7.
47 Note of the Czechoslovak delegation to the Joint Commission, dated 26 February 1982, RGAE, Fond 561 op. 53 d. 125 l. 131.

48 "Struktura Chekhoslovazkogo eksporta i importa v torgovle s Meksikoi v 1970–1976 gg.," RGAE, Fond 561 op. 53 d. 80 ll. 44–50.
49 "Soobrazehniia GDR po sushestvu punktov 1–3 povestki dnia u soveshchaniia ekspertov po vneshnei torgovle stran-chlenov SEV i Meksiki," RAGE, Fond 561 op. 53 d. 139 ll. 68–70.
50 "Soobrazheniia delegatsii PNR po voprosam razvitiia vneshnei torgovli s Meksikoi v ramkakh realizatsii Soglasheniia SEV-Meksika ot 13 avgusta 1975 goda," RGAE, Fond 561 op. 53 d. 80 ll. 52–5.
51 "Informatsiia o razvitii tovarooborota mezhdu stranami-chlenami SEV i Meksikoi v period 1970–1976 gg.," RGAE, Fond 561 op. 53 d. 85 ll. 7–8.
52 Ibid.
53 "Reunion De La Comision Mixta Mexico-CAME Cooperacion En Ciencia Y Tecnologia," RGAE, Fond 561 op. 53 d. 80 ll. 183–8.
54 "Acta Final de la Sexta Reunión de Expertos de Comercio Exterior de los Paises Miembros del CAME y los Estados Unidos Mexicanos," RGAE, Fond 561 op. 53 d. 151 ll. 22–33.
55 Letter from Dr. Schwierz to the Mexian Deputy Foreign Minister Jorge Eduardo Navarrete, dated 28.12.1981, RGAE, Fond 561 op. 53 d. 125 ll. 41–2.
56 Robinson and Dixon, *Aiding Afghanistan*, 47–8.
57 Robinson and Dixon, 49.
58 Robinson and Dixon, 50–1.
59 Robinson and Dixon, 60–70.
60 Robinson and Dixon, 75.
61 Robinson and Dixon, 95–8.
62 Directive for the conduct of the delegation of the GDR for the 29th meeting of the PCTA from 13-15 November1974 in Moscow, Barch Berlin, DL 2/6302.
63 Directive for the conduct of the delegation of the GDR for the 30th meeting of the PCTA from 04-06 June 1975 in Moscow, Barch Berlin, DL 2/6305.
64 "Zusammengefaßte Information über den Stand und die Perspektiven der wirtschaftlichen und technischen Zusammenarbeit der ML/RGW mit Syrien, Libyen, Afghanistan, der VDR Jemen und Iran," dated 12 February 1981, Barch Berlin, DL 2/16950.
65 Report on the 32nd meeting of the PCTA from 26-28 May 1976 in Moscow, Barch Berlin, DL 2/6316.
66 "Zapis' besedy Sekretaria Soveta V. Sycheva s Chrezvychainym i Polnomochnym Poslom Demokratisheskoi Respubliki Afganistan v SSSR Khabib Mangalom, sostoiavsheisia 9 dekrabria 1986 g.," RGAE, Fond 302 op. 2 d. 2251 ll. 54–5.
67 "Pamiatnaia Zapiska soveshaniia ekspertov stran-chelenov SEV (NRB, VNR, GDR, SSSR i ChSSR) 1–2 marta 1988g., Moskva," RGAE, Fond 561 op. 53 d. 169 l. 1.
68 "Protokol pervogo zasedaniia Smeshannoi komissii po sotrudnichestvu Soveta Ekonomicheskoi Vzaimopomoshchi i Respubliki Nikaragua 4–6 sentiabria 1984 g. g. Plovdiv," RGAE, Fond 561 op. 53 d. 141 ll. 75–80.
69 "Informatsiia o sostoiannii sotrudnichestva i okazannoi pomoshchi narodnoi respublikoi Bolgariei respublike Nikaragua," dated 05 July 1984, ibid. ll. 5–7; "Information der DDR über die Erweisung dringender ökonomischer Hilfe für die Republik Nikaragua, ausgehend vom Ersuchen der Leitung der Sandinistischen Front der Nationalen befreiung Nikaraguas (Punkt IX.2 des Protokolls der 110. Sitzung des Exekutivkomitees)," dated 02 July 1984, ibid. ll. 12–3.
70 "Osnovnoi dokument, podgotovlennyi Nikaraguanskoi storonoi dlia tret'ego zasedaniia Smeshannoi Komissii po sotrudnichestvu SEV i Respubliki Nikaragua (Budapesht, 22–24 oktiabria 1986 g.)," RGAE, Fond 561 op. 53 d. 155 ll. 125–167.
71 "Informatsiia o prodelannoi rabote po realizatsii ob"ektov mnogostroronnego sotrudnichestva v period posle pervogo zasedaniia Smeshannoi komissii SEV/Respubliki Nikaragua," dated 20 September 1985, RGAE, Fond 561 op. 53 d. 150 ll. 38–41.

72 “Zapis’ Besedy Sekretaria Soveta N. Faddeeva s chlenom Postoiannogo komiteta Vremennogo voennogo administrativnogo soveta Sotsialisticheskoi Efiopii Gessesse Vol’de Kidanom 4 aprelia 1978 g.,” RGAE, Fond 302 op. 2 d. 1666 ll. 6–10.
73 Letter to the Secretary of the CMEA, dated 16.02.1986, RGAE, Fond 302 op. 2 d. 2312 ll. 7–8.
74 Founding document of the Joint Commission CMEA-Ethiopia, dated 13 October 1986, ibid. ll. 53–75.
75 Letter from Iu. Vasianin to Antonov, dated 04 June 1986, ibid. ll. 9–11.
76 Zwass, *Der Rat Für Gegenseitige Wirtschaftshilfe*, 128.
77 Zwass, 128.
78 Letter from Andrei Lukanov to N. V. Faddeev, dated 22 October 1980, RGAE, Fond 302 op. 2 d. 1827 ll. 76–9.
79 Ibid.
80 Letter from the Soviet Ministry for Foreign Trade, dated 19 November 1980, ibid. l. 93; letter from the Permanent Representative of Hungary Istvan Terek, dated 27 November 1980, ibid. l. 101; letter from the Permanent Representative of the CSSR, dated 27 November 1980, ibid. l. 108.
81 Letter from George Louison to V. Libit, dated 24 July 1982, RGAE, Fond 302 op. 2 d. 2024 l. 4.
82 Letter from A. Zademidko to Talyzin, dated 13 September 1982, ibid. ll. 21–2.
83 Letter from Carlos Rafael Rodriges, dated 23 September 1982, ibid. l. 30.
84 Letter from the Soviet representative in the Joint Commission CMEA-Mozambique P. Ia. Koshelev to the Permanent Representative of the Soviet Union to the CMEA A. K. Antonov, dated 19 March 1987, RGAE, Fond 302 op. 2 d. 2401 ll. 1–3.
85 “Kratkosrochnoe sotrudnichestvo Narodnoi Respubliki Angola so stranami-chlenami SEV,” dated 19 October 1984, RGAE, Fond 302 op. 2 d. 2126 ll. 47–59.
86 “Zapis’ Besedy Sekretaria Soveta V. Sycheva s upravliaiushchim Bankom Mozambika Prakash Ratilalom,” sostoiavsheisia 19 aprelia 1984 g., ibid. ll. 5–7.

# 7 The view of the South

## CMEA stipends

When looking at the archival material of the Secretariat of the CMEA, there can be no doubt that the Complex-Program and its aftermath aroused a significant deal of curiosity in many countries of the Global South. The CMEA member countries furthermore actively tried to raise the attractiveness of their organization for the Global South. This should not only be achieved by concluding treaties of cooperation or by forming a new bank in the form of the International Investment Bank. Part of the deal included working out a stipend program for students from the Global South that were handed out not in the name of a particular member state of the CMEA but in the name of the organization itself.

The members of the CMEA were already exchanging information on the different education systems in the Global South in the mid-1960s. One can read in the shared material, what university courses were offered at the universities of Aleppo and Damascus or which educational certificates could be obtained in Uganda.[1] This information exchange was accelerated and became more refined in the early 1970s with the Soviet side providing the most detailed information due to their direct contacts with most countries from the Global South.[2] Furthermore, they were discussing the benefits and stipends they were offering to students from the Global South in detail with the aim to harmonize them to a certain degree. The documents indicate a caretaker attitude, as they include detailed information on reduced rents, tickets for public transport, and a special down payment for students from tropical countries, so that they won't freeze during the European winter.[3]

Forming a stipend program of the CMEA was an issue during the 25th meeting of the PCTA in late October and early November 1972. The draft version of the stipend program was approved by all delegations, even though the Romanian delegation had some reservations about it. The East German report on the meeting states:

> The draft of the statute for the stipend fund of the CMEA as well as the subsequent resolution by the Executive Committee was approved by the 25th session of the PCTA and the declaration of the delegation of the SRR [Romania] has been taken note of "that they are not interested in the formation

> of and participation in the above mentioned fund and they therefore won't participate in elaborating on the statute; that they are of the opinion that their attitude is not hindering the interested countries of the CMEA to form this fund".[4]

The motivation of the Romanian delegation in contrast to the motives of the other member states is clear from the report on the 24th meeting of the PCTA that had taken place four months before:

> The majority of delegations spoke out in favor of forming a stipend fund and judged it as a tool to strengthen the international authority of the CMEA as well as a new form to support the developing countries in educating national cadres. The delegation of the SRR [Romania] regarded the formation of this fund as inappropriate. Although the Romanian delegation cited a lack of possibilities to grant university places as a reason, it can be assumed that they don't want to provide a precedent for forming supranational organs.[5]

Romanian reservations proved in vain, as the precedent for a supranational organ was formed, indeed. The mutual exchange on technical assistance in the form of providing education and vocational training to young students from the Global South also served the important task of educating these young people politically. Providing political education was also used to get to know how the youth of the Global South was thinking and how easily their hearts could be won for socialism. This kind of information was exchanged via the PCTA. Obligatory training in Marxism-Leninism was introduced in 1969 in the GDR, to make a case in point.[6] An East German report on educating students from the Global South, and sent via the channels of the PCTA in 1974, reads:

> The teachers responsible for education in basic questions of Marxism-Leninism have foremost to understand the great enthusiasm of students from developing countries to discuss political-ideological questions, have to focus on the systematic study of Marxist-Leninist theory and have to develop the already present progressive attitude of a big part of the students, which is only founded emotionally, into a scientifically founded conviction . . .
>
> A growing number of students from all regions is judging the parties and governments today according to their attitude towards the Soviet Union and the socialist community of states in international politics . . .
>
> Through tenacious discussions it was possible to reach progress in the understanding of politics of peaceful coexistence. By now, most Arab students understand the politics of peaceful coexistence as class struggle on the basis of a balance of power increasingly changing in favor of socialism . . .
>
> Maoism is rejected by an overwhelming majority of students from the developing countries.[7]

As today's students could be tomorrow's leaders, sharing such information could be helpful for the prospects of the Eastern Bloc in the Global South in the long run. Studying the attitudes of the young could also serve as an early indicator of shifts in society. The teachers of Marxism-Leninism of the Eastern Bloc were not only fighting influences from the West, they also had to fight against Maoist tendencies after the breakup of the Sino-Soviet alliance which was already an issue looming over the foundation of the PCTA and remained one in the 1970s, as is clear from this document. The doctrine of peaceful coexistence, stipulated by Khrushchev, had to be taught to the students from the Global South who were sometimes more revolutionary minded and militant than was approved of by the leaders of the Eastern Bloc and therefore potentially susceptible to Maoism. Ideological and political education for students from the Global South also touched upon the issue of development aid. This was an intelligent, if selfish move, as an engineer thoroughly educated in Dresden, Debrecen, or Leningrad, would be more inclined to cooperate with partners from the Eastern Bloc when serving in a management position at a state factory or planning agency at home.

## Quantifying the stipend program

In the educational year 1975–6 a total of 406 CMEA stipends were handed out. Of these 300 were granted by the Soviet Union, 28 by the GDR, 24 by the CSSR, 17 by Cuba, 15 by Bulgaria, 11 by Poland, and 9 by Hungary. One hundred eighty each were granted to African and Asian countries, 46 to Latin American ones. The country that received most CMEA stipends during this year was Bangladesh with 51 stipends.[8] The Soviet Union clearly outpaced the other members of the CMEA by granting three-fourths of all stipends. To put the numbers into perspective, at the same time 20,821 people from the Global South were studying in Soviet education facilities alone in 1975–6.[9] This shows that the program was still small in the beginning but it was a program that could be expanded at any time. By early January 1984, more than 3,000 scholarship holders of the CMEA were receiving university and vocational training in the member states.[10] The yearly intake of students with a CMEA scholarship was close to 1,000 at the end of the 1980s.[11]

In June 1982 the Secretariat of the CMEA was informing the member states that in relation with granting technical assistance, more than one million people from the Global South had received some kind of education and vocational training by the CMEA member states since the end of the 1950s.[12] This was a sizable number. However, this training didn't necessarily have to take place in Europe but could also have been provided by courses given on site of newly built plants to train craftsmen who could then train future generations themselves.

Although the number of CMEA stipends remained rather small, it was nevertheless at least a public relations success. This can be seen by several letters stored in the archives in which students from the Global South asked the CMEA Secretariat to grant them one of the stipends, like the letter by the Angolan student Pembele Ze Lubienga who was writing to the Secretariat from Kinshasa, or the 24-year-old Foncham Feh from Cameroon who asked for a stipend to study Marxism-Leninism at the university of Leipzig.[13] This didn't apply just to single students but also to whole state institutions. In May 1975, the Tanzanian embassy in Moscow was asking the Secretariat for an appointment to discuss the possibility of granting stipends to Tanzanian students.[14] The stipend program was not exactly an Erasmus Program of the East, not only because of the lower number of students but also because it was directed at the "outside world" and not at the youth of the member countries. Despite these differences, the aims were to a certain degree similar, as the CMEA stipend program aimed at popularizing the organization.

## Letters to the Secretariat

In the years following the adoption of the Complex-Program and expansion of CMEA institutions, the Secretariat was receiving requests not only by representatives from left-leaning countries but also by other countries that were hitherto not closely associated with the Eastern Bloc. One of these representatives who was traveling to the Soviet Union as a private man was the former president of Columbia, Carlos Lleras Restrepo. Restrepo had been elected on the ticket of the Liberal Party in 1966 and had served as president until 1970. In early 1973, he was asking for a meeting with the Deputy Secretary of the CMEA, T. Angelov-Todorov, while being in the Soviet Union on the invitation of the Soviet Friendship Society. The meeting took place on 27 April 1973 and Mr. Restrepo, who was still the leader of the Liberal Party, was informed on the structure and objectives of the CMEA.[15]

These talks became more official two years later. In the meantime, the Liberal Party had gained power again after the election of its candidate, Alfonso López Michelsen. On 22 May 1975, the Colombian ambassador, U. Munos, was meeting the Secretary of the CMEA himself to discuss the establishment of formal ties between his country and the CMEA. The Colombian ambassador was hinting at a cooperation agreement that had been concluded between Finland and the CMEA in 1973 as a role model.[16] The treaty between Mexico and the CMEA was signed only a few months later so it is unclear if the ambassador was informed about the ongoing negotiations. Since the Mexican side was urging the Secretary of the CMEA to shield negotiations from public, it could well be that the ambassador was unaware of the Mexican endeavors.

Even if no treaty materialized between Colombia and the CMEA in the end, it is clear that the CMEA was regarded as an attractive trading partner for non-aligned countries in the Global South which were seeking to develop their countries economically and receive access to new technologies. Furthermore, Colombia was, like Mexico, a country traditionally inside the sphere of influence of the US. The Colombian political leaders therefore must have calculated the benefits and potential backlash of cooperating with the CMEA beforehand. They considered the CMEA attractive enough to engage in negotiations. The prevailing spirit of détente most likely shifted the balance in favor of negotiations with the CMEA, as long as the Columbian leaders wouldn't go down Salvador Allende's path.

Another unexpected guest who appeared in the Secretariat of the CMEA on Kalinin Prospekt in the 1970s was the Jordanian Hashemite prince Hassan Ben Talal who was joined by the Jordanian Minister of Transport. He met for discussions with Secretary Faddeev to elaborate on cooperation schemes for Jordan's chemical industry.[17] Although no technical details are mentioned in the protocol of the meeting that occurred in mid-October 1978, the Jordanian prince and his minister most likely wanted to create an equivalent of the Israeli Death Sea Works which was a very successful chemical company on the world market. The Jordanians mentioned a cooperation in extracting Jordan's resources and marketing them. They were arguing, since they had already concluded a treaty with the European Community, that they wanted to negotiate a similar agreement with the CMEA and profit from the technical cooperation the CMEA could provide.

Faddeev mentioned that the CMEA would only be too eager to provide that kind of assistance to expand Jordan's chemical industry. Faddeev was arguing that economic cooperation with the CMEA was not only beneficial for the recipient economically but also politically, since the CMEA was careful to preserve and strengthen the political independence of its partners in the Global South. This statement was probably directed against the European Community. In 1978, Faddeev could already refer to the treaties the CMEA had successfully negotiated not only with Finland but also with Iraq and Mexico. Again, even if no treaty emerged in the end, the Jordanian prince and his minister would not have engaged in negotiations with the Secretariat of the CMEA, if they hadn't hoped for an agreement that would benefit their country significantly. Hashemite princes and Soviet-style bureaucrats were not necessarily partners by nature. Furthermore, they were comparing the CMEA with the European Community and regarding the CMEA to a certain extent as the European Community of the East.

## Insights into a prospective member

The leadership of the People's Republic of Congo, otherwise known as Brazzaville-Congo, wanted to establish close ties with the CMEA in the late 1970s. Congolese representatives were repeatedly urging the Secretariat to establish stronger ties with their country. On one such occasion, a Congolese representative was presenting an official of the Secretariat with a plan for multilateral cooperation worked out by the government of the PR Congo. The Congolese side was promising mutually beneficial cooperation in the agrarian sector of the economy, expanding the production of rice, cocoa, and coffee for the Eastern market. They were also bringing forward the argument that they wanted nothing more than had been promised to the revolutionary leaders of Angola. However, the representative of the Secretariat reacted in a very reserved way to the Congolese proposals and mentioned that the Congolese side was already receiving significant and sufficient amounts of economic assistance on a bilateral level from the CMEA member states.[18]

This meeting that occurred in June 1978 was not the last of its kind, as the Congolese representatives didn't give up. On 31 October 1980, the Congolese ambassador was meeting Secretary Faddeev to discuss further cooperation measures with his country. The ambassador was urging Faddeev to establish closer ties with the PR Congo. He furthermore mentioned the possibility of his country becoming a full member of the CMEA. The ambassador therefore wanted Faddeev's approval to send a sizable Congolese delegation to the Secretariat to elaborate on further steps of cooperation and integration. Faddeev didn't oppose the ambassador's proposals but was criticizing them indirectly by mentioning that – in contrast to Western organizations – it is not the declared aim of the CMEA to force its members to give up their sovereignty. The aim of the CMEA was to foster true and equal cooperation.[19] This statement can be understood as a reference to the fact that the PR Congo was no suitable partner.

Nevertheless, a Congolese delegation was sent to the Secretariat. The Congolese filed a report on their visit which they were also handing to the Secretariat. This report can be read in the archives and provides valuable insights into the view of a country from the Global South, even if it is unclear, how "authentic" the report is, since it could already have been filed with prior knowledge of it being sent to the Secretariat afterwards. The Secretariat didn't keep the report secret but sent copies to the member states. The discussions in the Secretariat in Moscow weren't yet centered on taking up the PR Congo as a full member, as the Congolese leadership most likely had wished for, but on a cooperation treaty and the status of an observer in the CMEA. At least the East German experts in the Ministry for Foreign Affairs considered the Congolese report insightful and telling on the views of a country of the Global South.[20]

The mutual discussions had taken place between 13 and 22 April 1981. The Congolese delegates, led by the former Prime Minister Ambroise Noumazalay,[21] wrote about their negotiations in the Secretariat of the CMEA and their impressions of the organization:

> 5. Our Impressions of the CMEA
> 5.1. Political Viewpoint
> Every economic organization has political implications. By participating in the EEC [European Economic Community], the PR Congo is integrated in the international capitalist division of labor with all of its contradictions.
>
> If the PR Congo became an observer in the CMEA, it would enter the international socialist division of labor which is nothing else than a part of the international division of labor which is currently determined by the capitalist production mode . . .
>
> Although it is true that the admission of the PR Congo to the CMEA would integrate it in one way or another into the international division of labor of this organization, the fears of many Congolese that they would become a military or economic satellite of these countries in general and of the USSR in particular seem baseless. An integration into the EEC is an integration of tighter control [by the EEC] than into the CMEA.
>
> Even if the principles [of the CMEA] are well founded, one has to point out that in practice the power of a country like the USSR or the industrialized countries like the GDR or CSSR is greater than of all the other ones.[22]

The Congolese delegation scrutinized the organization quite openly in their report. Many of the statements were in opposition to the self-perception of the CMEA.

The Secretariat of the CMEA always proved eager to emphasize the equality of all members of the organization. This was, of course, mostly propaganda or theory, but the fact that the Congolese report doesn't reproduce this kind of rhetoric hints at its authenticity. The Congolese also made very realistic assessments of the power relations prevailing inside the CMEA. They were not regarding the CMEA as an organization dominated by the Soviet Union in a strict sense. The CMEA had more than one power center which they identified in the Soviets on the one side, and the industrialized smaller member states on the other. They were expressing their opinion straightforwardly when they stated that the socialist division of labor was in fact dominated by the capitalist one and actually a part of it.

The report also included a section on the economic implications of being associated with the CMEA:

> 5.2 Economic Viewpoint
>
> The consideration expressed in point 5.1 show their true value in the following deliberation. This economic integration [of the PR Congo] does not lead to a loss of our economic independence. The CMEA is no supranational organization (unlike the EEC which is trending this way and which is therefore opposed by the Gaullists in France).
>
> Every member state is free to participate in this or that organism or project approved by the CMEA. . . .
>
> The second aspect is the following:
>
> The aim of the socialist integration is to level the economic development of all nations, the backward nations are to catch up with the developed ones. That means, it is obligatory to industrialize the backward nations, so that they reach the development level of the most developed nations. For example: Bulgaria, Mongolia, and so forth. This possibility is only partially offered by the European Community.[23]

The section on economics in the report was most likely more in line with the self-perception of the CMEA. The Congolese delegation praised the efforts of the CMEA member countries to bring all members up to the same level of economic development. Although this statement contains a slight contradiction, since the part on political implications included a statement about the differences between the GDR and CSSR on the one side, and countries like Bulgaria and Romania on the other, there is a grain of truth in it. The CMEA could claim for itself to have leveled economic inequality inside the organization to a certain extent. From the point of view of the early 1980s, this was also true in comparison to the European Community which had just started to integrate Greece and the Iberian countries. The Congolese delegation furthermore approved of the organizational flexibility of the CMEA in the sense that they could cherry-pick the areas of mutual cooperation that were of greatest interest for them. One could therefore claim that Romanian obstructionism – as analyzed in chapter 5 – had also contributed to the attractiveness of the CMEA for countries of the Global South.

## An Ethiopian wish list

Two months before the meeting between Secretary Faddeev and the Ethiopian representative Gessesse Volde Kidan took place in the CMEA building in Moscow in early April 1978, the Provisional Military Government of Socialist Ethiopia had sent a 109 pages long book to the Secretariat titled "Request for Economic and Technical Assistance from Socialist Countries." Gessesse Volde Kidan served as a member of the Permanent Committee of the Provisional Military Administrative Council of Ethiopia in the late 1970s and had repeatedly led Ethiopian delegations to European socialist countries before his meeting with Faddeev.[24] This document that was passed around by the Secretariat to the Permanent Representatives of the CMEA member states contained a long list of projects that the Ethiopian government wanted the socialist countries to execute. The content of the book was divided into seven sections. The first section dealt with agriculture, the next with industry, followed by mining, transport, and communication, electric power and water supply, housing, and technical assistance.[25]

The authors of the book stated the following in their introduction:

> The present document attempts to spell out in a greater detail major economic problems and assistance requirements that were outlined in the October [1977] document in terms of specific projects, project ideas and the nature, extent and quality of assistance required. . . .
>
> The selection of projects included in this document is based on a number of criteria; some of these are: a) an increase in the supply of goods and services of general consumption; b) removal or mitigation of certain bottlenecks with respect to the production and distribution of goods and services; c) formation of a firm foundation for the long-term development of a strong national economy; and d) possibility of implementation under the concrete existing conditions. The projects include those that are ready for implementation immediately and those projects whose implementation will spread over a number of years.[26]

This document gives the impression of an Ethiopian wish list with the CMEA member countries having to choose which of the projects they would like to conduct for the Ethiopian side. The investment need for all projects was estimated by the Ethiopian authors to amount to one billion rubles. However, this sum excluded the projects, the investment value of which could not yet have been assessed properly.[27] The Ethiopians thus presented the CMEA member countries an investment plan that wasn't fully worked out but actually rudimentary. Forty-five percent of the sum should be invested in agriculture, 18.1 % in transport and communication, 17.9 % in manufacturing industry, 12.2 % in mining, 5 % in power generation, and 1.6 % in housing.[28]

These numbers already indicate severe imbalances in the development plan as envisioned by the Ethiopian authors of this large-scale proposal for their country.

It is unclear, why the Ethiopian leadership proposed the investment program the way they did. However, it seems unlikely that they were directly guided by Soviet or other socialist economic experts from the Eastern Bloc. It is more likely that the plan represented their own visions of a future socialist Ethiopia at least to a significant extent. What is striking in the investment plan are the relatively low numbers proposed for housing and agriculture. Ethiopia was an overwhelmingly agrarian society in the late 1970s and the housing situation of the rural poor abysmal. To invest 1.6 % in housing means that, even if all the projects were executed successfully, the housing situation and sanitary standards would have hardly improved at all. This is the more striking, since the CMEA member countries possessed some kind of expertise in providing housing of modest quality cheaply and fast. But the Ethiopian side didn't seem interested in that kind of expertise.

One should not be diverted by the fact that almost half of the proposed investment sum was earmarked for agriculture. More than 30 % were simultaneously earmarked for mining and manufacturing. Since Ethiopia didn't possess a sizable industrial sector in the late 1970s, this allocation of investment resources had the undeniable aim to build up an industrial sector fast without caring too much for the prospects of the hitherto single economic sector able to market its goods abroad. The authors were well aware of the fact that the agricultural sector of Ethiopia employed more than 85 % of the population and was responsible for more than 90 % of total exports. However, due to high population growth on the order of 2.5 % annually, the country had ceased producing food surpluses. This was to be overcome by organizing the agricultural sector "along socialist lines" which meant the introduction of large-scale state farms, amelioration schemes, and massive population resettlement from densely populated to thinly populated rural areas.[29]

Furthermore, the plan indicates that the Ethiopian leadership was not very much interested in raising the living standards in the short-term but actually in establishing an industrial sector first. Agriculture was important insofar as it was connected with industry and peasants were to give up their subsistence mode of production prevailing in most rural areas of the country.[30] This didn't change the fact that agricultural development was led by industrial development. The development model they were at last implicitly emulating was thus the Stalinist model of development, not necessarily the model practiced by the advanced European members of the CMEA in the late 1970s. Nevertheless, this demonstrates that the Soviet development model could still be attractive to local elites in the Global South.

Crunching the numbers casts doubts on the investment resources allocated for power generation. As Ethiopia didn't possess a developed energy infrastructure and large-scale industrialization demanded huge inputs of electricity, in particular in heavy industries, 5 % seems too low and reveals a potential bottleneck in the plan, as no viable electrical grid was in existence either. These 5 % also included spending on water supply. The Ethiopian authors of the investment plan were quite frank on their goals:

> The priorities indicated in terms of the allocation of investment funds are dictated by the objective conditions of the economy and are in conformity with

> the much broader objectives spelled out in the National Democratic Revolution Programme of Ethiopia. Obviously, the orders of priority will change dynamically as the economy undergoes fundamental transformations, and as light and heavy industries take their place as the dominant and leading sectors of the economy in place of agriculture, through conscious efforts and policies.[31]

This made clear that the Ethiopian leadership equated progress and development with heavy and light industries, though one can safely assume that the former prevailed over the latter. The system the Ethiopian revolutionaries had inherited in their country and which they wanted to overcome was called "feudo-capitalist mode of production" by them.[32] They were claiming that this system had led to stagnation and constituted a dead-end model of development. They acknowledged that former governments had embarked on small-scale efforts of industrialization by import substitution in the urban centers of the country but that these efforts had not weakened Ethiopia's ties with "imperialist economies."

The authors of the book also mentioned the difficulties of their task and the basic problems they encountered, while trying to assess the state of Ethiopia's economy:

> The characteristics of present-day Ethiopian economy are such that statistical data are not available, or that only some and inaccurate data are available; that statisticians and planners in general are in short supply; and that the existing organizational capacity is deficient. Along with many other characteristics of an underdeveloped economy, these factors remain the main obstacles for the elaboration of a comprehensive development plan in Ethiopia.[33]

The Ethiopian leadership was thus urging the CMEA members to make a leap of faith by simply trusting their Ethiopian partners that everything will work out well in the end. It is therefore understandable that Secretary Faddeev promised support for the Ethiopian revolution in spring 1978 but that negotiations on any formal association of Ethiopia with the CMEA lasted till the mid-1980s. The Ethiopian authors of the investment plan had a vision of how their country should look like in the mid- or long-term but they hardly knew much about the real state of their country, a fact they quite openly acknowledged and that most likely caused severe headaches in Moscow and the other capitals of the CMEA member states.

## Conclusion

By the late 1970s the CMEA had become an attractive partner for the Global South. The CMEA was not only actively on the lookout for new partners in the Global South, others were increasingly taking notice of its endeavors, as well. These requests for cooperation have left a significant paper trail in the archives. They were not limited to ideological allies of the Eastern Bloc but were authored by a wide range of political and economic actors, be it Hashemite princes, Latin American liberal opposition leaders, or African revolutionaries. This emphasizes the notion that the Complex-Program and the years that followed can be seen as a success for the relations of the CMEA with the outside world.

The European archives holding CMEA documents are furthermore in possession of documents that give valuable insights into the view of the Southern partners of the CMEA, like the Ethiopian investment plan of 1978 or the report by a delegation from the People's Republic of Congo on mutual negotiations on prospective membership in the headquarters of the CMEA. The Congolese document assesses the power relations inside the CMEA and between the CMEA and the West. Its authors came to the conclusion that the CMEA was no organization of true equals but actually entertained two power centers, while the international socialist division of labor was actually a subordinated part of the world capitalist system. Nevertheless, they approved of cooperation with the CMEA. The authors of the Ethiopian investment plan, on the other hand, saw in the CMEA an organization, the members of which could solve its economic problems and transform the country into an African economic powerhouse. However, as the 1980s were commencing, the prospects of the Eastern Bloc as well as of the Global South started to falter.

## Notes

1 Shared material of the delegations to the PCTA, dated 1967, RGAE, Fond 561 op. 53 d. 29 ll. 1–182.
2 Official letter from the East German government to the Permanent Representative of the Soviet Union to the CMEA Berezin, dated 03 November 1973, RGAE, Fond 561 op. 53 d. 60 ll. 126–8.
3 "Information über die materielle Versorgung der Bürger aus Entwicklungsländern, die an Fachschulen/Hochschulen der Deutschen Demokratischen Republik studieren," dated 1970, RGAE, Fond 561 op. 53 d. 45 ll. 185–202.
4 "Bericht über die 25. Tagung der SKTU (31.10.-3.11.72, Moskau)," dated 07 November 1972, Barch Berlin, DE 1/55319.
5 Report on the 24th session of the PCTA from 31 May -01 June 1972, ibid.
6 "Information über Erfahrungen in der Lehre der gesellschaftswissenschaftlichen Disziplinen für Studenten aus Entwicklungsländern als grundlegende Form der Organisation und Durchführung der politisch-erzieherischen Arbeit," dated 15 July 1974, RGAE, Fond 561 op. 53 d. 64 ll. 20–4.
7 Ibid.
8 "Spravka o kolichestve stipendiatov SEV iz razvivaiushchikhsia stran, priniatykh v vusy stran-chlenov SEV na 1975/76 uchebnyi god," RGAE, Fond 561 op. 53 d. 76 l. 6.
9 "Kolichestvo i raspredelenie po gruppam spetsial'nostei uchashchikhsia v vysshikh i srednikh spetsial'nykh uchebnykh savedeniiakh, aspirantov i stazherov iz razvivaiushchikhsia stran, obuchaiushchikhsia v vysshikh i srednikh spetsial'nykh uchebnykh zavedeniiakh SSSR (po sostoianiiu na 1.1.1976g.)," ibid. ll. 42–6.
10 "Informatsiia o funktsionirovanii Stipendial'nogo fonda Soveta Ekonomicheskoi Vzaimopomoshchi," dated 1984, RGAE, Fond 561 op. 53 d. 136 ll. 97–115.
11 "Informatsiia o funktsionirovanii Stipendial'nogo fonda Soveta Ekonomicheskoi Vzaimoposhchi," dated 39 September 1987, RGAE, Fond 561 op. 53 d. 161 ll. 238–250.
12 "Informtsiia o funktsionirovanii stipendial'nogo fonda Soveta Ekonomicheskoi Vzaimopomoshchi," dated 23 June 1982, RGAE, Fond 302 op. 2 d. 1994 ll. 57–62.

13 Letter by Pembele Ze Lubienga to the Secretariat of the CMEA, dated 04 April 1974, RGAE, Fond 561 op. 53 d. 64 l. 54; letter by Foncham Feh to the Secretariat of the CMEA, dated 11 February 1975, RGAE, Fond 561 op. 53 d. 70 l. 19.
14 Letter by the Tanzanian embassy to the CMEA Secretariat, dated 28 May 1974, RGAE, Fond 561 op. 53 d. 64 l. 61.
15 "Zapis' besedy zamestitelia Sekretaria SEV T. Angelova-Todorova s politicheskim deiatelem Kolumbii K. L'erosom Restrepo, sostoiavsheisia 27 aprelia 1973 g.," RGAE, Fond 302 op. 2 d. 954 ll. 64–6.
16 "Zapis' Besedy Sekretaria N. Faddeeva s Poslom Kolumbii v SSSR U. Mun'osom, sostoiavshcheisia 22 maia 1975g.," RGAE, Fond 302 op. 2 d. 1303 ll. 51–3.
17 "Zapis' Besedy s Naslednym printsem Iordanskogo Khashimitskogo Korolevstva Khasanom Ben Talalom i ministrom transporta Iordanii A. Sukheimatom, sostoiavshikhsia 18 i 19 oktiabria 1978 g. v Sekretariate SEV," RGAE, Fond 302 op. 2 d. 1666 ll. 82–6.
18 "Zapis' Besedy rukovoditelia gruppy Sekretariata SEV A. Popova s ekonomicheskim i torgovym sovetnikom Posol'stva Narodnoi Respubliki Kongo v SSSR E. Oko, sostoiavsheisia 27 iiunia 1978 g.," ibid. ll. 40–2.
19 "Zapis' Besedy Sekretaria Soveta N. Faddeeva s Poslom Narodnoi Respubliki Kongo v SSSR Zh. Okansa, sostoiavsheisia 31 oktiabria 1980 g.," RGAE, Fond 302 op. 2 d. 1818 ll. 80–2.
20 Letter by the East German ambassador to the PR Congo Pohl to Mr. Bayerlacher in the Ministry for Foreign Affairs, dated 25 July 1981, PA AA, MFAA ZR 2511/89.
21 Ambroise Noumazalay, born in 1933, had been Prime Minister of the Republic of Congo, as the PR Congo was then called, from 1966 to 1968. He later joined the Parti Congolais du Travail and served as the general secretary of the party during the 1990s. He died in 2007.
22 "Rechenschaftsbericht der beim Rat für gegenseitige Wirtschaftshilfe (RGW) in Moskau vom 13.-22.4.1981 durchgeführten Mission," PA AA, MFAA ZR 2511/89.
23 Ibid.
24 "Äthiopische Delegation bei Autowerkern in Ludwigsfelde," *Neues Deutschland*, 15 June 1977, 1.
25 "Request for Economic and Technical Assistance from Socialist Countries," dated February 1978, PA AA, MFAA ZR 5299/90.
26 Ibid.
27 Ibid.
28 Ibid.
29 Ibid.
30 Ibid.
31 Ibid.
32 Ibid.
33 Ibid.

# Part IV

# Financial shockwaves

# 8 The crisis of the 1980s

## The bubble bursts

The 1970s had been – in an economic sense – a rather blessed era for many developing countries despite political upheavals like the overthrow of the Allende administration in Chile or the dissolution of the Portuguese colonial empire leading to violent power struggles in Mozambique and Angola. This applied particularly to resource-rich countries in the Global South that benefited from a mixture of high commodity prices and a global inflation combined with low interest rates making it comparatively easy for them to borrow at almost no cost.[1] The export revenues of the OPEC countries alone had increased between 1970 and 1974 by 1,100 % due to higher oil prices.[2] But price increases didn't just apply to crude oil, other commodities like coffee, copper, and rubber became increasingly expensive, too.[3]

Also, countries previously known as only minor exporters of natural resources, like Mexico, found themselves amid a glut of foreign exchange earnings. This meant that a significant part of the so called "Third World" profited from the boom.[4] The temptation was imminent for them to use the money for a spending spree and to take loans from Western banks that were only to eager to grant them. This was a new development, because prior to the 1970s "developing countries" had almost exclusively borrowed money from public development banks. In the 1970s – and for the first time since the 1920s – they could tap the funds of the big Western commercial banks.[5] With credits backed by ever increasing foreign exchange earnings, the risks attached seemed to be negligible.[6] It is no coincidence that the CMEA countries tried to increase trade with the Global South during the 1970s to profit politically and economically from stronger mutual ties and the newly acquired wealth of formerly cash-stripped countries.

Not all developing countries profited equally from the political and economic trends of the 1970s, but the prospects of the Global South during this decade seemed to be promising. During the 1970s the underdevelopment gap between North and South seemed to be narrowing for the first time in history, thereby indicating the nearing of the end of "underdevelopment," since income per capita rose on an unprecedented scale in the Global South during the 1970s and at a much higher rate than in either the West or the East.[7] However, the 1980s proved to be a severe disappointment compared to the high hopes that prevailed during the 1970s. The "boom" of the 1970s in the Global South was fueled by high commodity prices and cheap credit, both vanished in the decade that followed. In 1981 alone, the Latin American countries increased their borrowings by 50 billion US dollars. At that point, the Global South owed 750 billion US dollars to foreigners.[8]

In August 1982, Mexico's minister of finance had to declare his country's insolvency and negotiated a debt moratorium for Mexico. This was only the beginning of a much larger economic reckoning. The flow of money to the South halted and reversed causing political, economic, and social calamities which led observers to speak of a "lost decade."[9] Even if the respective governments had wanted to pay back their debts immediately at all costs, they could not have done it. As is true for developing countries by definition, they were depending on capital inflows to bridge the development gap and to approach Western living standards. While growth rates of GPD per capita had averaged 2.5 % for the developing countries between 1960 and 1979, in the period from 1980 till the end of the century it amounted to nil percent on average.[10] For Latin America and Sub-Saharan Africa growth rates per capita during the 1980s were negative.[11] Their debt surpassed one trillion US dollars by the late 1980s.[12] The CMEA countries could not escape the consequences of a radically altered environment, as they were already strongly integrated in international flows of goods and money by the end of the 1970s.

In this chapter, the role of the socialist East as a lender to the Global South is highlighted. More often than not (economic) historians have regarded the Eastern bloc almost exclusively in relation to developments in the West. Contemporary scholars – like Yegor Gaidar – hardly mentioned "developing countries" at all in their works, in spite of their empirical material pointing in a different direction.[13] Gaidar stated in *Collapse of an Empire* that the combination of high costs for importing grain, an uncompetitive manufacturing sector, and the unpredictability of commodity prices proved fatal for the Soviet economy. Although Gaidar's argument is by and large convincing, it has to be amended when it comes to the manufacturing sector: whereas most of the goods manufactured by the CMEA countries could hardly be sold in the West, the situation looked somewhat different in the Global South. The late socialist countries have been mainly seen as capital importers relying on Western credit to import Western technology in the 1970s and 1980s.[14] However, they proved quite active capital exporters at the same time, too. This capital often came in a very tangible form like machines and industrial equipment.

The sharp increase of interest rates under the leadership of the newly appointed governor of the Federal Reserve Bank, Paul Volcker, together with the slump of commodity prices in the early 1980s, sparked off an economic crisis, the consequences of which were felt not only in South America, Africa, and the oil exporting countries of the Middle East. The crisis subsequently spread out to all "developing countries" of the Global South and hit the weakest links of the Eastern bloc, Poland and Romania, already in 1980–81. This dynamic of the crisis has hardly been recognized in scholarship. The literature on financial history is mainly focused on the 19th century and the period of globalization between 1815 and 1914. Latin America figures very prominently in this research, because of its close economic and financial ties to the UK and US from early on. Eastern Europe is often not more than a side note in the literature with the exception of maybe Ceausescu's regime and its – even from the point of view of IMF experts – harsh austerity.[15] Insufficient attention has been paid to the core countries of the CMEA and their reaction to the crisis of the 1980s.

CMEA documents of the 1980s will be used to scrutinize the role of the East as a lender of the South and search for mutual dependencies. The East felt the impact of monetary tightening in the West strongly and the CMEA members had to react to the changed environment. The reaction of the East says something about the contours of a "socialist world system." It is argued that the CMEA countries were hit not only directly by the policies of the West – due to their role as capital importer – but also indirectly via the Global South which could not repay its loans and therefore aggravated the impending crisis of the socialist countries in the 1980s. The mid-1980s are taken as the main reference point, since they were rightfully defined as pivotal for the collapse of state socialism by Yegor Gaidar.

## First problems

The CMEA countries had established close political and economic contacts with the former "boom" countries already in the 1970s. The mutual trade did not reach the same volume as East–West trade had but it served as an important link. The CMEA member states could import urgently needed raw materials, found more or less thankful customers for their industrial output, and could accumulate trade surpluses. This kind of trade had two significant downsides which became clear during the 1980s: it was based on credits and the socialist countries of Eastern Europe used the surplus they achieved and the convertible currencies they obtained to counterbalance their imports of Western technology.[16]

At first glance, decreasing commodity prices seemed to be a blessing for the smaller CMEA members. With the exception of coal none of the smaller CMEA countries possessed large quantities of raw materials. Thus, they had, ceteris paribus, to export less for the same amount of imports and thus could have either increased their imports or improved their balance of trade. To put it differently: the terms of trade[17] seemed to develop in their favor. But the reality looked differently: the East European countries had also gone borrowing in the 1970s and taken huge loans from Western banks. The net debt of the CMEA countries to Western creditors amounted to 83.2 billion US dollars in 1981 and despite a short period of deleveraging surpassed 100 billion US dollars by the end of 1986.[18]

The interest rate hikes by Western central banks were soon passed on to their customers by commercial banks and hit Eastern Europe hard leading to a balance of payments crisis in the People's Republic of Poland in 1980 and in the Socialist Republic of Romania one year later.[19] The combination of high interest rates, failed industrial policies, and still high import prices especially for crude oil, the price of which started to fall significantly only in 1982–83, proved fatal for them.

Even if Romania had been a country of dubious reputation inside the CMEA, and both countries, Poland and Romania, belonged to the least developed in Eastern Europe compared to Hungary, the GDR, or CSSR, Western banks started to have second thoughts about the credit-worthiness of the other CMEA member states, as well.[20] This distrust stood in sharp contrast to their previous practice of lending unanimously to the socialist countries of Eastern Europe.

The situation was aggravated further by the fact that those countries which had exported raw materials at high prices before got less and less revenue per unit exported from 1982 on. Among them were Syria and Iraq, two of the best customers of the Eastern bloc in the 1970s. On top of that, Iraq was involved in a bloody war against Iran. Even during the best times, Hafiz al-Asad and Saddam Hussein relied on credits from the East and paid their bills only to a small degree in cash.[21]

## Crisis meetings

Since all Eastern European countries faced increasing refinancing costs for Western credits, they were in no position anymore to grant advantageous conditions as creditors of many "developing countries." This led to an intensified economization of their relations with the South, to an adoption of Western banking culture and standards, and to an amplified level of mutual consultations within the CMEA. Talks about credit conditions had already taken place in the preceding decade. Their aim was not so much to agree on exact interest rates to be charged and to discuss the credit ratings of particular countries, but to avoid a bottomless competition among the socialist countries and to prevent them from outbidding each other, since a lack of understanding among the CMEA member states could easily be exploited by others, foremost by the recipients of their economic assistance. During the 1980s, these consultations gained a new quality and a deep look at the books revealed the true dimensions of the crisis for all bloc members. The gravity and urgency of the crisis made a closer cooperation inside CMEA imminent:

> The analysis of the economic situation of the developing countries leads to the assumption that the solvency problem of the developing countries will not only not be solved in the near future but, on the contrary, will actually worsen. In this situation it can be expected that other developing countries will also approach the CMEA member states and ask for a deferment of payments. For the preparation of negotiations and agreements on the delay of payments, it is advisable that the experts of the CMEA member states have full access to the content and the conditions of the agreements already concluded by other member countries with the respective developing country concerning the extension of credits.
>
> Practical experience shows that by coordinating the conditions for extending credits it is possible to agree on more advantageous terms for the creditors.[22]

In April 1985 a meeting of an expert delegation of the CMEA members took place in the Bulgarian town of Plovdiv to discuss a revision of the hitherto existing credit guidelines. A report on the meeting reads as follows:

> The economic situation of the developing countries has deteriorated in the last years as a consequence of the policies enforced by the leading capitalist countries. As a consequence, the valuta and financial relations destabilized. This had negative repercussions on the development of credit relations of the CMEA countries with those [developing] countries. . . . The expert meeting of the CMEA member states in Plovdiv, after having discussed the regulation of minimum interest rates for commercial credits, agreed to strive further for the closest possible approximation to the interest rates applied in world credit practice. The expert meeting defined a minimum floor for commercial credits of 6 to 8%.[23]

The document invokes a certain sense of irony that probably escaped its author. After stating – quite truly – that the financial policies of the industrialized countries of the West had destabilized the South, the announcement is made that the CMEA countries will follow exactly the same policies. Naturally, such measures could only worsen the situation of the South. Exceptions from this hard line were only allowed for countries "that align themselves to the socialist development path."[24] Other alternatives would have been imaginable. The CMEA countries could have maintained their policies of the 1970s as a sign of stability and solidarity and thus could have tried to gain political prestige. They could have also followed the rapid turn from mostly negative real interest rates during the 1970s to positive real interest rates till interest rates matched the expected inflation level as a kind of compromise. Prior to the crisis of the 1980s it was not uncommon to find interest rates of 2.5% in credit agreements between a CMEA member state and a "developing country."[25] There is no hint in the files that any alternatives to replicating the policies of the West had been considered.

## The East learns from the West

The planned economies of Eastern Europe, which have often been rightfully criticized as inert and slow, did not only learn to adapt to the quick interplay of Western central banks, they also demonstrated an astonishing agility by incorporating new financial innovations during the 1980s. The People's Republic of Poland reported to its CMEA partners in early 1986 that it had applied the Libor with a surcharge of 1 % for refinancing a governmental credit to Nigeria worth 24 mil US dollars.[26] This may sound trivial, but it hints at a changed "governmentality" inside the CMEA. The Libor or "London Interbank Offered Rate" was introduced just one year earlier. It depicted the interest rate at which the most important banks in London were lending money to each other. The introduction of such a reference was necessitated by deregulation and the expansion of the banking industry.[27] The credit granted to

Nigeria had a term of six years, while the Libor could be obtained for not more than a year. This meant that the Polish government passed the interest change risk on to the Nigerian government. If the interbank rate increased the following year, Nigeria's government would have had to increase its payments to the People's Republic of Poland. This was, of course, the same mechanism applied by Western lenders to their customers in the South that proved fatal during the whole decade, since long-term investments were not really financed long-term, because of the extremely volatile interest payments on the principal indexed to short-term rates like the Libor.[28]

This was a new instrument for Warsaw. A credit granted to Iraq the same year worth 200 million US dollars had to be paid only partially in cash. Most of it had to be paid back by deliveries of crude oil.[29] This deal was more representative of the 1970s. The Hungarian government used another financial innovation in the 1980s called "forfaiting." This meant that a claim against a debtor was transferred to a third party by the creditor against a discount on the nominal value of the claim. In the case of the Hungarian People's Republic a claim against a debtor from the Global South had been sold to a Western bank.[30] This was applied exclusively to commercial credits granted to public or private enterprises.[31] The advantage for the Hungarian government was that it received a significant amount of its claim back – immediately and in cash. It thus provided an immediate inflow of much needed convertible currency, even if the deal had to be closed with a loss. The reason why Hungary and Poland in particular were so eager to apply Western financial instruments could be their proximity to the IMF and therefore to Western financial practices. Another reason could be that they belonged to the most active borrowers of the 1970s.[32] Their close contact to Western financial institutions necessitated a group of experts familiar with Western economics and able to stand their ground in the negotiations.

The Hungarian People's Republic had already joined the IMF in 1982, while their Polish counterpart first aspired to become a member in 1981 and finally joined in 1986. It is likely that the process of becoming a member was accompanied by an ideological convergence, not in the realm of politics in general, but on the level of finances thereby prompting an adoption of knowledge and techniques. Despite the 1980s being a time of increasing cooperation inside the CMEA, there were also clear signs of frictions and boiling tensions inside the bloc related to its fiscal and monetary policies. This became clear on the 34th extraordinary session of the International Investment Bank (IIB) – one of the two banks of the CMEA – on 23 June 1983 in Moscow. The day after the session had taken place, the president of the East German State Bank, Horst Kaminsky, wrote to Willi Stoph, head of the Council of Ministers in East Berlin:

> The head of the Soviet delegation, comrade Alkhimov, presented his view on the current situation in the field of international financial relations to the bank council . . . Alkhimov told the bank council that the HPR [Hungarian People's Republic] has become a member of the International Monetary Fund and is still being "petted" by them. But this is a transitory condition that won't last long. "When the honeymoon is over, they will be tough on the HPR again, as they were with Romania."[33]

Those were quite harsh words for any banker to say. But the words of the Soviet head of delegation can't disguise the fact, that actually all CMEA countries strove for an increased influx of convertible currency.

It is clear for the Hungarian case that those reformers who wanted to initiate market reforms and to work on the basis of the reforms of the 1960s which abruptly came to a halt in Hungary in 1968, were on the upswing from 1983 on.[34] The growing debt pile and the contact to the IMF as a potential donor of money and ideas created a fruitful climate for the young generation of the Hungarian Socialist Workers' Party (MSZMP), even if János Kádár, as he did in a meeting of the Politburo in September 1983, still rejected these new ideas and reform proposals.[35] In 1984, a diluted reform program was passed. Radical reforms were not yet possible even in the more liberal environment of Hungary. Hungary's debts to the West doubled between 1984 and 1989 from ca. 10 billion US dollars to 20 billion US dollars.[36] Nevertheless, it seems appropriate to state that the intensified contacts with Western institutions in the early 1980s had practical consequences particularly among the new generation of state and party elites.

## Expansion of CMEA institutions

The "Permanent Commission for the Coordination of Technical Assistance and Cooperation with Developing Countries" (PCTAC) was the forum for talking about the credit relations of the CMEA countries.[37] This expansion of scope was in line with the development of the commission founded in 1961 under the name PCTA and underlined the increasing importance of the relations with the countries of the South and of cooperation inside the CMEA. The importance of these relations didn't decrease during the 1980s, but intensified, even if crisis symptoms were highly visible. A report of the PCTAC titled "Information on measures taken to activate the multilateral cooperation of the CMEA countries with developing countries" from 23 January 1987 read:

> At the same time the Commission asserts on the basis of an analysis of the situation that the conditions for a development of a multilateral economic and technical cooperation of the CMEA countries with developing countries have worsened. This is caused mainly by a deterioration of the valuta and financial situation, and insolvency of most developing countries and an increased indebtedness towards capitalist countries. As a consequence, investments in the development of the economy were lowered and demands by the developing countries for cheaper credits to build objects and pay for achievements have soared.[38]

In the mid-1980s the same mechanism applied to resource-rich "developing countries" as well, as follows from the same report:

> The strong decline of oil prices resulted in a deterioration of the economic situation of the oil- and gas-exporting developing countries, leading to a cutback of investments in the economy of those countries.[39]

Despite this negative outlook, representatives of the member states – in the case of the PCTAC the ministers for foreign trade and their staff – saw a promising solution in a more intense internal cooperation and a common appearance in the Global South. The Eastern European countries should combine their expertise and implement projects together instead of acting alone.[40] Since debts to the West were stated to be an important factor for the crisis, a look at the role of the East as creditor of the South seems worthwhile.

## The debts of the South

The debts of the "developing countries" didn't decrease during the 1980s, as could be expected in the economic environment of rising interest rates making it less attractive to borrow; they actually rose between South and West, and South and East as well. In 1983 alone, the amount of credits granted by the socialist bloc to the Global South increased by 20 %.[41] Their value still increased in 1984 and 1985 by 4 and 11.4 %, respectively.[42] On 1 January 1987, the debts defined as the sum of governmental and commercial credits amounted to 36.56 billion rubles.[43] According to the official exchange rate of that time this sum was the equivalent to ca. 54 billion US dollars.[44] This equation is, of course, dubious but nevertheless it shows that the sum was significant.

The role of the largest debtor had been occupied by India in 1986. India had played a significant part in East–South economic relations before but didn't figure as prominently as the key countries of the 1970s.[45] It is therefore not surprising to find Iraq, Egypt, and Syria as number two, three, and four on the list in 1987. Their debts amounted to 4.5 billion rubles in the case of Iraq and ca. 2.5 billion rubles for Egypt and Syria. Afghanistan and Nicaragua, which were not significant prior to 1979, were on position six and eleven with 2.01 billion rubles granted to Afghanistan and 1.094 billion rubles given to Nicaragua.[46] It is noticeable that countries which were interesting for the CMEA states primarily for political reasons, like Afghanistan or Nicaragua, almost exclusively received governmental loans that featured lower interest rates and longer terms. Countries like Nigeria and Turkey, on the other hand, received mainly commercial loans with more unfavorable conditions for the debtor.[47] Although there were several reasons for this, it shows that relations were structured according to two categories of countries: those that were more interesting economically and those deemed important for rather political reasons. This system was further differentiated during the 1980s. Certain "developing countries" were important to generate a stream of valuta, others were to be drawn into the orbit of the CMEA in the long term.[48]

This poses the question why the CMEA countries continued to lend to states like Syria and Iraq, and why the credit pile increased further in the 1980s. Loyalty and friendship might have played a role, albeit a marginal one. The reasons were probably the same as in similar crises: they were hoping for better days to come after a period of muddling through. This meant to bind more and more of their own financial and industrial resources to the South, while it would have been more suitable from a long-term perspective to cut losses and concentrate on more promising endeavors. But this would have meant to acknowledge the failed policies and realize the losses.

The example of Iraq shows how the crisis of the South reached the East with delay. The war that Saddam Hussein was waging against his neighbor Iran did not impair relations to the CMEA on paper. On the contrary, the trade volume was still increasing. As long as oil prices remained high, the Iraqi regime could pay for the war as well as for their national development plans. In 1972, Iraq had earned one billion US dollars through oil exports. This number increased to an annualized 33 billion US dollars in the month preceding the outbreak of the war with Iran in 1979.[49] This naturally changed with the decline of export prices. But it took more than a year for this change to have repercussions on the trade relations with the CMEA. The mutual trade volume peaked in 1983 at 3.3 billion rubles which equated to ca. 4.78 billion US dollars.[50] In 1984, the picture changed and trade decreased by a third to 2.3 billion rubles or 3.3 billion US dollars.[51] However, these numbers were still higher than in the mid-1970s.[52]

The continued war with Iran and the decline in foreign exchange earnings forced the regime to enact austerity measures for its civilian projects and to concentrate on the military.[53] The experts of the CMEA described the situation as follows:

> The Iraqi side is striving for measures to stabilize its economy and to improve its currency and financial situation with an emphasis on the needs of the military. This led to a deterioration of the economic cooperation between the CMEA countries and Iraq. This is mainly caused by two factors:
>
> - A drop in investments and the cancellation or delay of objects that have no strategic character, and a definition of new main tasks;
> - Iraqi demands for more favorable terms, preferred treatment and in particular for deferred payments for credits already granted, for cheaper credits for new objects and equipment and for the redemption of credits with deliveries of Iraqi oil in some cases.[54]

It is interesting that from an Eastern European perspective the slump of oil prices seemed to be a more dramatic event for CMEA-Iraq relations than the war between Iraq and Iran. The experts emphasized the long-term potential of Iraq in the mid-1980s and the possibilities for the CMEA states on the Iraqi market, but the short-term perspectives looked grim.[55] Iraq may be a rather extreme example, since the crisis of the "developing countries" and war came together in this case, but the Eastern European countries were confronted with similar problems all over the Global South: even if trade volumes could be stabilized, trade generated less valuta, needed a higher capital input and was more risky than in the preceding decade. If the CMEA countries wanted to muddle through the crisis and wait for better days to come, they thus had to lend more and more. If they had insisted on a timely redemption of the debts, the whole dimension of the disaster would have become visible. The dilemma for the CMEA countries was that their strategy proved to be more favorable in the short-term but used up more and more valuable capital that could – and with hindsight should – have been invested more sensibly in the 1980s.

## Differences among the creditors

A look at the creditors is as important as a look at the debtors. A comparison of the Eastern European countries shows significant differences among them. The respective data had been shared inside the CMEA regularly since the mid-1980s, the only exception next to Mongolia and Vietnam being Ceausescu's Romania that didn't share any data out of tradition. Vietnam and Mongolia not being mentioned in the files is probably due to the fact that they – in comparison to Cuba – were only recipients of credits by other CMEA states and didn't become involved as creditors. It is not surprising that out of 26.193 billion rubles granted as governmental loans, ca. 19 billion were lent out by the Soviet Union. More surprising are its followers on the list: Bulgaria came second, then the CSSR and – despite its own financial problems – Poland. Concerning governmental credits, Bulgaria was a far more active lender than the CSSR or the most developed economy inside the CMEA, the GDR, which came in fifth and proved a more rigorous lender.[56] The volume of its governmental loans was just one-third of the Bulgarian one. The GDR was also just barely ahead of Hungary. Cuba played only a symbolic role as a lender.[57]

A different picture evolves concerning commercial credits: their volume amounted to 10.367 billion rubles with the Soviet Union placed second with 2.235 billion rubles. The leading position was taken by the CSSR with its credit volume 1.3 billion rubles higher. The GDR was placed third, barely behind the Soviets.[58] Bulgaria, on the other hand, was of only marginal importance with regard to commercial credits and took the last place among the European CMEA members.[59] The People's Republic of Poland was also in the realm of commercial credits an important player and lent out more money than Hungary.[60] The commercial credits of Poland equated to roughly two billion US dollars and thus proved a major asset in the Polish books.

There are primarily three reasons for the differences among the Eastern European countries with regard to their lending practice: one reason is their export structure. For example, products of the electrical industry were delivered on the basis of short-term, high-yielding commercial credits, while whole factories were often assembled on the basis of governmental loans which had longer terms and lower interest rates attached.[61] This practice was in line with internal CMEA agreements of the 1970s and was advantageous for countries like the CSSR and GDR which could command a capable industrial sector and disadvantageous for countries like Bulgaria which were considered industrial late-comers inside the bloc.

## The relevance of Libya for the less developed CMEA countries

The second and more important reason besides the export structure is the different competitiveness of the CMEA economies. An attempt to compensate for these differences was made by a risky lending practice to gain market shares in the Global South. The People's Republic of Bulgaria is a good example for this: Sofia gave a governmental loan of 1.072 billion rubles to Gaddafi's Libya in 1984.[62] This was a huge sum for two small and economically not so capable countries. Although Libya possessed huge oil reserves and used its high export revenues of the 1970s to become a regional power, the country was a pariah on the international stage and suffered from the deteriorating prices of crude oil in the 1980s.[63] It became clear to the Bulgarian delegate that granting money to Gaddafi was not necessarily a good idea when all representatives of the CMEA countries declared at a joint conference that they didn't loan to Libya for quite some time because of its bad payment record.[64]

Gaddafi, who had come to power following a coup in 1969, cemented his power during the 1970s and used the windfall in oil revenues to implement ever more ambitious economic development plans for Libya and to finance his interventionist foreign policy.[65] In March 1977, he renamed Libya "The Socialist People's Libyan Arab Jamahiriyya."[66] He defined his ideological views, which were a mixture of socialism and an imagined tribal community without the need for a state bureaucracy, in "The Green Book."[67] Some common ground existed in ideological terms between the CMEA countries and Libya, in particular since Gaddafi had embarked on a wave of nationalization in the 1970s. Still, his government had only intensified its contacts with the East after an oil embargo by the Reagan administration in 1981 and a sharp decrease in foreign exchange reserves from 15.5 to 2.4 billion US dollars.[68]

Despite this drawback, the Libyan government still pursued its ambitious development plans up to the late 1980s. The five-year-plan for the late 1970s alone had encompassed investments of 26.3 billion US dollars.[69] But since Western firms were more reluctant to conclude long-term agreements with Libya as the 1980s proceeded, and the regime faced ever more difficulties to pay its bills, it had to look for other partners that were maybe not as splendid but wanted to contribute. Thus, it made sense that two pariahs on the international stage, Gaddafi's Libya and the socialist East, in particular Poland and Bulgaria, forged deals. Libya – in theory – had huge oil reserves and some crumbs of foreign exchange on offer, the East could supply Libya with its technology for the country's development plan. Furthermore, Libya needed huge amounts of expatriates for its economy, as a third of its technicians and more than half of its unskilled labor had to be provided by foreigners.[70] So Eastern technicians could fill the gaps left by the West.

At a financial conference of the CMEA in Prague in April 1986, the summoned experts concluded that the state of Libya's finances was constantly deteriorating and that Libya was pleading for new loans just in order to survive. Except for Bulgaria, no one had responded to the Libyan demands.[71] On the 53rd session of the PCTAC from 14–15 January 1987, the problems were disclosed, since Libya was among the main topics of the meeting. The conference report stated:

> The commission asserts that the Libyan economy showed signs of trouble recently which can be traced back to a great extent to the discriminatory measures taken by the USA and some of its Western allies against Libya.

> The decline of foreign currency revenues caused by the slump of oil prices led to a deterioration of the economic, valuta and financial situation of the country and necessitated a revision of the national development plans, and a cutback in investment goods imports. Despite the mentioned problems, Libya remains an important trading and economic partner for the CMEA.[72]

Despite the crisis, the sectors of engineering, metallurgy, and nuclear energy were regarded as promising. Soviet experts had erected a nuclear research center called "Tashura" in Libya in 1985 with Bulgarian help.[73] They had also promised to build 1,200 km of electrical grid till 1990.[74] On 1 January 1986, 11,643 experts from the CMEA countries were working in Libya, one-fifth the amount of CMEA personnel working in the Global South.[75] Most of the personnel were Bulgarian builders. Among the 11,643 CMEA specialists, 8,000 came from Bulgaria.[76] The list of prospective objects the Soviets wanted to build with Bulgarian help in Libya until 2000 included a steel works in Misrata,[77] a fertilizer factory, several power stations, gas pipes, railways, and a nuclear power plant in Gaddafi's home town Sirt that was supposed to have much bigger dimensions than the testing reactor already built close to the capital in 1985.[78]

Only a fraction out of these projects was executed until 1991. It seems logical that the Polish leadership also wanted to jump on the bandwagon to do business with Gaddafi. The Polish representative wrote:

> Poland – like other CMEA countries – has increasing difficulties to maintain the level of deliveries to this market. Simultaneously, the Libyan government is deferring payments for construction works and services considerably. Nevertheless, Libya is considered to be one of the most important partners of the PRP [People's Republic of Poland] among the developing countries.[79]

The Libyan government delayed payments up to 12 months.[80] This leads to the question why Bulgaria and Poland in particular made deals with Gaddafi, with the Bulgarian government being supported by the Soviets as they were authorized to erect many of their objects. The answer is that both countries – due to their comparatively low competitiveness within the CMEA – were reliant on such business, while the GDR and CSSR didn't feel the necessity to concentrate their efforts on such risky deals. The Bulgarian government had agreed with their Libyan counterpart in 1983 that all engineering services by the Bulgarians were to be paid half in crude oil and half in US dollars, while all deliveries of goods were to be paid completely in US dollars.[81] Usually the guest country had to pay much higher rates for CMEA experts than skilled Bulgarian workers or engineers were paid in their home countries. The Bulgarian assembly of the nuclear research center "Tashura" alone was worth 113 million US dollars.[82]

The rates, the People's Republic of Bulgaria was asking for their experts, fluctuated heavily. While Soviet-friendly Afghanistan had to pay just 914 US dollars a month for a senior engineer, the sum was raised to 1,800 US dollars for Egypt, and 4,000 US dollars for Iraq.[83] Since Libya could hardly be called a poor, socialist-minded country but was rather seen as a source of foreign exchange earnings with big oil reserves, the rates were probably very close to the ones Iraq had to pay. Iraq served a double function for the CMEA: it was a country with close economic and political ties to the CMEA and its member states and had deep pockets – at least up to 1982. It is clear from this comparison that even the bills presented to the Afghans should have been sufficient to cover the costs. Even if the Libyan payments were made up mainly of crude oil, the deliveries were calculated according to their value in US dollars. Thus, they proved a big asset for the Bulgarian planned economy despite the bad payment behavior of its contract partner. The same mechanism applied to Poland.

## Differences on the "developed" Western periphery of the CMEA

These two points are not sufficient to explain the differences between the GDR and CSSR, both of which contained a similar export structure and level of economic development. Despite their similarities, the lending practice towards the Global South of the CSSR was much more aggressive and the volume of their lending higher than was true for the GDR. This leads to the assumption that the experts of the CSSR regarded loans as an important tool to gain and secure market shares and that they used this tool more often than their CMEA partners, even if they didn't have to rely on loans as strongly as Bulgaria and Poland. A comparison of the numbers provided for the CMEA makes the difference clear: while the CSSR had given loans to the Global South worth 8.55 billion US dollars, the GDR had lent out just half of that sum, 4.41 billion US dollars.

The different behavior of the Eastern European countries as creditors of the South is well illustrated by comparing the payment structures. In 1985, East Berlin was proudly reporting to its CMEA partners:

> In 1985, the payment structure could be mainly maintained on the level of 1984, despite increasing economic and financial difficulties in the developing countries. The share of realized agreements with developing countries that were paid immediately obtained 43.3% . . .
>
> This unaltered high level of payment conditions was influenced by raising exports in the area of basic materials, of the food processing and light industry, and by a further decline in exports of factories.[84]

By adapting its export structure to the new environment, the GDR could at least mitigate the consequences of the crisis. Nevertheless, the following year the payment structure worsened and in 1986 only 39.7 % of the contracts concluded were paid immediately. For other CMEA countries, the situation was even worse: Hungary reported to its CMEA partners that during the first half of the 1980s, only 18 % of its trade with the South were paid immediately by their customers.[85] This was just half of what the GDR experts for foreign trade had reported. The rest had to be financed on credit.

The problems of this trading strategy are obvious: at first glance, it doesn't make a difference on paper, whether goods and services are sold on credit or paid immediately in cash. The profit remains the same, only payment structure and cash-flows are altered. As long as credits are being serviced by the customers, there is no reason to start worrying. But if debtors experience a liquidity crisis, the constant stream of revenue for the creditor is running dry. Applied to East–South relations, this meant that the CMEA countries could have either written off the debts of their Southern customers or hoped to get paid with delay.

This kind of slow-motion implosion was happening inside the CMEA. The Czechoslovak delegation was reporting to its socialist partners:

> The developing countries are a key market for Czechoslovak exports. 90% of our long-term loans (governmental and commercial), tied mainly to engineering exports, are made up of loans to developing countries.
>
> This highlights the significance that credit relations with developing countries bear for the economy of the CSSR. All assets of the state valuta position towards the NSE [non-socialist economies=non-CMEA economies] and 90% of the valuta assets of the FTO [Foreign Trade Organizations] are made up of debts of the developing countries. The redemption of these locked-up funds is at risk under the currently extremely complicated conditions of the capitalist economic, financial and valuta system.[86]

The message attached was clear and applied – with differing degree – to all CMEA countries: the crisis of the South was hitting Eastern Europe hard. The CMEA countries – at least partially – realized with the South the trade gains that were needed to balance their deficit with the West. The East was therefore in a certain sense "dependent" on the South. Recent scholarship is mainly in line with the old view and states that the role of the South for Eastern Europe had been (economically) marginal at best during the Cold War.[87] This assessment may be justified, if one considers only the trade volume that lay mainly between 10 and 13 % from the mid-1960s on till the end of the Eastern bloc.[88] The qualitative significance of this trade was much higher than can be argued for with a first look at published trade statistics.

## Polányi's heritage

Questioning Eastern Europe's role in the post-1945 world leads directly to Polányi's considerations on the Soviet Union, published by him in 1944. He had the idea that the Soviet Union actually mirrored the developments of the world system from 1917 to 1944. The driving force behind these developments had not been the Soviet Union itself but the West. War Communism ended exactly at the same time, when the rest of the world returned to the old pre-war market order. Although a Communist country, the Soviet Union had introduced the gold standard and integrated into the Western world trade system.[89]

After the rediscovery of Polányi's works and their popularization following the world economic crisis of 2007, an attempt has been made by Oscar Sanchez-Sibony to apply his ideas in a simplified form to the post-1945 Soviet Union.[90] This led to the thesis that the Cold War world actually had never been a bipolar one. Its true character had always been unipolar. The Soviet Union had tried repeatedly after the Second World War to integrate again into the Western system. This system had been dominated by the US which excluded the Soviet Union from any participation in it. After 1991 a final reconciliation took place. In fact, following this narrative, there never was an attempt to establish a competing socioeconomic system.[91]

This approach deserves scrutiny. It seems more promising to return to Polányi's original thesis and to apply it to the CMEA states: hence, the 1950s can be characterized as a time of a parallel Western integration of Western Europe and America, and an Eastern integration between the Soviet Union and its "satellites" which was intended to form an autonomous system. These two social and economic orders tried to expand their reach in the 1960s and to export their systems. This led to the emergence of a dense web of mutual relations between West, East, and South in which Eastern Europe in particular was very keen to link itself with both other areas.

Similarly to the 1920s, it can be argued that the Eastern realm inevitably adapted to the West to the same degree the old order of the long 19th century was restored in the 1970s and 1980s. In accordance with the developments of the 1920s, when the Soviet Union implemented the gold standard, the socialist countries of Eastern Europe implemented the innovations of high finance that – 30 years after the war had ended – began to shine as brightly as during its previous heyday. Dollar, Libor, and credit volumes were their clear indicators. The internal CMEA material of the 1980s can be cited as proof for this particular development.

But this interpretation proves just one side of the story and stands for one direction of the post-1945 developments. Simultaneously, the socialist countries of Eastern Europe tried to expand and to reform their own model. Even in the late 1980s, when the crisis of the South – triggered by developments on the Western financial markets – threatened to draw Eastern Europe into the maelstrom, the CMEA countries still pursued their aim to bring other countries closer to the CMEA and to integrate them economically and politically in the long term, to bind them to the inner logic of the socialist market. This illustrates the Janus-faced character of the post-1945 development of the CMEA and Eastern Europe. The South was to be brought closer to the East in the long run. The directive for the 49th session of the PCTAC, taking place from 20–21 March 1985 in Moscow, reads as follows:

> By designing the long-term and complex relations with developing countries of socialist orientation, the preconditions should be reached for their integration into the international socialist division of labor and their participation in the CMEA as fully entitled partners.[92]

As shown previously, concrete discussions were held to integrate Angola and Mozambique closely in the framework of the CMEA in the mid-1980s, to make a case in point. This is evidenced by the material of the Permanent Soviet Representative to the CMEA, Mikhail Lesechko. When the Secretary of the CMEA, Viacheslav Sychev, and the head of the Mozambiquan national bank, Prakash Ratilal, met both agreed that as long as the bulk of Mozambiquan trade occurred with the West, full membership in the CMEA was no viable policy option. That Mozambiquan trade with the CMEA never surpassed its trade volume with the West was not so much due to lack of trying, but to the relative unattractiveness of Eastern goods combined with prevailing power structures in global markets that could never be broken up by the institutional framework of the CMEA.

## Conclusion

The explosion of commodity prices in the 1970s sparked a booming demand for Eastern European goods in the Global South, especially the resource-rich countries. The decision-makers inside the CMEA were only too eager to jump on the bandwagon and to offer cheap credit on a long-term basis. The developments of the 1980s led to a breakdown of this trade system and the CMEA economies lost some of their most valuable customers. The necessity of often loss-making trade with the West and of paying back their own credits remained. All CMEA countries collapsed due to the developments of the 1980s. The reasons for this collapse may not necessarily be the ones typically provided. The war in Afghanistan, the armaments race, and the procrastination of reforms are essential parts of the story to understand the dismantling of the Eastern bloc. But one highly underrated phenomenon, that was not consciously induced by the Reagan or Thatcher administration but by the independent central banks of the US and other Western central banks, has to be considered, too, together with general developments in the Southern hemisphere.

The primary goal of raising interest rates dramatically was to tackle inflation and to overcome stagnation in the US The unholy alliance of these two economic evils was coined "stagflation." This intensified an already looming crisis in many "developing countries" which had pursued public development programs on credit and tried to improve living standards with state interventionism. It took up to the second half of the 1980s, till the aftermath of this crisis had encompassed the Eastern bloc in full. The gravity of the crisis is best illustrated by the reports of the Czechoslovak delegation inside the CMEA. The trade with the "developing countries" plummeted, the payment structure worsened, which meant a deteriorating solvency of the East that had to take much higher risks than before to market its products in the South. This constellation, together with the high real interest rates that also applied to the CMEA economies made the looming crisis threatening and accelerated a debt spiral. This debt spiral – in Hungary alone – led to a doubling of its external debt which increased from ca. 10 billion US dollars to 20 billion US dollars in just five years between 1984 and 1989.[93] But it had taken Hungary 35 years to raise its external debt from 0 to 10 billion US dollars. This shows that the increased borrowing of the CMEA economies during the 1970s did not necessarily mean the beginning of the end. The problem was that the economic and financial order of the 1980s showed one big difference in comparison to the preceding decade: the division of labor of the 1970s didn't work anymore.

The role of the South in the bankruptcy of the East has hitherto been underrated. The CMEA material also shows that the term "bankruptcy," at least in an economic sense, is misleading. The Eastern European states had never been bankrupted in a technical or financial sense, since they paid their dues in the end, even in the case of Romania. It is more suitable to talk about a liquidity crisis. It is the fear of a liquidity crisis that first appears in internal documents, long before the threat of bankruptcy was on the agenda.[94] But even in 1989, all countries of the Eastern bloc "commanded" significant foreign assets. It is even questionable, if – on paper – the net debt of the socialist countries was considerable. For example, the Soviet Union had, according to CMEA material cited previously, granted credits to "developing countries" worth 30 billion US dollars. For a complete assessment, the loans given to North Korea and the "developing countries" inside the CMEA, namely Cuba, Vietnam, and Mongolia, have to be added. The liability section of the Soviet books contained outstanding loans with a nominal value of 54 billion US dollars at the end of 1989.[95] The debt pile therefore seems to be rather small on paper since liabilities – at a first glance – were balanced. The problem of the debt pile was not necessarily that it was unbearable but that the loans denominated in US dollars were almost exclusively short-term and thus had to be refinanced continuously.[96] While the Soviet Union had to pay interest and refinance loans worth 5.9 billion US dollars in 1984, this sum had already increased to 15.1 billion US dollars in 1986.[97] The payments on servicing Soviet debts most likely decreased to less than 9 billion US dollars in 1989, but this was still a huge sum.[98]

In this situation, any payments on loans granted by the Soviet Union would have been urgently needed. Yegor Gaidar cites a very telling source on this issue which – in a sense also very telling – he doesn't use for his analysis. The protocol of the Politburo meeting that had taken place on 23 August 1989 states:

> The basic interests of the USSR as creditor are tied to the loans of developing countries. . . . On January 1, 1989, it was more than 61 billion rubles (or approximately 85 % of the entire "third world" debt to the USSR), including more than 32 billion rubles to socialist developing countries – Vietnam, Cuba, China, and Mongolia. . . . Bearing in mind the real creditworthiness of our partners, the USSR periodically is forced to ease their debt burden. In the most recent period, payments by Algeria, Angola, Vietnam, Iraq, Cuba, China, Libya, Mongolia, and Nicaragua were postponed from 1989–90, for a total of more than 7 billion rubles.[99]

It is interesting that in the political environment of 1989–90 when IMF, World Bank, IECD, and EBRD were proposing reform solutions for the Soviet Union on an initiative of the G7, they didn't mention the South or "developing countries" with a single word in their report that strongly recommended implementing a "shock therapy." They focused on the debts of the Soviet Union to the West but did not mention the assets of the Soviet Union abroad.[100] Of course, these assets were pretty much frozen in the economic environment of the late 1980s. But even after writing off 50 or 75 % of the debt, taking their "real" value into account alters the picture and shifts the balance more to a political and moral breakdown than to an economic one. The economic outcome of the crisis of the 1980s was by no means determined. Scenarios would have been possible, e.g., different interest rates and commodity prices, in which the economic policies pursued by the East in the 1970s were not doomed to fail ultimately but actually could have worked out and in which the South could have serviced its debts.

## Notes

1 Reinhart and Rogoff, *This Time Is Different*, 17–8.
2 Gaidar, *Collapse of an Empire*, 57–8.
3 Frieden, *Global Capitalism*, 364.
4 Reinhart and Rogoff, *This Time Is Different*, 17–8.
5 Frieden, *Global Capitalism*, 370.
6 Gaidar, *Collapse of an Empire*, 64–7.
7 Arndt, *Economic Development*, 144.
8 Frieden, *Global Capitalism*, 370. It is unlikely, that Frieden included credits granted by CMEA countries in his calculation.
9 Frieden, 375.
10 Easterly, "The Lost Decades," 135.
11 Walle, *African Economies*, 5.
12 Moyo, *Dead Aid*, 22.
13 See e.g. Gaidar, *Collapse of an Empire*, 123, 146–7.
14 See Kotkin, "The Kiss of Debt."
15 See Reinhart and Rogoff, *This Time Is Different*. Only the socialist countries of Romania and the Soviet Union are mentioned as side notes in this standard textbook among economic historians.
16 This is clear by looking at the respective trade statistics as cited by Yegor Gaidar for the Soviet Union in: Gaidar, *Collapse of an Empire*, 123. Gaidar doesn't draw this conclusion but his numbers clearly indicate a multi-billion-dollar surplus achieved by trade with the South during the whole 1980s.
17 Defined as relation between export and import prices.
18 Gaidar, *Collapse of an Empire*, 128.
19 See Ban, "Sovereign Debt, Austerity, and Regime Change."
20 Mong, *Kádár Hitele*, 172.
21 This becomes clearer when we look at the CMEA material and the documents in the respective ministries' archives of the CMEA members.
22 "Untersuchung der Möglichkeit der Schaffung eines Systems des Informationsaustausches und der Koordinierung des Vorgehens interessierter Mitgliedsländer des RGW in der Frage des Zahlungsaufschubs für Entwicklungsländer," dated 06 March 1986, Barch Berlin DL 2/16969.
23 "Information über die Entwicklung der Kreditbeziehungen der RGW-Länder mit EL," dated 12 March 1986, ibid.
24 Ibid.
25 "Perechen' i Annotatsii soglashenii ob ekonomicheskom i tekhnicheskom sotrudnichestve stranami-chlenami SEV i rasvivaiushchimsia stranami, postupivshikh v Sekretariat SEV v 1965 godu," RGAE f. 561 op. 53 d. 18. ll. 55–71.

26 "Information über die von den Mitgliedsländern des RGW den Entwicklungsländern gewährten Regierungs- und kommerziellen Kredite, ihre Auslastung und Tilgung per 1.1.1986 sowie über die Abstimmung von Maßnahmen zur Sicherung der rechtzeitigen Tilgung der Kredite und der Garantien gegen Währungsverluste," dated 29 April 1986, Barch Berlin DL 2/16970.
27 Frieden, *Global Capitalism*, 397–9.
28 Reinhart and Rogoff, *This Time Is Different*, 17–8.
29 "Information über die von den Mitgliedsländern des RGW den Entwicklungsländern gewährten Regierungs- und kommerziellen Kredite, ihre Auslastung und Tilgung per 1.1.1986 sowie über die Abstimmung von Maßnahmen zur Sicherung der rechtzeitigen Tilgung der Kredite und der Garantien gegen Währungsverluste," dated 29 April 1986, Barch Berlin DL 2/16970.
30 "Information über die Entwicklung der Kreditbeziehungen der RGW-Länder zu den Entwicklungsländern, Studium der Währungs- und Finanzlage einzelner Entwicklungsländer, Festlegung der Höhe der Mindestzinssätze und andere Bedingungen für Firmenkredite im nachfolgenden Zeitraum, gegenseitige Information über die Verrechnungsmethoden mit den Entwicklungsländern," dated 19 March 1987, Barch Berlin, DL 2/16975.
31 Ibid.
32 Kotkin, "The Kiss of Debt," 85.
33 Letter by Horst Kaminsky to Willi Stoph, dated 24.06.1983, KfW Company Archive, Staba 2814.
34 Mong, *Kádár Hitele*, 221–3.
35 Mong, 223.
36 Mong, 224.
37 "Direktive zur 52. Tagung der SKTUZ vom 27.05.-29.05.1986 in Moskau," Barch Berlin DL 2/16970.
38 "Information über die ergriffenen Maßnahmen zur Aktivierung der mehrseitigen Zusammenarbeit der RGW-Länder mit Entwicklungsländern," dated 23 January 1987, Barch Berlin, DL 2/16974.
39 Ibid.
40 Ibid.
41 Material of the PCTAC inside the Ministry for Foreign Trade of the GDR, Barch Berlin, DL 2/16975.
42 Ibid.
43 "Information über Regierungs- und kommerzielle Kredite, die die RGW-Länder den Entwicklungsländern gewährt haben, deren Inanspruchnahme und Tilgung per 1 January 1987 und Maßnahmen zur Sicherung der rechtzeitigen Tilgung der Kredite und von Garantien in bezug auf Valutaverluste," dated 29 April 1987, ibid.
44 The internal exchange rate inside the CMEA was 1:1,45 in 1987, statistical material of the PCTAC, Barch Berlin, DL 2/16976.
45 The new role played by India is directly connected to the policies of Gorbachev who put livelier political and economic relations with India high up on his agenda.
46 "Information über Regierungs- und kommerzielle Kredite, die die RGW-Länder den Entwicklungsländern gewährt haben, deren Inanspruchnahme und Tilgung per 1 January 1987 und Maßnahmen zur Sicherung der rechtzeitigen Tilgung der Kredite und von Garantien in bezug auf Valutaverluste," dated 29 April 1987, Barch Berlin, DL 2/16975.
47 Ibid.
48 "Direktive 49. Tagung SKTUZ," Barch Berlin, DL 2/16965.
49 Gaidar, *Collapse of an Empire*, 57–8.
50 "Protokoll der Tagung der Leiter der handelspolitischen Verwaltungen der Ministerien für Außenhandel und der staatlichen Komitees für Außenwirtschaftsbeziehungen der ML/RGW (15.-18. April 1986, Plovdiv)," dated 29.04.1986, Barch Berlin DL 2/16970. The numbers presented inside the CMEA to the ministers for foreign trade most likely do not include arms sells.

51 Ibid.
52 "Spravka o sostoianii sotrudnichestva stran-chlenov SEV s Irakom, osushchestvliaemogo v ramkakh Sovmestnoi komissii SEV i Irakskoi Respubliki," dated 20 April 1982, RGAE f. 561 op. 53 d. 123 ll. 20–5.
53 "Protokoll der Tagung der Leiter der handelspolitischen Verwaltungen der Ministerien für Außenhandel und der staatlichen Komitees für Außenwirtschaftsbeziehungen der ML/RGW (15.-18. April 1986, Plovdiv)," dated 29 April 1986, Barch Berlin DL 2/16970.
54 Ibid.
55 Ibid.
56 2.417 billion rubles for the People's Republic of Bulgaria and 2.319 billion rubles for the CSSR.
57 All numbers concerning governmental credits as of 01 January 1987 are taken from the document "Information über Regierungs- und kommerzielle Kredite, die die RGW-Länder den Entwicklungsländern gewährt haben, deren Inanspruchnahme und Tilgung per 1.1.1987 und Maßnahmen zur Sicherung der rechtzeitigen Tilgung der Kredite und von Garantien in bezug auf Valutaverluste," dated 29 April 1987, Barch Berlin DL 2/16975.
58 CSSR 3.577 billion rubles, GDR 2.179 billion rubles.
59 Bulgaria 0.312 billion rubles, Cuba 0.059 billion rubles.
60 Poland 1.299 billion rubles. All numbers concerning commercial credits as of 01 January 1987 are taken from the document "Information über Regierungs- und kommerzielle Kredite, die die RGW-Länder den Entwicklungsländern gewährt haben, deren Inanspruchnahme und Tilgung per 1 January 1987 und Maßnahmen zur Sicherung der rechtzeitigen Tilgung der Kredite und von Garantien in Bezug auf Valutaverluste," dated 29 April 1987, Barch Berlin DL 2/16975.
61 "Information über die Entwicklung der Kreditbeziehungen der RGW-Länder mit EL," dated 12 March 1986, Barch Berlin DL 2/16969.
62 "Information über den Stand der Kreditbeziehungen der ML/RGW mit Algerien, Libyen, Libanon, VDRJ, Nikaragua, Afghanistan," dated 06 March 86, ibid.
63 Vandewalle, *A History of Modern Libya*, 98.
64 "Information über den Stand der Kreditbeziehungen der ML/RGW mit Algerien, Libyen, Libanon, VDRJ, Nikaragua, Afghanistan," dated 06 March 86, Barch Berlin, DL 2/16969.
65 Vandewalle, *A History of Modern Libya*, 92–6.
66 Vandewalle, 103.
67 Vandewalle, 101.
68 Vandewalle, 112.
69 Vandewalle, 110.
70 Vandewalle, 110.
71 "Protokoll der Expertentagung der RGW-Länder für Valuta- und Finanzfragen (1.-3. April 1986, Prag)," Barch Berlin DL 2/16970.
72 "Bericht über 53. Tagung der SKTUZ vom 14.-15 January 1987 in Moskau," Barch Berlin DL 2/16974.
73 The research reactor in Tashura seems to be still operating.
74 "Information über die ergriffenen Maßnahmen zur Aktivierung der mehrseitigen Zusammenarbeit der RGW-Länder mit Entwicklungsländern," dated 23 January 1987, Barch Berlin DL 2/16974.
75 Statistical material of the PCTAC, Barch Berlin DL 2/16976.
76 "Zusammengefaßte Information über die Festigung und Stärkung der Positionen der RGW-Länder auf dem libyschen Markt und die Erhöhung der Effektivität der Zusammenarbeit durch eine Reihe von Koordinierungsmaßnahmen," dated 29 October 1986, Barch Berlin DL 2/16973.

77 The Misrata steelworks was meant to form the backbone for industrializing the whole area and was thus a project of some significance.
78 "Zusammengefaßte Information über die Festigung und Stärkung der Positionen der RGW-Länder auf dem libyschen Markt und die Erhöhung der Effektivität der Zusammenarbeit durch eine Reihe von Koordinierungsmaßnahmen," dated 29 October 1986, Barch Berlin DL 2/16973.
79 Ibid.
80 Ibid.
81 Ibid.
82 "Zusammengefaßte Information über die Ergebnisse der Realisierung des 'Verzeichnisses der Objekte der möglichen mehrseitigen Zusammenarbeit der ML/RGW mit EL im Zeitraum 1981–1985'," dated 02 August 1985, Barch Berlin DL 2/16967.
83 Statistical material of the PCTAC, ibid.
84 "Jahresinformation über die Gewährung von Regierungskrediten und kommerziellen Krediten an Entwicklungsländer sowie die Inanspruchnahme und Tilgung der Kredite per 1 January 1986," Barch Berlin DL 2/16969.
85 "Information über die Entwicklung der Kreditbeziehungen zwischen den ML/RGW und den Entwicklungsländern," dated 28 March 85, Barch Berlin DL 2/16966.
86 Ibid.
87 Sanchez-Sibony, *Red Globalization*, 19.
88 Number for the Soviet Union, Sanchez-Sibony, 94.
89 Polányi, *The Great Transformation*, 327–8.
90 Sanchez-Sibony, *Red Globalization.*
91 Sanchez-Sibony, 59.
92 "Direktive 49. Tagung SKTUZ," Barch Berlin DL 2/16965.
93 Mong, *Kádár Hitele*, 304–5.
94 E.g. in Hungary at the end of 1982: Mong, 227.
95 International Monetary Fund, The World Bank, Organisation for Economic Co-Operations and Development, and European Bank for Reconstruction and Development, *The Economy of the Soviet Union*, 7.
96 International Monetary Fund, The World Bank, Organisation for Economic Co-Operations and Development, and European Bank for Reconstruction and Development, 7.
97 Gaidar, "The Inevitability of Collapse," 28–9.
98 Gaidar, *Collapse of an Empire*, 146.
99 As cited in: Gaidar, 146–7.
100 International Monetary Fund, The World Bank, Organisation for Economic Co-Operations and Development, and European Bank for Reconstruction and Development, *The Economy of the Soviet Union.*

# 9 Who belongs to the "Third World", who to the "Second"? Mutual dependencies

## Decreasing competitiveness

The basic problem of the CMEA member states concerning economic cooperation with the countries of the Global South was that the export of their development model depended on a specific promise: that they could offer more sophisticated and more efficient technologies and management styles to run the economy than were already present in the Global South. This promise was indirectly threatened by the West offering its own model to run the economy, even if the development projects were often of the same character as their Eastern equivalents. A more imminent threat originated from the South itself. If economic cooperation and "development aid" were successful, at least to a certain degree, building heavy industries in the Global South could threaten the competitiveness of the Eastern Bloc's industry at least in the long-term. As Indian or Brazilian engineers were appropriating the necessary know-how to manage a steel factory efficiently, they could come up with the idea of building one themselves and – if this endeavor proved successful – exporting it to other markets. This, in turn, threatened the position of the East, if the East was unable to keep pace and stay at least one step ahead of their former disciples turned competitors.

This problem logically became more urgent with time. Since it is easier to master already existing technologies than to invent entirely new ones, the "development gap" was likely to close as the years passed by, at least for some countries. The East could not go on selling the same type of only slightly modernized and adjusted projects over several decades again and again. This problem gained momentum in the files of the CMEA and the PCTA in particular in the mid- and late 1970s. A report on a meeting of the heads of the foreign trade organizations of the CMEA member states that took place in 1976 reads:

> It has been made clear that many different tendencies come together on the market of the developing countries: on the one hand, customers are demanding the delivery of turnkey objects, on the other hand, there is the desire of those countries, the industry of which is relatively developed, which want to reduce their imports to a minimum and which want to limit their exchange [with the CMEA] to the most complicated part of full deliveries and which

> want to participate in the building process with own deliveries, thereby partially trying to conduct project planning with their own means.[1]

More than 20 years after Stalin's death and the subsequent endeavors of the Eastern Bloc to cooperate with the Global South, a new dynamic was unfolding. As is clear from the document, some countries were still demanding projects on a turnkey basis. These were the kind of projects predominant during the 1960s. Entire factory complexes and branches of industry were erected with only minor participation of locals. These projects proved very complex in nature, as many things had to be coordinated. The cooperation of several state combines was already a delicate matter at home, becoming even more difficult in a country of the Global South like Syria or Iraq. Although the needs of the Southern customer had to be respected, the typical development project of the 1960s was mainly an intrabloc affair, as Eastern state combines performed the overwhelming majority of the respective steps needed to assemble factories themselves.

However, more and more partners in the Global South insisted on a direct participation of their national industrial champions. The role of state combines from the Eastern Bloc was to be limited to assemble the parts that could not yet be produced in the recipient country, while still being responsible for the success of the project in the end. This threatened to increase the complexity of cooperation with the Global South dramatically, since the number of variables and therefore possible problems was increasing exponentially. State combines had to stay in touch with companies from the Global South that most likely entertained different management styles, in particular if cooperation occurred with private or semi-private companies. Therefore, cooperation with countries from the Global South that were advancing the technological ladder, put a strain on the managerial capacity of the state combines of the East, possibly overburdening socialist managers.

The situation was furthermore complicated by the fact that the spending spree of most CMEA member states in the 1970s had not significantly increased the competitiveness and technological level of their respective economies. What remained were the debts with which Western technology had been bought but not well integrated in the socialist production processes and state combines.[2] The European members of the CMEA had therefore to enact austerity measures to stay afloat. This meant scaling back imports from the West and cutting investments in the capital stock which, in turn, threatened to erode the competitiveness of the socialist economies further. Despite most countries in the Global South facing the same problems, a dilapidating capital stock in the East proved no good omen to keep the "development gap" between East and South intact and to prevent potential customers from the South to turn increasingly to the West for development schemes.

## ISI under fire

The situation was further aggravated by the West increasingly abandoning the propagation of the traditional development model prevailing in the immediate post-war decades. While up to the late 1970s, Western and Eastern development strategies had enjoyed a significant degree of similarity, the situation changed in the 1980s. Western partners and donors of the Global South rejected industrialization by import substitution (ISI) as outdated and as a failed theory. Although the Reagan administration itself was not a shining example for free-trade thinking at home, it promoted free trade abroad and in the international organizations it had a significant say in, such as the Bretton Woods institutions.[3] Since ISI was based on protectionism and a strict control of trade flows, the new development model propagated in the West took an opposite position towards the one still prevalent in the East and in a majority of Southern societies.

Countries like Singapore, Hongkong, South Korea, and Taiwan had always pursued a different development path than the majority of the countries of the Global South. Since the mid-1960s they were following a strategy of export-oriented industrialization (EOI).[4] This in no way meant that their respective governments were allowing the forces of free enterprise to flow freely. Their economic policies were no less interventionist and dirigiste than those of the majority of the governments in the Global South pursuing an import substituting development model. The difference was that they encouraged their public and private companies to produce for the world market instead of the domestic market.[5] The East Asian countries which embarked on EOI didn't have much of a choice. Since they possessed few marketable raw materials to pay for imports of technology needed for ISI, they had to focus on exporting manufactures instead of raw materials to earn foreign exchange.[6]

ISI had come under pressure already in the 1970s to a certain degree. The huge imports of technology and the expansion of the industrial base of many countries of the Global South were financed on credit. This led to the crisis of the 1980s. Even if the 1980s had not been marked by crisis, the debts of the South had to be repaid anyhow. The only possibility to do so were rapidly increasing exports. Therefore, the governments of countries like Brazil had started to encourage exports before the immediate outbreak of the crisis triggered by the Mexican default in 1982.[7] Nevertheless, ISI remained the model favored by a majority of countries till the early 1980s.[8]

When credit flows from the West to the South stalled in the early 1980s, many countries were forced to abandon ISI rapidly, since they could no longer afford to pay for the necessary imports like machines, production licenses, or raw materials for their industrial base. In the ten years following the outbreak of the crisis of 1982, most countries of the Global South liberalized trade, and opened their economies for foreign investors.[9] This was much to the liking of Western donors and institutions like the IMF and the World Bank. The adjustment programs of these two institutions in particular often involved policy agreements which obliged the recipient of their financial aid to abandon their former development path and focus on increasing export revenues, while limiting imports. The resulting trade surplus was to guarantee that debts to Western lenders would be paid back.

However, such developments could hardly be to the liking of the CMEA member countries. They relied on exporting their machinery to the Global South based on a more or less explicit agreement that East and South were following the same development model. The change is noticeable in the documents on the CMEA–Mexico Joint Commission. As Mexico happened to be at the epicenter of the crisis, the consequences for cooperation were swift and decisive. The trade directive for the East German delegation to the 45th meeting of the PCTA in early December 1983 in Moscow states:

> Since the 4th session of the Joint Commission CMEA/Mexico (September 1981) there has been no progress at all in multilateral cooperation between the CMEA member countries with Mexico, or rather has the Mexican side not reacted to the proposals made by the CMEA side in the commission to activate this cooperation.[10]

Although a meeting of the working group for industry of the CMEA–Mexico Joint Commission did take place in 1986, its members couldn't agree on any future projects.[11] Trade between them was collapsing. Particularly GDR trade, while amounting to 70 million US dollars in 1981, declined sharply to 34 million US dollars two years later.[12] This drop was almost entirely due to shrinking Mexican imports, as the GDR itself continued to import goods from Mexico on the same scale as in 1980–81. The GDR was no exception in the CMEA. Czechoslovak exports to Mexico shrank by more than 50 % between 1981 and 1983, while trade between Bulgaria and Mexico was almost totally wiped out in the same time, amounting to 17 million US dollars in 1981 and only 0.057 million US dollars in 1983.[13] This meant that Mexican actors had stopped buying Eastern machines and equipment abruptly. Even if Mexico was a secondary trading partner for the CMEA, the European members of the organization lost export income between ca. 10 and 30 million US dollars each; and Mexico was only the beginning.

The only area in the Global South that still enjoyed untainted growth rates and looked like paradise was East Asia, where the countries following an EOI strategy were rapidly advancing on the economic ladder and were joined by China. The non-socialist countries of the region were growing by 7 % annually with the PR China experiencing even higher growth rates during the 1980s. This made other leaders from the Global South take a look at the East Asian "miracle." While most of them had looked to the socialist countries of Eastern Europe or Cuba before, they were now starting to study the East Asian model.[14] This was also true for leaders who stayed in close contact with the CMEA during the 1980s like Denis Sassou-Nguesso of the PR Congo, or Jerry Rawlings of Ghana.[15] Since EOI had worked only under very special circumstances in East Asia and severe state interventionism, the implementation of EOI and free trade enforced by the Bretton Wood institutions and Western governments could not replicate the successes of the East Asian countries and led to disastrous socioeconomic consequences.

## Penny pinchers

Valuable insight into how the CMEA member states considered handling the new developments is delivered by the general East German trade directive for fulfilling the economic plan in 1982 and laying the groundwork for 1983. This document contains the following initial statement on the Global South and the aims of mutual trade:

> The economic and scientific-technical relations with developing countries are to deepen on a long-term and stable basis with the aim to improve and maximize export surpluses. Hereby in particular
>
> - the countries which pursue a socialist development path should be supported in strengthening their economic independence and the industrialization of their countries;
> - by a concentration of exports and market work on focus countries as well as financially strong developing countries, above average growth in freely disposable foreign currency income should be guaranteed;
> - the complex connection of export and import should be hedged with scientific-technical cooperation, the training of cadres, consulting activities, and customer service.[16]

The aim of trading with the South was clear: export revenues had to increase and had to exceed the costs of imports from the South. Nevertheless, socialist countries should be exempted from maximizing the economic benefit for the GDR, as their industrial base and "economic independence" in the sense of independence from Western trading partners had to be strengthened. Technical assistance in the direct sense of providing auxiliary services and vocational training served the same purpose to increase export revenues and to train prospective craftsmen and engineers in East European facilities with machines made in the CMEA member countries. The non-socialist countries of the Global South were further differentiated by their relative financial strength with a clear preference for the ones with high reserves of foreign exchange.

However, this category could prove highly volatile. The trade directive for 1982 and 1983, drafted in 1981, still listed Mexico as a financially attractive country next to Arab oil exporting countries like Saudi Arabia or Kuwait.[17] Further measures to increase the cash in hand of the East German state included curtailing long-term issuance of credits to the Global South. Instead, credit issuance to finance the export businesses of the GDR was to be minimized by increasing exports of the food processing industry, and light industry which could be paid in advance or immediately at the time of delivery. Electronic industries and machine building were supposed to focus on delivering equipment and not necessarily whole factories to avoid granting long-term credits which could put a strain on East German cash-flows. Deliveries of plants to the Global South were to be increased on a multilateral basis by cooperating with other CMEA partners as well as with "capable national partners in developing countries."[18] The last point in particular took the wishes of the economically more advanced countries of the Global South into account.

It is interesting to note that the trade directive urged for more sophisticated supply chains for the East German economy. Imports were to serve the purpose of maximally stimulating East German exports.[19] But imports were not to be limited to raw materials and tropical goods anymore. The authors of the directive stated the following by relating to a resolution of the Presidium of the Council of Minister from January 1979 and a resolution of the Governmental Commission for Uniformly Steering Import and Export (RKEI) from 31 October 1980:

- concrete proposals have to be worked out and proposals have to be made to selected developing countries for long-term and stable relations based on the division of labor for expanding production, in particular of foreign exchange lucrative marketable products for NSE-export [non-socialist economic area=non-CMEA] by setting free production capacities in the GDR and outsourcing this production to developing countries;
- the inclusion of deliveries from partners in developing countries has to be implemented in GDR exports of plants for which there are no or no sufficient preconditions in the GDR (in particular construction and assembly, spare parts production, electronical equipment, tools, simple cutting machine tools) and
- the inclusion of semi-finished and finished goods of industrial plants erected by the GDR in developing countries has to be included in the NSE-import plan and thereby production capacities in the GDR have to be unlocked for foreign exchange lucrative NSE-exports and further exports of plants by the GDR.[20]

This signaled a change from the old economic policies pursued in the preceding decades. The passage cited previously can be interpreted as softening the socialist version of ISI by acknowledging that sophisticated supply chains and import structures could enhance domestic wealth and free economic capacities at home to increase labor productivity. In theory, such a strategy could have proved an escape from the predominantly extensive growth strategies of the East that were exhausted by the late 1970s in favor of intensive growth. Intensive growth in general means to improve output with given levels of inputs of labor and resources by streamlining production processes, thereby making them more efficient and providing better training and technology for workers.

To a certain degree this was already practiced, as can be seen in the Syrian cement example. Bulgarian and later also Lebanese workers had built factories on behalf of East German plans under the guidance of only a few East German engineers, while the machine parts and equipment were produced in the GDR and other bloc countries like the Soviet Union. This meant that East German workers could be used for other projects in the meantime. However, this division of labor had already proved precarious in the Syrian case. As more and more steps, particularly in manufacturing, were delegated to other partners, the number of problems would hardly decrease, without changes in management style and management capacities.

These aims of trade with the Global South didn't change during the 1980s, even if the goals were not reached. In the case of long-term credits, the authorities of the CMEA member states, including the GDR, proved unable to curtail credit growth. An East German document on trade with non-CMEA countries from 1987 provides concrete numbers on the surpluses that actually should have been achieved. Trade outside CMEA in 1987 was expected to generate a surplus of 2.6 billion Valutamark (VM), 1.625 billion of which directly as freely disposable foreign exchange surplus.[21] This 2.6 billion VM equaled ca. 1.4 billion US dollars in 1987. This sum was further differentiated: 748 million VM were to be earned in the category of exports that didn't need any imports as prior input and could thus be booked immediately as surplus.

Products for export that didn't need any imports were not the most sophisticated things the economy of the GDR was producing. This type of goods was delivered to 28 countries as the main East German export line. According to the plan, this category consisted exclusively of countries from the Global South like Libya, Ghana, and Congo.[22] Furthermore, the plan explicitly stated two more countries from the Global South, Egypt and Algeria, where a trade surplus of 135 million VM each was to be achieved in 1987.[23] Thus, the Global South provided the East Germans with a surplus in freely disposable foreign exchange of 1.016 billion VM. As is clear from the documents cited in chapter 8, the same tendencies applied to the other European members of the CMEA, as well, even if concrete numbers are not available. A customer like the Libyan state was attractive, because products of questionable competitiveness could be sold for at least partial payment in foreign exchange. This trade pattern was emulated by other CMEA member states, as well. Hungary, to make a case in point, achieved an annual surplus in excess of 100 million US dollars in its trade relations with the Global South in the late 1970s.[24] Although this was less than the sum the GDR achieved, considering the smaller size of Hungary's economy, these numbers were not significantly lower.

It is interesting to note that at least in the East German case foreign trade relations became more embedded in a system of "checks and balances" in the sense that state commissions started supervising the foreign trade organizations and state combines much more rigorously in the 1980s than in the preceding decade. This is exemplified by the Governmental Commission for Uniformly Steering Import and Export (RKEI).[25] This commission doesn't appear in the files on projects conducted in the 1970s. It was headed by Gerhard Beil. Beil, born in 1926, had worked as a clerk and as a miner in his youth before embarking on studying economic planning in 1952. After his graduation, he had started working in several East German foreign trade agencies and finished his dissertation in 1968. He had already become deputy of the Minister for Foreign Trade in 1965 and was taken up into the Central Committee of the SED in 1981. In March 1986, he became the successor of Horst Sölle as Minister for Foreign Trade.[26] Horst Sölle changed for a position in Moscow at the CMEA, as he became the new Permanent Representative of the GDR to the CMEA.[27] Connected with this post was the position of deputy head of government of the GDR. As Sölle was an experienced trade official, this change signals that his expertise was valued and needed in the CMEA to preserve East German interests.

## Still an attractive partner?

The 1980s brought some institutional changes to the PCTA, as well. These were not limited to renaming the commission and expanding its agenda but included personal changes, as well. Its longstanding chair, Skachkov, was replaced by Mikhail Alekseevich Sergeiichik on the 48th meeting of the PCTAC that took place in Moscow from 12–13 December 1984.[28] Sergeiichik served as head of the Governmental Committee for Foreign Economic Relations (GKES) of the Soviet Union. He held onto his post only till the end of 1986. This coincided with other changes in personnel taking place inside the Gorbachev administration. The Soviet foreign trade minister, Nikolai S. Patolichev, who had served as foreign trade minister since 1958, was replaced at the end of 1985, as well.

The crisis of the 1980s didn't mean that no new partners approached the CMEA for cooperation but such attempts became much rarer than in the 1970s and it was clear that the CMEA had lost attractiveness. One such country was Ghana. Despite its own grave economic and political problems or just because of them, as it was in need of any support the country's leadership could obtain. The government of Ghana had called for the CMEA to send a delegation of economic experts to evaluate a set of projects for economic cooperation. The report of this delegation was on the agenda of the 53rd meeting of the PCTAC that took place from 14–15. January 1987 in Moscow.[29] Although the CMEA was in essence no supranational organization, it is remarkable that the experts were sent in the name of the CMEA and not in the name of the countries they were originally from. As was also true for the stipend program, the sending of experts in the name of the CMEA pointed at the direction of slowly developing supranational structures, even if these were only small initial steps. The Romanian government still disapproved of such development in the 1980s.[30]

Before contacting the CMEA, the Ghanaian government had been in close contact with Czechoslovak economic advisers. The projects the Czechoslovak experts had proposed were not very innovative, as they consisted mainly of rebuilding factories that had gone bankrupt due to the economic crisis of Ghana and had been built by Eastern companies in the 1960s and 1970s.[31] Nevertheless, the CMEA delegation judged the long-term prospects of the Ghanaian economy positively in its report. Its role as the world's largest producer of cocoa beans and one of the ten largest producers of gold and industrial diamonds was acknowledged next to its rich deposits of iron ore, bauxite, and manganese. The economic potential of its forests and the potential of using its rivers for electricity production were mentioned, as well.[32] On the negative side were the current economic problems of Ghana and its high debts. The authors of the document clearly stated that economic relations between the CMEA member countries and Ghana had cooled down significantly after the downfall of Nkrumah in 1966. They explained the renewed interest of the Ghanaian leadership in the socialist East with the will of the new government to counterbalance its economic relations and to profit from trading with the West as well as with the East.[33]

Interestingly, the files list the Iran of the ayatollah as a more attractive partner for the CMEA member countries than the Iran of the Shah had ever been, in particular for the smaller members. This was true despite the close relationship of the Eastern Bloc with Iraq and the cooperation treaty with the CMEA. In early March 1981, the departmental heads of the members of the CMEA states for the Global South in the Ministries for Foreign Trade met in Budapest, where they discussed the prospects of economic cooperation with a selection of countries from the Global South, one being Iran under its new leadership.[34] The section on Iran reads:

> The Iraqi-Iranian conflict that started in September 1980 led to a further aggravation of economic difficulties of Iran and to a deterioration of the trade situation for the activities of the CMEA member states on the Iranian market. . . .
>
> It has been asserted on the conference that, despite the complicated trade situation of the FTOs of the socialist countries on the Iranian market, they have continued their activities. Most CMEA member states increased their exports to Iran in 1980 in comparison with 1979 foremost by deliveries of food and consumer goods, rolling stock, steel products etc.[35]

This excerpt of the conference protocol sounds highly ambiguous. The Iranian economy was obviously in severe trouble due to the revolution and the war with its neighboring country Iraq. Nevertheless, the CMEA member states could increase their exports to Iran. This was due to the changing structure of Iranian imports and – counterintuitively – to the economic problems of the country. The new Iranian leadership had to save hard currency and curtail imports of goods that were not necessarily needed like luxury goods and the most advanced civilian technologies. More often than not these could not be provided by the Eastern economies, anyhow. What they could provide were basic consumer goods, products of heavy industries, and sturdy equipment.

These deliveries could be obtained by the Iranians mostly without paying in US dollars. The experts of the Ministries for Foreign Trade of the CMEA member states complained about the fact that trade with Iran of the ayatollahs had to be settled by clearing accounts, but they were confident that their exports could increase significantly during the 1980s.[36] The GDR trade experts in Iran stated in their reports that 14 % of East German exports were paid in US dollars, the rest was settled via a clearing account.[37] What they could get in return was mainly Iranian oil. The departmental heads assembled in Budapest agreed to intensify their cooperation in Iran and to closely monitor any policy initiatives of the Iranian leadership as concerned their trade policies, since they couldn't see a clear agenda in 1981. Furthermore, they agreed to closely watch the solvency of Iran to avoid a situation where the credits given for development projects weren't repaid.[38]

One large-scale project that reveals what kind of business could be conducted with Iran, was the erection of transformer stations and the expansion of the electrical grid of Iran. This project was executed by East German state combines with deliveries from other intrabloc partners. Sixteen contracts concluded between East German and Iranian state agencies called for the erection of 110 transformer stations in Iran between 1980 and 1987. The aggregated value of the contracts amounted to 250.3 million valutamark, thus ca. 120 million US dollars.[39] The dollar value was only of theoretical importance, as payment was most likely due by oil deliveries. A report of the RKEI filed in late June 1989 stated that only three of the 16 contracts had been executed according to plan. All the other ones had incurred delays of up to four years.[40] Responsible for the projects were the state combines Heavy Current Plant Assembly Leipzig-Halle[41] and Heavy Current Plant Assembly Dresden.[42]

The delays were partly due to the war between Iran and Iraq. However, this was only a minor issue compared with other deficiencies. East German deliveries were incomplete, some deliveries were dysfunctional, inputs from contractors from inside the bloc were flawed,[43] the assembly could not be completed according to schedule by the building teams and engineers. The situation was further complicated by the dilapidating energy infrastructure of East Germany. Although not explicitly stated, the protocols convey the impression that the state combines responsible for the deliveries had to conduct emergency repairs in East Germany which further delayed deliveries to Iran.[44]

Many of the components delivered by the East Germans had to be replaced. On one occasion, a whole transformer station had to be shipped back to the GDR for repairs only to be delivered back to Iran without being fully repaired. Thus, the engineers had to send the station back again once more. Needless to say, the Iranian customer was not pleased with that behavior.[45] The East Germans were well aware that their technology was increasingly out of date and stated this explicitly in the files. They could only sell energy infrastructure to countries from the Global South like Syria, Ethiopia, and Iran:

> A third market besides the ARE [Egypt] and the SAR [Syria] was to be created in Iran for energy distribution facilities. While realizing the 16 contracts, an extremely complicated situation arose due to a multitude of omissions by the GDR, difficulties created by the contract partner, and war damages. The situation was further aggravated by significant energy problems in the GDR in this time. . . . It is evident that similar to all plant objects in the NSE [non-socialist economic area=non-CMEA] cardinal problems in the realization phase have led to a complicated situation and economic losses (in foreign exchange and mark):
>
> GDR:
> - repeated change of the general contractor
> - extreme delays of deliveries
> - incomplete, flawed, and technologically unexact partial deliveries

- noncompliance with the assembly plan
- quality problems with GDR and imported equipment
- underestimation of transport and storage problems
- too frequent change of cadres on the construction side

Iran:
- delays in the construction process
- difficulties in visa issuance for GDR cadres
- war damage and its implications . . .
- the technological level of the energy equipment of the GDR is of only limited competitiveness . . .
- selling GDR equipment on other markets [than Iran, Syria, and Ethiopia] can hardly be guaranteed anymore[46]

All in all, trade between the GDR and Iran peaked in 1983 at 562.4 million valutamark, ca. 300 million US dollars. Back in 1979 when the regime of the Shah was collapsing, the volume of mutual trade amounted to a mere 71.5 million valutamark. The East German trade officials secured options to buy up to 1 million tons of Iranian oil but according the documents they never imported more than 0.445 million tons.[47] In 1985 trade with Iran was at only 60 % of its 1983 level.[48] There is reason to assume that the high numbers of the early 1980s were due to the Iranian war efforts, as the GDR was also selling dual-use goods like trucks that could also be used in the desert for military purposes. These imports could not be maintained by the Iranians at a high level in the late 1980s due to the third oil shock.[49]

The documents furthermore illustrate the difficulties and problems of socialist accounting. On 30 June 1989, the RKEI decided that part of the losses of the projects that amounted to 20.2 million valutamark, were due to war damages and the rest was due to deficiencies of the East German state combines. The state combines were thus able to state higher profits in their accounting of the project. Their profits increased by 5.1 million valutamark.[50] This involved a certain degree of bookcooking. The 5.1 million valutamark were in reality still a loss, not a profit, as the state combines didn't actually receive higher payments by the Iranian side for the war damage. Therefore, the state combines could in theory have stated profit after profit in their books and still go bust in the end, as they would have run out of cash. This could be called creative socialist accounting.

The project in Iran wasn't supervised by SKET, the main East German state combine for projects in the area of heavy industries. This proves that the Syrian example with all its ups and downs was neither unique nor were the problems of economic cooperation with the Global South in East Germany limited to one state combine that for whatever reason couldn't manage such projects well. It is also safe to assume that problems were not limited to East German state combines, as some of the problems experienced in projects under East German auspices were due to insufficient deliveries and services of CMEA partner organizations. Having said that, SKET was still troubled by the same kind of problems in the 1980s. This becomes evident and was also acknowledged by East German economic experts when SKET and ZAB tried to build cement factories in Ethiopia, modeled on the Syrian example. The hope of the economic planners was that SKET and ZAB had been able to learn their lessons in Syria. Reality proved them wrong as a report on the second stage of the cement factory in New Mugher shows:

> 1 The customer knows our performance/weaknesses very well from the cement factory I (technical problems, delays, missing assembly steps, accident of the main gear mechanism, compromises on foreign exchange questions, technological and quality issues two years after the final handover . . .).
> 2 Previous controls showed the same problems at cement factory II.[51]

Direct comparison with the Syrian projects was also drawn in the files:

> Right from the start, greatest attention has been given to a timely and preemptive control of the object in evaluation of our experiences with prior deliveries of cement factories to Syria (Tartous and Adra) and Ethiopia (New Mugher I) to avoid the recurrence of economic damage in foreign currency and [East German] mark, a further damage to our reputation and the loss of markets.[52]

## New projects

Although the competitiveness of many parts of the economies of the East was tumbling, the members of the CMEA pursued new initiatives, as well. The example of the expansion of the electrical grid and infrastructure in Iran shows that the old kind of projects relying on intrabloc cooperation and coordination of imports had not gained in efficiency in the late 1970s and 1980s. Quite on the contrary, problems seemed to become even more frequent. The technical components had not become more reliable, as could be expected after an ongoing period of economic integration. Imports from Yugoslavia or Bulgaria still didn't fit well combined with, among others, East German technology. Declining investments in the own capital stock of the East and the industrial base were taking their toll.

One project meant to provide a shining example for the future of economic cooperation with the Global South occurred in Algeria. On the same conference in Budapest in March 1981 of the heads of the departments for "developing countries" in the foreign trade ministries of the CMEA member states, not only Iran had been on the agenda but also Algeria. The "active, antiimperialist policies" of the Algerian government and its "progressive socioeconomic transformation" were mentioned positively in the protocol.[53] One year before, the state party of Algeria had urged for strengthening economic planning mechanisms in the country on its party congress, and thus propagated an increased role of the state in the economy. The orators of the party congress emphasized the potential role of the CMEA in fostering the independence of Algeria.[54]

Trade with Algeria had already increased threefold during the 1970s but was still judged as "all in all not big" by the departmental heads of the East. However, improving mutual trade in the 1980s wasn't only rooted in ideological commitment, it was furthermore fed by economic arguments. Algeria was not only exporting raw materials like iron ore and oil; the Algerian government was changing its trade regime with the East from settling trade by clearing accounts to convertible currency. This measure was judged decisive in the protocol as having prepared the ground for a new, more sophisticated level of mutual economic relations.[55]

A treaty between the GDR and Algeria had been signed on 7 March 1979 to build a cables factory in the Algerian town of Biskra between 1 June 1980 and 31 January 1986. The project was worth 435 million VM, thus ca. 200 million US dollars.[56] It consisted of three stages. The plant's first production line was to produce household cables, the second and third cables for industrial customers.[57] The project was complicated as it included not only the cooperation between three East German state combines, SKET, the combine for automated plants,[58] and the Cables Plant Oberspree[59] situated in Berlin, but also had a multinational component. SKET was head of a consortium consisting of four other companies from four different countries: TGE from Algeria, the Yugoslav company Invest-Import, the West German firm Warimex, and Nokia from Finland.[60] While Nokia and the West German partner were delivering highly sophisticated machinery and chemicals, the roles of the Algerian and Yugoslav subcontractors were mostly limited to providing building services.[61]

In early December 1984, the collective of the building side had written a letter to the General Secretary of the East German state party (SED), Erich Honecker, promising to finish the assembly of the factory till the end of 1985. They had further promised to take up the production of the first cables and to open the training side for the future Algerian craftsmen on "the day of liberation", 8 May 1985. The second stage of production was to open on the day of the Revolution in Algeria, 2 November 1985. The last stage of cables production was set to begin immediately before the opening of the 11th SED Party Congress.[62] Most likely the builders didn't have much of a say in the promises made in their name. The project in Algeria was the most significant executed by the East German heavy industries branch in the 1980s.[63] The deadlines could not be honored.

The protocol of the meeting of the RKEI that had taken place in early October 1987 on the issue reads:

> [this project] could have become a guiding example for the GDR on how the experiences and skills of the GDR together with equipment could be sold on economically favorable conditions. Instead, the object has become a contested case due to deficiencies of both partners with severe consequences for both and intricate legal relationships.[64]

Several things were going wrong in Algeria. By early 1986, when the project originally was due to be finished, the consortium headed by the GDR was 24 months behind schedules. According to the documents, the problems weren't due to the Western subcontractors but to relations between the East German state combines involved in the project and their intrabloc and Algerian building personnel.[65]

In early May 1986 the East German trade representative in Algeria, Dr. Schütz, wrote an alarming telegram to the East German state combines responsible for the cables plant as well as to the Ministry for Foreign Trade and the Ministry for Heavy Machine and Plant Building:

> 11 cadres of the introductive management are missing on the spot and the deployed cadres, in particular comrade Siegel, are ineffective because of missing language skills. According to estimations, 50 percent of the deployed cadres of the introductive management are technically not able to fulfill the tasks in technology transfer demanded of them . . . some cadres declared to the Algerian side officially that they had never before fulfilled such tasks in the GDR and due to language difficulties, GDR cadres and Algerian cadres are avoiding each other. This situation has already led to significant operating errors and accidents with the machines employed in the production process.[66]

The first stage of production in the factory had already started in March 1986 and cables production in the plant amounted to 954 tons till year's end.[67] It was the task of East German technicians and engineers to train Algerian personnel that could later operate the factory on their own. The situation described in the telegram by Dr. Schütz has comic qualities and, luckily, no injured workers are mentioned in any protocol. The East Germans meant to train the Algerians told them quite openly that they had no clue how to fulfill their task despite being sent to Algeria for exactly that purpose. Instead, they were trying not to get into contact with the Algerians. The state combines of the GDR didn't possess enough trained personnel themselves to send to Algeria to work in an international context and train local craftsmen.

The Algerian side reacted by simply starting up the machines in the semi-finished plant on their own. Since the Algerians employed in the plant didn't know how to use the machines, many of them were destroyed in the process, as described in the report by Dr. Schütz cited previously. The East Germans reacted by stopping all ongoing works.[68] This action was later approved of by the RKEI and its head, Dr. Beil, to save at least parts of the machinery and already finished objects, as well as to deny responsibility for any accidents.[69] Nevertheless, the RKEI was quite critical of the behavior of the East German state combines and scrutinized their explanations. In the case of the cables plant, the East German state combines were criticized for claiming that the delay in assembling the plant was solely the fault of their Algerian partners. It wasn't until 1985 that they admitted partial responsibility for the delays, as well.[70] However, this enhanced system of internal checks and balances didn't prove successful. The problems in Algeria were still an issue in the RKEI in 1989.[71]

## Who has the power?

On 27 February 1985, the Central Committee of the SED, the state party of the GDR, approved of a directive for discussing trade with Soviet representatives on a bilateral basis. The document clearly states the aims of doing business with the non-socialist world:

> The foreign trade relations with capitalist countries and developing countries are directed at generating foreign exchange by exports to get the necessary resources and country products for the GDR that can't be obtained or not fully obtained in the socialist economic area and to secure the solvency of the GDR, as well as its economic invulnerability.
>
> It is advisable, by making use of the contradictions between capitalist countries and between capitalist companies and their governments, to acquire technological know-how in economically decisive areas to advance as soon as possible to the international top level.[72]

This extract contains some bold statements such as the assumption that Western governments and companies could be played off against each other easily. Furthermore, to talk about economic invulnerability in intrabloc negotiations and consultations during the mid-1980s showed a level of confidence that could hardly be justified by the facts. The leadership of the GDR wanted to use trade with the outside world including the Global South to generate the foreign exchange needed to buy the most advanced technologies to belong to the most developed countries in the end. So were the countries of the Global South by doing business with foreigners. The strategy of the GDR which was also the strategy inherent in the economic policies of all other members of the bloc was therefore in essence a kind of game depending on the smartness of the respective participants. Since everyone, East and South alike, wanted the same, success depended on who could outsmart the others. Seen from the angle of the archival material, there is good reason to assume that the members of the Eastern Bloc were not the smartest in the game and if the system was rigged, it was not rigged in their favor.

One problem was that countries from the Global South could simply turn to the West. This is also an imminent problem in the files. It applied even to socialist-minded states like Iraq in the 1970s. When the Iraqi leadership could employ only modest means and was diplomatically rather isolated, as had been the case in the early 1970s, the East was an appropriate partner. When the boom of the first oil shock provided the Iraqi leaders with unprecedented amounts of foreign exchange, they still continued to enjoy relations with the Eastern Bloc countries but couldn't resist the temptation to import Western technology and sell their oil to Western partners. Western companies with support from their respective government at home were only waiting to make deals with an Iraq that seemed strong and an emergent power like in the mid-1970s. One example for this is a report for the PCTA on Iraq filed in 1981:

> 95% of the oil production have been exported in 1980, more than 65% of which to the CIL [Capitalist Industrialized States], 26% to the DC [developing countries], and 8.1% to the SC [socialist countries] . . .
>
> The Iraqi leadership has repeatedly stated that Iraq will look to the Soviet Union and the socialist countries to realize its program of economic

> development. At the same time, Iraq is expanding its cooperation with companies from capitalist industrialized countries, which have intensified their economic relations with Iraq significantly since 1973.[73]

The CMEA countries couldn't do much to prevent such things from happening. They could use diplomatic means to remind Iraqi leaders of their good relations with the bloc but they could hardly pressure or threaten a regional Middle Eastern power that was, at least in the mid-1970s, politically relatively stable and awash with foreign exchange. However, this was not the only kind of problems the Eastern countries were facing while trying to trade with the Global South to maximize their own economic advantage. The case of Iraq illustrates another set of problems well. They could simply stop to deliver promised goods as in the following example:

> The payments for the assistance and the payments to redeem the taken-up loans are conducted by Iraq in convertible currency as well as by oil deliveries. It hereby has to be emphasized that Iraq has almost completely ceased its oil deliveries to the CMEA countries in 1981.[74]

## Debts and power

The Iraqi leadership stopping oil deliveries connects the question of who enjoyed the upper hand in East–South economic relations directly with the debt issue. The CMEA countries had given huge loans to countries of the Global South which were used to pay for the equipment and plants of the East. Thus, when the factories were completed, more often than not had the recipient countries only paid back a tiny fraction of the credits. The big payoff was yet to come. The trade strategy of the CMEA countries to generate foreign exchange with which to pay for imports of Western technology could only work out, if the credits were completely repaid. This gave the countries of the Global South significant leverage in dealing with the East. As they were already in possession of the factories and machinery, they could employ delaying tactics to maximize their own economic benefit and serve their perceived national interests. In the context of the economic crisis of the 1980s for many societies and governments in the Global South this was not only a question of maximizing their own benefits, but actually a question of economic survival, as well.

How bad the situation of the closest partners of the CMEA countries had become by the mid-1980s didn't escape Eastern observers. They furthermore clearly noted who received a preferential treatment. The annual report of the East German trade representation in Damascus for 1986 stated that it was not Syria's CMEA partners that were served first. Rather did the Syrian leadership try to squeeze them:

> The debts, 2.7 billion US-$ towards capitalist countries, 12.3 billion US-$ towards socialist countries, equal roughly six times the value of the annual exports of the SAR. Therefore, the SAR, in relation to its economic potential, belongs to the group of the highest indebted developing countries. The

> payment behavior of the SAR allows to draw the conclusion that [the SAR] is trying to solve its complicated economic situation to the detriment of the socialist countries by using its good political relations.[75]

The Syrian government and Syrian companies had debts in late 1986 amounting to ca. 15 billion US dollars according to the archival material with the overwhelming majority of these debts, more than 12 billion US dollars, owed to the East. The same report stated that the Syrian foreign exchange reserves had sunk to below 50 million US dollars in the course of 1986. By the end of 1986 ca. 200 million US dollars of Syrian debts towards the GDR were overdue and 240 million US dollars had to be repaid between 1987 and 1991.[76]

A similar situation emerged in Iraq, one of the first countries to conclude a treaty of economic cooperation with the CMEA. One could therefore expect some kind of goodwill behavior. The annual report of the East German trade representation for 1989 observed no difference to the behavior of the Syrian leadership:

> The hopes and expectations for a fast improvement of the economic situation of Iraq, raised by the surprising cease fire in summer 1988, have not come to pass . . .
>
> In 1989 Iraqi debts to the GDR of 159.8 million USD have come due which had to be deferred completely and for which the GDR received payments in 1989 of 2.3 million USD only . . .
>
> Due to the non-realization of agreed payments and new export treaties, the claims of the GDR rose from 622 million USD to ca. 640 million USD.[77]

According to the payment schedule negotiated between the GDR and the Iraqi government in 1989 the Iraqi government was obliged to pay 199.7 million US dollars in 1990 and 153.6 million US dollars in 1991 alone. Even if the GDR had continued to exist in the following years, it is unlikely that the Iraqi state agencies would have kept their word. In 1989, when the East German leadership needed any injection of cash it could obtain, it received not even 2 % of the Iraqi payments due that year.

## Who is whose periphery?

If one combines the East German claims towards Syria and Iraq, these two countries owed the East Germans close to one billion US dollars by the late 1980s. The net debts of the GDR to the West at the time the Berlin Wall fell amounted to 8.2 billion US dollars.[78] Thus, the Syrian and Iraqi debts to the GDR combined would have been enough to pay off more than 10 % of the East German net debts in the West, if the economic climate of the 1970s had persisted in the 1980s. As the East Germans were not the only ones in the bloc to have conducted trade with Saddam Hussein's regime, the same picture emerged for the other European members of the CMEA, as well.

Furthermore, attention should be given to the institutional framework on which the CMEA member states relied when it came to accounting for their credits and business with the South. This is revealed by taking a closer look at the credit agreements negotiated between CMEA member countries like the GDR and a government in the Global South like Syria:

> 10% of the entire value fob [free on board] GDR harbor rate payable within 60 days after the treaty has been ratified to an account of the DABA[79] in the USA in favor of the FTO [Foreign Trade Organization] Rail Vehicles. The Bank American International, New York, is being considered or the Irving Trust Company, New York.[80]

This was not an exception but seems to have been the norm. In a similar treaty negotiated in summer 1983, the GDR granted the Syrian government a commercial credit at 10 % interest worth 4.587 million US dollars for equipment for one of its cement factories erected by East German state combines. The account the Syrians had to use for the repayments of the credit was at the First National City Bank, New York, one of the predecessors of Citi Bank.[81] This exposes the deep contradictions of the CMEA member states in dealing with the outside world.

While the socialist world of the Eastern Bloc – at least in theory – wanted to present an alternative to the capitalist world, they were deeply integrated in the global division of labor. This proves the accuracy of the observations made by the delegates from the PR Congo during their negotiations of a cooperation treaty with the CMEA in the early 1980s. The financial infrastructure of the West was so attractive that the CMEA countries chose to rely on Western institutions rather than trying to assemble a strong counterweight. Not that these institutions weren't potentially in the making, one should think of the potential of the International Investment Bank and the International Bank for Economic Cooperation in this respect that could have challenged the Western institutional framework, if the CMEA member countries had pushed harder for it.

One should not forget that the early 1980s constituted the high tide of the Global Cold War. This was the first term of Reagan's presidency with a heated international political atmosphere and economic sanctions by the West, while proxy wars were fought in Africa and Latin America and the Soviet army got bogged down in Afghanistan. There is a certain irony in the East German documents sincerely demanding their Syrian partners, themselves rather disliked by Western leaders, to pay their debts in US dollars to an East German account at some big American bank situated in Manhattan at the height of the Cold War. It is likely that the East Germans and the Syrians contributed markedly with their deposits and banking fees to the income of Western banks, as they were probably treated like any other customer. The East could not live without the Western financial framework dominated by the USA The attempts of the CMEA member countries to combine their economic power to do business with the outside world, notably the Global South, rather strengthened their dependence on Western economic institutions, even if there were factors at work that also contributed to intrabloc cohesion.

During the Cold War, the model of three worlds had enjoyed a significant level of popularity. While the developed West constituted the First World, the socialist countries of Eastern Europe constituted the Second. The rest, the so called Third World, was comprised of the Global South. This model explicitly implied an internal hierarchy with the West at the top followed by the East and the South at the bottom. Judging by indicators for economic development such a model could by and large be justified. Even in the late 1980s, most CMEA member states could provide higher living standards for their population than the average society in the Global South.

However, this model of the three worlds is rather inflexible and not dynamic enough to analyze the situation of the 1970s and 1980s. A better alternative is provided by Immanuel Wallerstein and his model of core, semi-periphery, and periphery. While the core is economically and militarily well developed with a complex institutional framework underwriting its power, the semi-peripheral countries are sandwiched in between the core and the periphery, often possessing partially competitive economic, military, and political structures but dependent on protectionism and not able to exercise a significant level of power in international trade relations. Nevertheless, the semi-periphery is striving to become tomorrow's core in the prevalent world system. The periphery, on the other hand, is economically often dependent on exporting commodities, and enjoys only weak political, economic, and military institutions that are not sufficient to push forward an agenda that would enable the respective societies to overcome this situation.

This categorization fits into the 1970s and 1980s. The core in the world system of this period was constituted by the West with the East being in a semi-peripheral status marked by protectionism and a weak influence on international trade, even if their economies were partially competitive on the world market. The Global South constituted the periphery. Nevertheless, this model has to be dynamized, as these categories are of increased analytical value, if they are understood as being exposed to change. Furthermore, as the situation of the 1980s shows, a country or area could take up two positions at the same time in relations to other areas of the world.

The European members of the CMEA were taking up a rather peripheral position towards Western Europe and North America. They were supplying these areas mainly with commodities and were themselves highly reliant on imports of sophisticated Western technology. Towards the Global South the European members of the CMEA rather appeared to belong to the semi-periphery or in the case of the GDR, Soviet Union, and CSSR even could be perceived as belonging to the core. While the Soviet Union was in military terms the second most powerful nation on earth, the GDR and CSSR – seen from an outside perspective – could provide sophisticated technologies to countries in the Global South that seemed to be roughly on par with the West. Otherwise, Southern leaders would not have actively sought industrial cooperation with these countries.

However, if one looks at financial and political relations, in particular in the 1980s, the East appears to be the periphery with the South as semi-periphery. The Eastern state agencies were in no way as effective as their Western counterparts in collecting their money. They were even tricked by their Southern partners who enjoyed the upper hand. Southern governments paid their Western debtors but they didn't feel obliged to do so vis-à-vis their Eastern partners. The East in return never considered itself as being able to do the same the South did with them with their Western debtors. They were in an inferior position towards the West as well as towards the South. While the West could rely on the Bretton Woods institutions to enforce their own agenda and interests, the East couldn't. The CMEA, IIB, and IBEC were too weak to function as counterweights. In practice, the East relied heavily on Western institutions and not on a strong institutional framework of its own making.

When a country like Iraq didn't pay its debts, the East could do nothing, as there was no possible action in between writing a letter urging for payment and an armed intervention. The latter neither constituted a viable option, because of the unforeseeable risks attached to an invasion, even if such a move had been in line with 19th century diplomacy, as exercised by the Great European Powers. The Western core could rely on a very nuanced set of political action provided by its control over the world economy, its main currency, and the Bretton Woods institutions in the 1980s. It is also important to visualize the political situation: Hafiz al-Assad and Saddam Hussein both survived the crisis of the 1980s. With them did many other leaders of the Global South. The Eastern Bloc, on the other hand, in particular its seemingly most developed European members, didn't. Honecker, Husak, Ceaucescu, and Jaruzelski had to step down dragging their political systems with them in the same world system that enabled the Southern leaders to retain control.

## Conclusion

One could claim that the projects of economic cooperation that left the biggest paper trail were necessarily the ones that went wrong. Furthermore, the cases that were investigated by organizations like the RKEI were not the ones that ran smoothly, as the RKEI was problem-oriented. However, the tone of many documents, like the one on the cement factories in Ethiopia, strongly suggests that these were no exemptions but that the same kind of deficiencies and problems were inherent to the Eastern economies when doing business with the Global South. The RKEI, to make a case in point, proved successful in critically reviewing the viewpoints of East German state combines, thereby exposing false statements and analyzing the problems causing failure. However, at best it could only make minor revisions to how the export economy was run.

If one scrutinizes the power imbalances prevalent in the 1980s, it is clear that the Eastern Bloc was not able to outsmart neither the West nor the South. The lack of control over its own financial entanglements combined with a weak institutional framework led to a situation in which Southern leaders found it advisable to largely obey the demands by Western donors, while ignoring Eastern partners. As Eastern leaders could not afford to pursue the same strategy towards their Western partners, they were worse off in this trilateral game. While traditionally referred to as the Second World, the East rather looked like the Third World in the 1980s, not economically but in relation to its standing in the international world system. The lack of institutional soft power contributed to the downfall of the Eastern Bloc.

In the next chapter, the reform proposals and measures for the CMEA during the early Gorbachev period will be analyzed with an emphasis on the Global South. The Gorbachev administration tried to improve political as well as economic relations with India. India didn't abandon ISI till the turning of the decade. Thus, India proved a promising partner due to the similarity of the economic models of the CMEA countries with India and the size of the Indian market. However, India, while being rather poor on average, was one of those countries that already insisted on a participation of its own national industrial champions in development projects. Therefore, the discussions inside the CMEA will be compared with the reality of erecting flagship projects of the CMEA in the mid and late 1980s. The CMEA files are supplemented by Indian archival documents.

## Notes

1 "Bericht über das Auftreten der DDR-Delegation zur Tagung der Leiter der Außenhandelsorganisationen der Mitgliedsländer des RGW zu Fragen der Erweisung technischer Unterstützung an Entwicklungsländer," dated 22 April 1976, Barch Berlin, DL 2/22846.
2 Besnik, *Globalization*, 103–6.
3 Westad, *The Global Cold War*, 360–1.
4 Frieden, *Global Capitalism*, 319.
5 Frieden, 319.
6 Frieden, 319.
7 Frieden, 370–1.
8 Arndt, *Economic Development*, 72–3, 87.
9 Frieden, *Global Capitalism*, 376.
10 Directive for the 45th meeting of the PCTA from 01–03 December 1983 in Moscow, Barch Berlin, DL 2/6396a.
11 "Information über die ergriffenen Maßnahmen zur Aktivierung der mehrseitigen Zusammenarbeit der RGW-Länder mit Entwicklungsländern," dated 23 January 1987, Barch Berlin, DL 2/16974.
12 "Soobrazheniia GDR po sushestvu punktov 1–3 povestki dnia u soveshchaniia ekspertov po vneshnei torgovle stran-chlenov SEV i Meksiki," RGAE, Fond 561 op. 53 d. 139 ll. 68–70.
13 "Razvitie torgovykh i ekonomicheskikh otnoshenii mezhdu ChSSR i meksikoi za period 1980–1983 gg.," RGAE, Fond 561 op. 53 d. 139 ll. 78–80; "Informatsiia po punktam 1–3 predvaritel'noi povestki dnia soveshchaniia ekspertov stran-chlenov SEV i Meksiki po vneshnei torgovle," ibid. ll. 85–6.
14 Westad, *The Global Cold War*, 361–2.
15 Westad, 361–2.
16 "Handelspolitische Direktive zur Plandurchführung 1982 und Vorbereitung 1983," Barch Berlin, DL 2/16951.
17 Ibid.
18 Ibid.
19 Ibid.
20 Ibid.

21 "Aufgaben der Bereiche des MAH zur Sicherung der Exportüberschüsse 1987 im Handel mit dem NSW," dated 23 January 1987, Barch Berlin, DL 2/6428.
22 Ibid.
23 Ibid.
24 "Information über die wichtigsten Ergebnisse der Wirtschaftsbeziehungen der UVR zu den Entwicklungsländern im Jahre 1980," dated 02 April 1981, Barch Berlin, DL 2/16950.
25 Regierungskommission für die einheitliche Steuerung von Export und Import.
26 Bundesstiftung Aufarbeitung Biographische Datenbanken, "Beil, Gerhard."
27 Bundesstiftung Aufarbeitung Biographische Datenbanken, "Sölle, Horst."
28 Protocol of the 48th meeting of the PCTAC in Moscow from 12–13 December 1984, Barch Berlin, DL 2/16965.
29 Protocol of the 53rd meeting of the PCTAC in Moscow from 14–15 January 1987, Barch Berlin, DL 2/16974.
30 Ibid.
31 "Zusammenarbeit mit der Republik Ghana," dated 19 February 1987, Barch Berlin, DL 2/16975.
32 "Über den Stand der Handels- und Wirtschaftsbeziehungen, einschl. der Kreditbeziehungen, der Perspektiven der Zusammenarbeit und der Koordinierung des Auftretens der interessierten RGW-Länder mit Ghana, Simbabwe, Kongo, Madagaskar und Nigeria," dated 20 March 1987, ibid.
33 Ibid.
34 "Protokoll der Tagung der Leiter der handelspolitischen Verwaltungen für Entwicklungsländer der Ministerien für Außenhandel der ML/RGW," dated 13 March 1981, Barch Berlin, DL 2/16950.
35 Ibid.
36 Ibid.
37 "Jahresanalyse 1986 HPA Teheran," dated 22 December 1986, DL 2/6426.
38 "Protokoll der Tagung der Leiter der handelspolitischen Verwaltungen für Entwicklungsländer der Ministerien für Außenhandel der ML/RGW," dated 13 March 1981, Barch Berlin, DL 2/16950.
39 Protocol of the meeting of the RKEI on 30 June 1989, dated 30 June 1989, Barch Berlin, DL 2/14972.
40 Ibid.
41 VEB Starkstromanlagenbau Leipzig-Halle/SALH.
42 VEB Otto Buchwitz Starkstromanlagenbau Dresden/OBSAD.
43 This applied in particular to deliveries of electrical equipment by Yugoslav companies. Other deliveries came from Bulgaria, and the CSSR.
44 Protocol of the meeting of the RKEI on 30 June 1989, dated 30 June 1989, Barch Berlin, DL 2/14972.
45 "Revisionsprotokoll Prüfungsobjekt Anlagenexportvorhaben 'Umspannwerke Iran'," dated 23 May 1989, ibid.
46 Protocol of the meeting of the RKEI on 02 December 1988, dated 02 December 1988, Barch Berlin, DL 2/14972.
47 "Jahresanalyse 1985 der HPA Teheran," dated 21 November 1985, Barch Berlin, DL 2/4368.
48 Ibid.
49 The Iranians canceled an import agreement of 2,950 W50 trucks that the GDR officials had thought safe due to a lack of foreign exchange caused by lower than expected oil revenues. Ibid.
50 "Beratung RKEI 30.06.1989," dated 30 June 1989, Barch Berlin, DL 2/14972.
51 Protocol of the meeting of the RKEI on 06 October 1989, dated 06 October 1989, ibid.

52 Protocol of the meeting of the RKEI on 23 September 1988, dated 23 September 1988, ibid.
53 "Protokoll der Tagung der Leiter der handelspolitischen Verwaltungen für Entwicklungsländer der Ministerien für Außenhandel der ML/RGW," dated 13 March 1981, Barch Berlin, DL 2/16950.
54 Ibid.
55 Ibid.
56 Protocol of the meeting of the RKEI on 02 October 1987, dated 02 October 1987, Barch Berlin, DL 2/14972.
57 "Abrechnung des Abbaus der Rückstände bei der Realisierung des Anlagenexportvorhabens Kabelwerk Biskra/DVR Algerien," dated 22 January 1986, ibid.
58 VEB Kombinat Automatisierungsanlagenbau Berlin.
59 Kabelwerk Oberspree.
60 Annex to the document "Bericht über Stand der Realisierung des Objektes Kabelwerk Biskra/DVR Algerien," dated 05 June 1985, Barch Berlin, DL 2/14972.
61 Ibid.
62 "Bericht zum Stand der Realisierung des Objektes Kabelwerk Biskra/DVR Algerien," ibid.
63 Ibid.
64 Protocol of the meeting of the RKEI on 02 October 1987, dated 02 October 1987, ibid.
65 "Abrechnung des Abbaus der Rückstände bei der Realisierung des Anlagenexportvorhabens Kabelwerk Biskra/DVR Algerien," dated 22 January 1986, ibid.
66 Telegram by Dr. Schütz HPA Algier, dated 05 May 1986, ibid.
67 "Abrechnung des Standes der Übernahme/Übergabe des Kabelwerks Biskra/DVR Algerien," dated 30 September 1987, ibid.
68 Protocol of the meeting of the RKEI on 02 October 1987, dated 02 October 1987, ibid.
69 Ibid.
70 Ibid.
71 Letter from the Ministry for Heavy Machine and Plant Building to the RKEI, dated 03 January 1989, ibid.
72 "Beschluß zur Direktive für eine bilaterale Beratung mit der UdSSR zur Gestaltung der außenwirtschaftlichen und wissenschaftlich-technischen Beziehungen mit kapitalistischen Ländern und Entwicklungsländern," dated 27 February 1985, Barch Berlin, DC 20 I/4/85415.
73 "Information über den Stand und die Perspektiven der Entwicklung der Zusammenarbeit der ML/RGW mit Irak," dated 14 October 1981, Barch Berlin, DL 2/16952.
74 Ibid.
75 "Jahresanalyse 1986 HPA Damaskus," dated 22 December 1986, Barch Berlin, DL 2/6426.
76 Ibid.
77 "Jahresanalyse 1989 der HPA Bagdad," dated 26 November 1989, Barch Berlin, DL 2/6449.
78 Steiner, *Von Plan Zu Plan*, 255.
79 The East German foreign trade bank.
80 "Kreditantrag vom 5 November 1984 Tender der Syrischen Eisenbahn Nr. 455 über 286 Güterwagen," dated 1984, DL 2/16424.
81 "Kreditvorauszusage zum Objekt Fahrbare Großbrechanlage Zementwerk SAR," dated 05 July 1983, Barch Berlin, DL 2/16448.

# 10 Gorbachev, India, and the CMEA

## CMEA reforms in the 1980s

The latest scholarly books written on the CMEA in the late 1980s show a great deal of sympathy and curiosity in relation to Gorbachev and the supposed changes to the stagnating system of state socialism he embodied. These books largely remain the best ones available on the CMEA up to this day but their enthusiasm should be taken with a grain of salt. This is advisable not only because it is clear with hindsight that Gorbachev's efforts were in vain or even accelerated the demise of state socialism, but because the scholarly literature of the late 1980s tells as much about the atmosphere in the Western intellectual community at that time, as it tells about the state of affairs inside the CMEA member countries. Even Jozef van Brabant, one of the most distinguished scholars on the CMEA and a political scientist by training, didn't mention the possibility of the dissolution of the Eastern Bloc in a single sentence in the version of his book on economic integration in Eastern Europe published in 1989.[1]

Scrutinizing the policies of the Gorbachev administration doesn't mean that there weren't attempts at radical reform in the late 1980s in the Eastern Bloc in general and in the Soviet Union in particular. But with regards to the CMEA and to economic relations with the Global South these reforms were – at least till 1989 – more often in line with prior reform measures than they constituted radical departures from preceding policies. The focus of the CMEA Council Sessions gradually shifted during the 1980s. The 1981 Session focused on integrating those countries from the Global South that had already become members of the CMEA more closely and discussed measures to forge closer ties between the CMEA and the non-member states from the Global South.[2] This discussion is reflected in the exchange of letters found in the Moscow archives and cited previously.

The Council Session that took place in Moscow in June 1984 constituted a "crisis meeting" that dealt with the financial and economic problems of the Eastern Bloc more closely, such as the deterioration of the terms of trade of the smaller socialist countries with the Soviet Union and Soviet demands for higher quality goods in exchange for its resources.[3] The Council Session had been preceded by several rounds of negotiations between high-ranking officials and economic experts.[4] This and subsequent meetings showed that the CMEA member states still regarded the organization as a vehicle to facilitate economic reform and to overcome their problems. Opposition to increasing the role of the CMEA and its institutions was uttered by the Romanian leadership, although the critique that short-term economic problems could hardly be solved by large-scale long-term reform of the CMEA was not fundamental by nature.[5]

The Council Session in June 1984 had concluded with a reform program that was approved by all member states. Discussions were centered on harmonizing pricing mechanisms inside the CMEA, strengthening the role of monetary and financial incentives and thus also the role of the Transferable Ruble, more cooperation between state combines across borders and greater responsibility for managers, a better coordination of East–West trade and the utilization of new technologies.[6] The program worked out in 1984 was drafted too late to be fully integrated into the five-year plan that started in 1986 and remained vague. Thus, even countries that would have liked to embark on new cooperation schemes, especially in the fields of science and technologically advanced sectors of the economy, like the GDR, pursued a timid approach.[7]

This shows that Gorbachev and his administration found something they could build on when he became General Secretary of the CPSU in March 1985. One of the first measures in the framework of the CMEA included drafting new large-scale investment projects inside the bloc. In contrast to the 1970s, these projects weren't confined to the territory of the Soviet Union anymore but included investments in the extractive industries of Poland, Cuba, the CSSR, and Vietnam, as well.[8] The 40th Council Session that took place in Moscow in June 1985 approved of a resolution to curtail the consumption of natural resources under the supervision of CMEA organs.[9] This was a step towards higher energy efficiency and intensive growth, as decreased levels of energy input for a given unit of output meant higher productivity.

The Soviet Chair of the Council of Ministers, Nikolai Tikhonov,[10] struck a different tone on the Global South on the 40th Council Session in the name of the Soviet leadership. He emphasized that future efforts should be aimed at increasing the economic benefit for both sides, particularly while dealing with Cuba, Mongolia, and Vietnam. This meant that in practice the benefits for the European members of the CMEA should be larger than had hitherto been the case.[11] Gorbachev himself was a proponent of supranational integration but not by orthodox supranational planning, as had been the traditional view of past Soviet leaders.[12] One step in this direction was the "Complex-Program for scientific-technical Cooperation till the Year 2000" approved by the 41st Council Session on 18 December 1985 in Moscow.[13] This new Complex-Program aimed at embracing the technological changes of the post-war era and utilizing them for the benefit of the economies of the CMEA. A stronger level of integration in the CMEA was to be reached by harmonizing economic policies inside the bloc and increased contacts between different state agencies and state combines, not by one economic development plan that was unilaterally applied to all member states.[14] The technological gap with the West was to be closed till the turn of the century.

To a certain extent this sounded more revolutionary than it actually was. The East German leadership, to make a case in point, could rightfully argue that it had already enacted some of the reforms proposed by the new Complex-Program like the delegation of (limited) powers to large state combines. Furthermore, the GDR and CSSR had already embarked on development paths of intensive growth, even if their successes were modest at best.[15] The reforms didn't stop there. The next Council Sessions took place in 1986 and in October 1987 to discuss the implementation of further steps of reform. The participants of the 44th Council Session in Prague in 1987 approved of a resolution that called for the establishment of a common market of the East.[16] This coincided with attempts to streamline the organization of the CMEA to make it more efficient and to abolish ineffective commissions and organs.[17]

However, these measures constituted merely declarations of intent rather than hard reform programs. The enthusiasm of the authors of the late 1980s was partially nurtured by the fact that the position of the Soviet leadership had changed. While being strongly opposed to market integration in the 1960s and 1970s, the Gorbachev administration embraced elements of market-oriented reforms. But the rest of the bloc had changed as well. The leaders of some of the small European member states of the CMEA had experimented with market reforms in the mid-1960s. Some of these like the East German and Czechoslovak nomenclature had become less receptive for such endeavors as time was commencing. Furthermore, the Complex-Program of 1971 was in essence as much of a broad declaration as the Complex-Program of 1985. Still its successes were mixed and mostly confined to the resource and energy sector. It is at least doubtful that Gorbachev's Complex-Program would have become more successful than Brezhnev's, even if the Eastern Bloc hadn't collapsed soon after the Prague Session of the CMEA.

## Gorbachev and the Global South

The Gorbachev administration changed the geographical distribution of Soviet economic aid which had repercussions for the CMEA, as well. In a book by Charles R. Dannehl on Soviet economic aid to non-socialist countries, published in 1995, the author states that 13.37 billion US dollars were handed out by the Soviet leadership in credits for economic cooperation schemes with these countries between 1986 and 1989.[18] While the Brezhnev administration had allocated the majority of funds to North Africa and the Middle East, hotspots of the Cold War in the Global South during the 1960s and 1970s, this region was largely ignored by the new administration in the Kremlin. The same applied to the non-socialist countries of Sub-Saharan Africa.[19]

In his analysis of the situation Gorbachev was building on the experiences of Soviet advisers who had worked in the Global South in the late 1970s and early 1980s and had developed a critical view of Soviet assistance.[20] By 1986 Gorbachev had received enough intelligence briefings by the KGB on Southern revolutionary leaders who had proved turncoats that he became uneasy with continuing the old policies of the Brezhnev and Andropov eras.[21] This didn't lead to a radical alteration of the Soviet approach to the Global South, as some of his foreign policy advisers like Anatoli Cherniaev had recommended, but to a change in focus. Southern leaders who were not ready to listen to Soviet advice and pursue more moderate paths to socialism, like Nicaragua's Daniel Ortega and Ethiopia's Mengistu, found their Soviet assistance curtailed.[22] However, these policies were neither completely understood nor followed by the other members of the bloc.[23] The net amount of Soviet assistance to the Global South started to decrease only in 1990.[24]

A region that gained in importance under the Gorbachev administration was Latin America which achieved 17 % of Soviet aid between 1986 and 1989 as defined by Dannehl.[25] The Soviet leadership shifted attention from the poor and overwhelmingly agrarian societies to already partially industrialized countries like Brazil.[26] However, the biggest beneficiary of Soviet aid in the Gorbachev period was India which received almost two thirds of Soviet credits to non-socialist countries.[27] This is also reflected in the CMEA materials on financial relations with the Global South. As of 1 January 1987, India was the largest debtor of the CMEA member states with handed out credits amounting to 5.885 billion rubles, more than one billion rubles more than Iraq which came in second.[28] According to the exchange rate used in the CMEA documents, the sum of credits granted to India was the equivalent of more than 8.5 billion US dollars. It is interesting to see that 90 % of these credits were handed out by the Soviet Union, while the small European members of the CMEA played no big role as creditors of India.[29] This didn't mean that they had no trade relations with India but that these were not based on large-scale credit flows.

A strong signal of Soviet–Indian friendship could be seen in Rajiv Gandhi, the Indian Prime Minister who took office in November 1984, making his first major trip abroad to Moscow in May 1985 to speak with Gorbachev.[30] During his stay, the two sides concluded two treaties. The first treaty comprised the first large-scale ruble's credit to be handed by the Gorbachev administration to India and economic cooperation schemes in the energy and machine building sectors for which the Soviet loan was supposed to be used. The second treaty set out guidelines for economic and scientific cooperation between the two countries.[31] As can be said in general of Gorbachev's policies to the Global South, his administration could build upon the achievements of their predecessors, since India had been a focus country of the Soviet Union and the Eastern Bloc in general since Stalin's death.

Gorbachev responded in kind to Rajiv Gandhi's visit one year later. His visit in November 1986 was his first to an Asian country as General Secretary which underscored the importance the Soviet leadership attached to India.[32] According to Soviet estimates, Soviet development schemes accounted for 36 % of India's steel production, 32 % of aluminum production, 77 % of its annual output in metallurgical equipment, more than 40 % of its production in power and mining equipment, and 10 % in overall energy production.[33] Most of these projects of economic cooperation preceded Gorbachev's tenure as General Secretary of the CPSU.

## We have a plan

There was already a link between the Indian territories and the Soviet Union in the interwar period, as the Communist Party of India had been founded in Tashkent in 1920.[34] However, Stalin's stance towards revolutionary movements in the Global South heavily contributed to the decimation of the party in the 1930s.[35] Khrushchev's trip to Asia and his stay in India shortly after Stalin's death led to stronger ties with Asian leaders.[36] In the ruling class of India, Soviet officials like him could find potential partners, like Jawaharlal Nehru, who were eager to learn from the Soviet experience. Nehru stated on the issue of economic planning:

> The idea of unrestricted private enterprise is out of date. . . . The State has to come in the picture in a big way. We cannot with our limited resources allow people just to go in any direction they like. We have to plan and planning has to include both the public and the private sector, leaving a great deal of room to private enterprise.[37]

Nehru's statement shows that what was later called Nehruvian socialism was similar to Bolshevik socialism at the first glance at best. The private sector continued to play a large role and big companies like Birla and Tata, which predated Indian independence, exercised considerable influence on policy-making.[38]

Prior to the mid-1950s the Eastern Bloc's economic cooperation with India had been of negligible importance for India's development plans.[39] The Indian National Congress (INC) that became India's ruling party at independence had set up a planning commission already in the late 1930.[40] To overcome the perceived backwardness of the country was one of the central topics in Indian politics.[41] Independent India's first five-year plan enacted in 1950 was not yet a comprehensive economic plan but a compendium of different investment projects, most of them dated back to the colonial era. Its focus lay on agriculture. Since 80 % of the Indian population lived on the countryside, increasing the production of food was essential for any later industrialization plan.[42]

The first five-year plan was financed with the surplus the British Raj had accumulated during the Second World War for its contribution to the British war effort and which later had been passed on to independent India.[43] The focus changed with the second five-year plan worked out under the supervision of P.C. Mahalanobis[44] that relied on the concept of industrialization by import substitution and comprised elements of W. Arthur Lewis's work.[45] The second and third five-year plan were successful according to the dogmas of development prevailing in the 1960s, as the savings rate improved, a heavy industrial base was founded, and an improvement in the agricultural sector occurred.[46] Nevertheless, in contrast to the first five-year plan, the second and third cost between two and three times as much and had to be financed on foreign credit to a considerable degree.[47]

This made India an attractive economic partner next to its political importance as one of the most significant countries inside the non-aligned movement. It is therefore no coincidence that India had already been on the agenda of the CMEA long before Gorbachev became General Secretary of the CPSU. The CMEA member states were exchanging their experiences on the Indian market in the 1960s. One East German document on economic cooperation with India to be found in Moscow reads:

> The delivery of complete plants depends on what can be produced in the respective area in India. For breweries and dairies, the share of Indian supplies amounts to 50–60% of the whole plant. The Indian government demands that supplies that can be produced by Indian companies are not allowed to be imported. No import license is issued for this purpose. . . . It is, of course, very difficult to assert in preliminary talks which parts can be produced in India. This does not mean that [Indian] machines and equipment fit into the specifications of the plant. On the other hand, Indian legislature demands that the [foreign] contractor issues guarantees for the entire plant, even if 50% or more of the supplies have been delivered by the Indian side.[48]

This report illustrates the difficulties the members of the CMEA were facing on the Indian market early on. Although the strong role of the state and of state planning in the Indian economy resembled their own economic approach, they found it difficult to abide by the rules of industrialization by import substitution. Indian officials were insistent that their economic partners resorted to Indian supplies as much as possible. Foreign exchange or even clearing currency were only to be spent on products and services that could not be produced at home. The document cited previously already hints at the fact that such a policy was not always sensible and not necessarily in the interest of the Indian customer. Since production standards and the specifics of individual products could differ sharply, Indian technology was not easy to integrate into East German, Czechoslovak, or Soviet designs. What proved rather manageable in a brewery or dairy could turn out difficult to achieve in more complex branches of the economy.

Some long-term agreements with India were concluded in the 1960s, the aim of which was to enable the Indian industry to manufacture equipment for certain branches of the economy by themselves. One such treaty was meant to make the Indian economy self-reliant in the sector of equipment for rice and flour mills within seven years.[49] The trade volume of the smaller European members on the Southern periphery of the CMEA with India remained rather small in the 1960s. The Romanian and Bulgarian trade volume with India during the early 1960s averaged between 11 and 16 million US dollars annually.[50]

While the purpose of information exchange and cooperation inside the CMEA was to improve the economic situation of the member countries, the early documents on India show that at least the CSSR was at times reluctant to discuss new cooperation schemes. There is a certain logic behind this, as the economy of the CSSR could produce sophisticated equipment in many branches of the economy without external assistance, in particular assistance from the lesser developed countries inside the CMEA. A letter by Technoexport Prague to the Secretariat of the CMEA exposes a questionable level of confidence:

> The markets of the UAR [Egypt], India, Iraq, and Syria are not new to us and we have sufficient experience. One could say that we are a traditional supplier for these countries, particularly in the field of the food processing industry. We are in no need of cooperation with other socialist countries in this area.[51]

The Indian government, on the other hand, saw clear advantages during the 1950s and 1960s in trading with the Eastern Bloc, as is clear from internal Indian documents:

> In a bid to expand the import capacity needed to meet the developmental demands generated by the efforts of economic planning in the decade of the fifties, India had launched a massive export expansion and diversification program. In this program, the central element of strategy was to explore new markets for Indian goods. The Soviet Union and other East European countries came to our special attention. The emphasis on this region also derived from an additional but equally important factor. These countries belonging to a different economic, social, and political system had not yet become an integral part of the world economic system . . .
>
> The period 1956–57 to 1968–69 as a whole may be taken as the period of India's construction of her industrial base, marked by the setting up of metallurgical, electrical, mining and fuel industries in which the import of Soviet equipment and technical know-how played a major role.[52]

After the death of Jawaharlal Nehru in 1964 and the short premiership of Lal Bahadur Shastri, who died in Tashkent during peace negotiations with Pakistan, Nehru's daughter, Indira Gandhi, became Indian premier in 1966.[53] The role of economic planning was maintained under her premiership. She focused in her economic policies on the fight against poverty which coincided with similar endeavors of the World Bank under McNamara. However, the fundamentals of industrialization by import substitution remained unchanged.[54] Her government even increased the role of the state in the economy.

## The Indo-Soviet treaty of 1971

India and the Soviet Union faced a common foe in Mao's China which had led a war against India in the past and was testing the Soviets on the Ussuri in the late 1960s which made any Sino-Soviet rapprochement unlikely.[55] The tensions in Pakistan in the late 1960s and the final breakup of Pakistan in 1971 had led to a closer cooperation between India and the Soviet Union that resulted in them signing a treaty of friendship and cooperation on 9 August 1971. This treaty, however, didn't mean that the Indian government had given up non-alignment.[56] Significant parts of the Indian public and the right wing of the INC saw the Soviet Union with suspicion.[57]

This treaty was not born out of immediate urgency, as the relations between the Soviet Union and India and the smaller European countries in the Eastern Bloc had developed positively since the early 1950s.[58] Internal documents of the CMEA state that the share of the CMEA member countries in India's foreign trade had doubled between 1965 and 1971 and amounted to 23 % in 1971.[59] While most countries of the CMEA enjoyed balanced trade accounts with India or even achieved a surplus, this didn't hold true for Poland. The Polish government was forced to switch from clearing accounts to conducting trade with India based on foreign exchange in the early 1980s. They had constantly imported more from India in the 1970s than they had exported which meant that India, one of the poorest countries on a per capita basis, had granted the Polish state the equivalent of a multimillion US dollar credit.[60] But this proved an exception to the rule and was punished by the Indian government. Since the Polish government had also granted credits to their Indian partners worth more than 100 million US dollars, it is likely that the Polish industry proved unable to deliver the promised capital goods for Indian imports of textiles, leather, foodstuff, and tea.[61]

In the early 1970s, the PCTA had organized consultations to elaborate on an "India-Program," the aim of which was to increase the economic ties between the CMEA and India. India was, to make a case in point, on the agenda of the 27th meeting of the PCTA that took place from 23–26 October 1973 in Moscow.[62] The delegates to the PCTA officially agreed on the India-Program in this session.[63] This cooperation plan was split up in several branches of the economy with at least one member state responsible for coordinating intrabloc activities. These included black iron metallurgy, the oil industry, chemical industry, power generation, machine building, transport, the construction industry, and others. The coordination work in most of these branches was supervised by the Soviet Union.

Interestingly, the CSSR came in second and took the lead in the chemical industry, and machine building, while the GDR played no big role in supervising the India-Program, although its state combines could employ significant amounts of industrial expertise.[64] As of 1 January 1974, India had taken the role of the most important partner for the CMEA's economic cooperation projects, as the value of these projects exceeded the ones to be conducted in other countries of the Global South like Egypt or Iraq. However, taken as a region, the Middle East was still more important economically as well as politically than India in the mid-1970s. Furthermore, the imbalance between the activities of the Soviet Union and of the smaller members of the CMEA was greater in India than in Iraq, Syria, and Egypt.[65] Despite the importance attached to the cooperation with India, it can be certainly said for the early 1970s that India was overshadowed by the Resource-Program in the PCTA.

Nevertheless, there was a familiar pattern at work here. Like in the case of Iraq, the Soviet leadership had concluded a treaty of friendship and cooperation with their peers from a Southern country that could function as a door opener for the rest of the bloc. After the treaty had been concluded, the CMEA organs were asked to facilitate cooperation programs with the respective country, be it Iraq or India. What followed was a treaty of cooperation with the CMEA, at least in the case of Iraq. The result was that up to 1983 trade between the CMEA member countries and Iraq expanded rapidly. This was partially due to the oil bonanza of the 1970s but it is highly unlikely that the common treaty had played no role in it. Therefore, the smaller members of the CMEA could profit from the political and diplomatic successes of the leader of the bloc and could convert this political capital into economic capital for themselves.

There is strong archival evidence that such a treaty was in the making with India, as well. An internal document of the CMEA stated that the Indian government was looking for ways to foster closer ties with the CMEA since the beginning of the 1970s.[66] Furthermore, there is a document on a meeting between the Secretary of the CMEA, Faddeev, and the Indian ambassador to the Soviet Union, Durga Prasad Dhar, that took place on 4 April 1975. The Indian ambassador urged the wish of his government to enter into an association agreement with the CMEA.[67] He emphasized the importance of the Eastern Bloc for the economy of India, since the East was responsible for a third of its foreign trade and said it was the personal wish of Indira Gandhi to raise the quality of mutual cooperation by expanding from bilateral trade deals to a multilateral treaty with the CMEA.[68] Furthermore, he expressed that his government wanted to pursue a non-capitalist path of development with a socialist society as eventual goal. However, this was no socialism in a Bolshevik sense but the socialism of the Fabian Society, as he mentioned to pursue the path opened up by Nehru.[69]

Nevertheless, Dhar would have been predestined to negotiate an association treaty with the CMEA. He had already served as ambassador to the USSR before in the crucial years of 1969–71 which saw the friendship treaty come into being. In September 1972, as India's Planning Minister, he was responsible for finalizing the agreement to found the "Intergovernmental Soviet-Indian Commission on Economic, Scientific, and Technical Cooperation" which met in New Delhi in February 1973 for its first session.[70] This commission could therefore have served as a blueprint for a cooperation treaty with the CMEA. More than 40 agreements on economic, scientific, and cultural cooperation between India and the Soviet Union were signed between 1972 and 1974.[71] He was responsible as well for establishing links with Gosplan. Together with the head of Gosplan, Nikolai Baibakov, he agreed to form a joint study group in which Soviet and Indian planners were to improve their abilities and exchange expertise on making economic forecasts and formulating investment projects for the five-year plans.[72]

Dhar concluded the meeting with Faddeev by stating that the growing public sector was a source of stability for the Indian economy and emphatically expressed his wish to meet with representatives of the International Investment Bank and the International Bank for Economic Cooperation.[73] The documents available don't give any reasons why this treaty of cooperation between India and the CMEA didn't come to pass. Several reasons are possible which are not mutually exclusive. The Indian ambassador died of a heart attack two months after his meeting with Nikolai Faddeev which could have delayed the preliminary negotiations significantly, as these needed to be conducted in secret to avoid controversy at home. Dhar was succeeded by Inder Kumar Gujral who held the post till 1980.[74] It is, however, more likely that the state of emergency declared by Indira Gandhi in 1975 and the loss of power of the INC two years later was a more decisive factor. There are no available archival documents showing that her government revived the plan to sign a treaty with the CMEA again when she became prime minister of India for the second time in 1980.

## Trade patterns with India

The short reign of the Janata government didn't impede relations with the CMEA countries. The mutual economic ties had become so strong that the repercussions of a radical breakup would have been detrimental to the Indian economy. This was clear to Indian officials and is evidenced in Indian archival documents:

> The Soviet Union is today India's third largest trading partner accounting for 13% of India's total trade and the third largest buyer of Indian goods accounting for 11% of India's total exports. Traditional goods such as tea, coffee, spices, tobacco, cashew nuts, jute and cotton textiles, still constitute important share in India's exports to USSR. Their share on an average is about 75–80 per cent of our total exports, while non-traditional manufactured products account for 20–25 per cent. For our traditional exports we have found in the USSR an assured additional market. It has contributed towards realization of a stable unit value in the international markets. In fact the USSR had been the principal market for many of our export goods.[75]

The India-Program of the CMEA was repeatedly updated and discussed in the PCTA. Its continuation was the topic of meetings of leading foreign trade officials under the umbrella of the CMEA as well.[76] Soviet trade officials were actively approaching their colleagues inside the CMEA to foster cooperation schemes. Thus, the East German delegation to the PCTA was asked in 1973 to contribute to the expansion of the metallurgical plants of Bhilai and Bokaro, a copper mine in Maladjhand, an oil refinery in Mathura, and the expansion of the electrical grid in India.[77] Indian documents on the Mathura oil refinery illustrate the ongoing discussions inside the Indian leadership on potential trade-offs between domestic and foreign technology, efficiency, and reliability. The Soviet Union offered to partially incorporate Western technology in its designs. The head of Engineers India Ltd. wrote a letter to the high-ranking official P.K. Dave in the Planning Commission and the Minister for Petroleum and Chemicals D.K. Barooah:

> My experience tells me that in our country we must use only that technology which gives maximum assurance of dependability. We do not have the resources to take chances, particularly in vital areas. The Mathura Refinery with a capacity of 6 million tonnes will represent a major portion of our total refining capacity and is backed up by heavy investments on a major pipeline

> and off-shore terminal. As you know, the fertilizer plants in Durgapur and Cochin have run into trouble because of the newness of the design employed for the associated waste heat recovery system. This is only one example where we have suffered because of relatively untried technology.[78]

In another letter to P.K. Dave and to the Secretary inside the Ministry of Heavy Industry, the advisor to the Planning Commission, L. Kumar, wrote:

> I understand that, during the visit of the Minister (P&C) to Moscow, the Soviet authorities had clearly agreed that as much Indian equipment as can be conveniently arranged should be incorporated in the project. I would seriously urge for your consideration that, in programming the Mathura Refinery, we should inform the Soviets that the requirements of structural will be met from within the country. The advantage of such an intimation is that the preparation of the detailed project report by the Soviet authorities would take into account this stipulation. We should also offer to supply such information as they may require regarding the Indian specifications and Indian capability.[79]

These two letters hint at some unique advantages cooperation with the Eastern Bloc comprised. Although Soviet designs were less efficient than the latest Western ones, they often could prove more reliable, whereby reliable most likely implicated that the machines were easier to use and required less skilled workers. For a country relying on state planning for industrialization, this proved advantageous, since it literally made planning easier. While Soviet-style economies had a well-deserved reputation for being inflexible, they showed a remarkable ability to accommodate to the needs of their Indian customers for large-scale projects, as they were ready to incorporate as much Indian supplies as possible in their designs. Subsequent examples in this chapter, particularly drawn from the steel industry, show that Western competitors could not match this flexibility. The reason for this was the ideological coherence between the Eastern Bloc and India in the Cold War. Although the economic system of India allowed for a significant role of the private sector, both areas were in essence pursuing a strategy of industrialization by import substitution. Thus, their approaches to the economy and their management styles were similar enough to provide for synergies between them.

The plans agreed upon in the PCTA demanded that the India-Program should be split up in two stages: the first one from 1974–75 should be marked by a coordination of Eastern imports from India, a strong cooperation between the different sales organizations of the CMEA member states operating in India and preliminary studies to introduce a system of multilateral payment between the CMEA and India. During the second stage from 1976–80 the delegates to the PCTA should draft a list of concrete proposals and objects for multilateral economic and technical assistance to build and expand factories in India particularly in agriculture and heavy industry. It is interesting to note that the delegates to the PCTA also talked about the possibility to buy manufactured goods from India.[80] This plan was later revised and updated on the 44th meeting of the PCTA 2–3 June 1982 in Moscow.[81]

Not all of the projects executed in India by the Eastern Bloc were successful. To give examples, the Barauni oil refinery could neither process Indian nor Gulf oil, the surgical instruments factory in Madras could only produce cutlery, and the lack of spare parts and a reliable after-sales service often angered Indian customers.[82] Despite occasional setbacks, the Soviet Union overtook the USA as India's largest trading partner for the first time in 1981.[83] In 1987, India accounted for 1.7 % of total trade turnover of the Soviet Union which was the highest share of any non-socialist country from the Global South. Nevertheless, trade with India was quantitatively less important for the Soviet Union than trade with West Germany, France, Finland, and Italy.[84] The economic importance of the Soviet Union for India was far greater than the other way around, as the Soviet Union stood for more than 10 % of India's imports and more than 14 % of its exports in the mid-1980s.[85] This supports the point that what the Gorbachev administration did in its approach to the Global South was to gradually shift the focus of aid and attention, without radically altering the policies of preceding Soviet leaders.

The smaller members of the CMEA had expanded their trade links with India as well but not on a scale comparable to the Soviet Union. Nevertheless, the participants of a conference of foreign trade representatives that took place in Moscow from 7–9 April 1987 stated on their economic relations with India:

> It has been emphasized that India is among the leading trade partners of the developing countries for most CMEA countries. . . .
>
> Coordination among the interested CMEA member states in the field of commercial and economic cooperation with India on a bilateral as well as on a multilateral basis is therefore gaining importance under these circumstances. The development of cooperation agreements to support the erection of complete objects of the CMEA countries in India, the cooperation with Indian organizations on third markets and the application of new forms and methods of industrial cooperation can contribute to increasing trade of the CMEA countries with India.[86]

The overall share of the CMEA countries in total Indian trade turnover amounted to roughly twenty percent in the mid-1980s.[87] If the Soviet numbers are deducted from this value, this shows that overall trade of the smaller CMEA countries with India was about half as much as Soviet–Indian trade. The share of India in trade turnover of the smaller CMEA countries was also less than that of India for the Soviet Union. The GDR, to make a case in point, stood for 0.8 % of India's trade with the outside world. It was the source of 0.6 % of its imports and 1.1 % of its exports.[88] For Hungary, India was as important a trade partner as Syria but less important than Iran and Iraq in the early 1980s.[89] The same holds true for the GDR.[90] Like the Soviets, the trade representatives from the smaller European CMEA countries agreed early on to import significant amounts of non-traditional goods from India which meant (semi-) manufactured goods. In the case of the CSSR, these already made up more than 40 % of Czechoslovak imports as agreed in the trade protocol for 1973.[91] One advantage that trade with India had over trade with Iran, Syria, and

Iraq was that it proved more stable. Trade with the Middle Eastern countries in the 1980s was highly volatile and partially inflated by the military conflict and the import of dual-use items like desert-going East German trucks.

## Steel for India

The second five-year plan of India supervised by Mahalanobis divided the economy mainly in two sectors, one producing consumer goods, the other one producing capital goods. According to Mahalanobis, the main problem of the Indian economy was that it produced insufficient amounts of capital goods which therefore had to be imported making the country dependent on Western credits.[92] Despite being overwhelmingly agrarian, the Indian economic planners could build on some pockets of industrialization already present in the country. There were some basic steel factories in the country which could be used as the backbone for expanding capital goods production. India's steel production, amounting to one million tons at the end of the Second World War, increased to three million tons in 1960 and six million tons in 1964.[93] Therefore, the economic plans worked out by Mahalanobis and his colleagues proved successful, as the country's industrial base was significantly expanded.[94] The Soviets had played a part in this plan, as they provided a significant amount of capital goods and built several factories in the heavy industries sector. Their work had often proved more suitable to Indian needs than similar Western projects.

Some of the projects, particularly with regards to erecting steel plants, were as contested as the Aswan Dam project. Soviet engineers built two steelworks in India between the mid-1950s and mid-1970s in Bhilai and Bokaro. They were not the only ones to do so, as two other major public steel works were erected during that time: one by the British in Durgapur and one by the West Germans in Rourkela, each of them with a planned capacity of one million tons annually.[95] These steel works were meant to serve as showcases for their builders and were financed with financial assistance of the respective country of origin.[96] While the steel works of the mid-1950s had been built largely by foreign companies, it was increasingly the aim of Indian planners to let Indian companies contribute more to the projects. This was already an issue in the meetings of the PCTA in the 1960s and became more and more relevant. To make a case in point, Indian planners rejected Czechoslovak designs for a steel factory to be built at Ranchi in the 1960s, because of its complexity which was beyond the production capacity of Indian industries. This would have resulted in a permanent dependency on Czechoslovak deliveries of spare parts for the factory.[97] This illustrates that the representatives of Skodaexport, while having sophisticated technology on offer, would have been well advised to cooperate more closely within the CMEA in the 1960s when it came to doing business in India. The building of steel factories in particular was no matter confined to a narrow circle of experts but for the Indian public as well which closely observed the projects.[98]

Soviet companies had built the steel plant at Bhilai almost simultaneously to a West German consortium headed by Krupp in Rourkela. Apparently, the Soviets could accommodate themselves better to local conditions. Soviet engineers and craftsmen were officially employed by the Indian government and therefore "Indianized," a move of great symbolical value.[99] The West German project of Rourkela had been ridiculed in the press as "the Stalingrad of German industry."[100] Sectarian violence broke out repeatedly at the construction side and the factory. In spring 1958 19 Sikhs had been beaten to death by militant Hindus. Six years later, an even greater tragedy took place when riots by parts of the Hindu population against Muslims left up to 2,000 people dead.[101] Whether by chance or thanks to a better understanding of potential ethnic tensions no such known incident happened at the Soviet-managed site in Bhilai, less than 500 km to the West of Rourkela.

Although the factory designed with West German engineering know-how could produce steel more efficiently than the Soviet factory at Bhilai and more efficiently than its British counterpart, as well, this was not what the whole endeavor was all about. More important than the latest Western technology and the highest economic efficiency were achievements that fit into the framework of industrialization by import substitution which was something the West German engineers didn't seem to understand. When the Indian government tried to expand the factory in the late 1960s from one to 1.8 million tons capacity, Indian planners could hardly handle the West German designs and the costs of expanding the factory were almost as high as building it, including the iron ore mine and the city of Rourkela. In the end, the Indian planners had to recruit West German engineers again which was considered a loss of face.[102] Expanding the Soviet steel factory at Bhilai proved much easier to accomplish for Indian planners.[103] The Soviets could repeat their success later at Bokaro, where they competed against a factory proposal designed by US steel and an Indian competitor named Dasturco. Interestingly, the Soviet proposal contained the highest share of Indian supplies, higher than the design by the domestic company Dasturco. Whereas Dasturco's engineers envisioned the share of domestic supplies to stand at 30 %, their value amounted to nearly two-thirds in the Soviet designs.[104]

This also meant that the share of imports was comparatively small in the Soviet proposal for the plant. The Soviet plans demanded imports worth 200 million US dollars, for Dasturco imports amounted to 318 million US dollars and US Steel calculated 512 million US dollars.[105] In addition, the Soviet offer was attractive, because trade was settled by clearing accounts. Thus, the credit didn't have to be paid back in US dollars but with Indian goods. This all contributed to the Indian government signing a treaty with the Soviets in the mid-1960s.[106] The Soviet engineers didn't use the most sophisticated technology for their designs and the production costs per unit of output were larger than for similar projects in Britain and Japan which were constructed at roughly the same time.[107] As was the case with Krupp in Rourkela, the design by US Steel most likely would have led to lower production costs per unit of output but efficiency was not the sole objective of the industrialization by import substitution strategy. The Soviet designs saved foreign exchange and used local industrial know-how to a large degree. Besides this, the high operating costs of the plant were also related exactly to the fact that Indian supplies were used so extensively, since these were not necessarily the most efficient available on the market either.[108]

However, as shown in Indian documents cited in this chapter, the emphasis of the Indian five-year plans changed in the 1970s, as an industrial base was already established by the late 1960s. This meant that the Soviets had to adapt their non-military export mix, if they wanted to enjoy strong trade relations with India in the future. This proved more difficult for them than for some of the smaller members of the CMEA like the GDR which exported equipment for branches of the economy with a more steady demand like equipment for printing presses.[109] Indian and Soviet officials concluded treaties on joint production whereby the Soviet would deliver raw materials to be processed in India and then exported to the Soviet Union again.[110] But this proved insufficient to stabilize or expand civilian trade in the 1970s.[111]

Therefore, the Soviet leadership decided to export crude oil to India. This was extraordinary for two reasons: first, the Soviet Union didn't receive foreign exchange in return due to the clearing agreement; second, at the same time the Soviet leadership was curtailing oil deliveries to Central Eastern Europe.[112] The Soviet leadership therefore valued its ties with India higher than with its European allies. The share of oil in Soviet exports to India peaked at 78 % in 1982 and decreased afterwards to 42 % in 1986 due to lower oil prices not to changes in volume.[113] Soviet trade with India was therefore unique, because it was the only country in the Global South from which it mainly imported manufactured goods in return for raw materials, a trade pattern that was more common in Soviet trade with the West. Since countries like Hungary, the CSSR, or GDR obviously had no crude oil to export, their trade pattern with India more closely resembled traditional East–South trade.

The India-Program of the CMEA was revised one year after Gorbachev had become General Secretary of the CPSU. A sensible push towards multilateral cooperation occurred. This new version of the India-Program would be valid till the end of 1990 and comprised objects that were meant to serve as prime examples for multilateral cooperation inside the bloc.[114] One of these objects was a prospect steel plant in Visakhapatnam. The plant was to have an annual capacity of 3.2 million tons of steel and to be erected as a joint project of the Soviet Union, the CSSR, GDR, Poland, Romania, Bulgaria, and Hungary.[115]

Other objects touched the branches of resource extraction, machine building, chemicals, and energy production.[116] All these projects give a hint at how the practical side of economic cooperation with the prime target of Soviet activities was to be conducted under the new administration in the Kremlin. Since the steel plant in Visakhapatnam was a large undertaking and included all European members of the CMEA, it is worthwhile to take a closer look at it. The more so, since building steel factories in India was a traditional strength of the Soviet export economy. Investments in the steel industry hadn't played as large a role in India in the 1970s as in the 1960s. Despite the difficulties Indo-Soviet trade and the Indian public sector in particular experienced in the 1970s, a narrative of constant decline is hardly in line with the facts. By the early 1980s, Indian planners anticipated a huge gap between supply and demand for steel. Steel production which stood at 14 million tons annually in the early 1980s was planned to expand to 45 million tons annually by the year 2000.[117] This plan once again provided ample opportunity for the heavy industry sector of the Eastern Bloc. Indian experts were making unflattering comparisons between the state of their steel industry and the one of countries like Brazil or South Korea as is clear from a letter by M.N. Dastur, the founder of Dasturco to P.N. Dhar, Principal Secretary to Indira Gandhi.[118]

The ideological underpinning for fruitful economic cooperation between India and the CMEA countries was still intact in the mid-1980s under the premiership of Rajiv Gandhi who had followed his mother in office after her assassination. This is evidenced by official statements like during his visit to Moscow but also from internal Indian material. The protocol of the 40th meeting of the National Development Council reads:

> The Prime Minister pointed out that every meeting of the NDC was a reaffirmation of our national commitment to planning, of the national consensus on planning. Planning was aimed at bringing to bear the powers of reason and the fruits of science and was the structural transformation of our society. Also, it promoted social change and reduced disparities. Development was the fostering of national self-reliance and of securing a gainful life for all. It was the modernization of our society and economy. Continuing, the Prime Minister stated that the key to the modernization of our economy lay in deepening the technological base of our society, placing the tools of modern technology in the hands of our people.[119]

## The long road to Visakhapatnam

Visakhapatnam was meant to repeat the successes at Bhilai and Bokaro. However, the fact that the Soviets so actively sought cooperation with all other European members of the CMEA for this project could either be interpreted as a sign of weakness or as a sign of a new spirit of cooperation. Most likely it was a mixture of both. While the Soviet economy on average was still more productive than the Indian one in the 1980s, they found it difficult to export their own equipment in exchange for non-traditional Indian goods. Cooperation, particularly with the more advanced CMEA countries on its Western periphery, therefore promised to overcome this deficiency of the Soviet export economy. In the end, this could work out as a win-win situation to all parties involved, since it meant more business for East German and Czechoslovak state combines, as well as for Soviet ones.

Internal documents of the Indian government give valuable insights into the decision-making process. Negotiations on the steel factory at Visakhapatnam predated the election of Gorbachev as General Secretary of the CPSU. The Public Investment Board was discussing the project as late as 1979.[120] In the same year an Indian delegation traveled to Moscow for negotiations.[121] It is interesting to note that at least during the 1970s Mr. Skachkov was involved in the negotiations with the Indians due to his position in the Soviet government.[122] This was the same Mr. Skachkov who headed the PCTA till the early 1980s. This shows the advantage the Soviets had in CMEA affairs. In many cases they could obtain information on new business proposals earlier and easier than their peers in the bloc due to their international position. They could then decide, if they wanted to execute the projects on their own or to offer parts of it to their CMEA partners.

Building another large public steel plant was already a contested issue in 1970, prior to the general elections that took place in 1971.[123] Indira Gandhi's government had announced the decision to build a steel factory in the Visakhapatnam area in April 1970 without any plan being worked out on the feasibility of the project.[124] This makes it likely that the decision was foremost a political one, the more so, since the government had announced the building of another steel plant in Karnataka in India's South the same day, as well.[125] This was a promise of regional development. Visakhapatnam was located on the Eastern coast of India and already contained a harbor that could be used for imports and exports. Nevertheless, the location had profound deficiencies for a steel factory, since the deposits of vital resources were far away. The coal deposits were 1,007 km, the iron ore deposits 768 km, and limestone deposits 455 km away from the planned factory site.[126] The Chief Minister of Andhra Pradesh wrote to Indira Gandhi in October 1970:

> The people of Andhra Pradesh have waited and worked long for the coming of the Steel Project which will mark a water-shed in the transformation of our preponderantly agricultural economy into a modern industrial State. You have more than anybody else made the fruition of the Steel Project possible for Andhra Pradesh.[127]

The foundation stone was laid by Indira Gandhi one year later but besides that not much happened after the announcement. On its session on 24 October 1973, the Public Investment Board asked Dasturco which had also played a role in the Bokaro project to prepare a detailed project report for the future steel plant.[128] The plans were beginning to take shape in the late 1970s. By that time, India had to increase its imports of steel, since domestic production proved insufficient to keep up with demand. As steel imports were costly and had to be paid with foreign exchange, the pressure on the planning authorities was increasing. This followed the logic of import substitution. The passage on the justification of the project reads as follows:

> Based on the March 1979 Report of the Working Group on Iron and Steel set-up by the Planning Commission for six years period 1978–84, there is considerable gap between demand and availability . . .
>
> In assessing the demand growth rate it also appears highly desirable to keep in view the fact that per capita consumption in the country is at present at a very low figure of 14 kg as compared to the figure of 700/800 kg in some of the developed countries. It would, therefore, be quite reasonable to expect

> and plan for at least doubling this figure in the next 5–7 years i.e., to 28 kg to 30 which again is a very low figure compared to some of the developed countries. Import during 1979–80 is likely to be about 1.74 MT at c.i.f. of about Rs 550 crores. Early establishment of additional capacity within the country is, therefore, essential to avoid continuous drain of foreign exchange resources on account of import of steel, and to prevent shortages and black market.[129]

The total planned investment costs for the steel plant at Visakhapatnam were estimated at Rs 2693.5 crores.[130] Therefore, under the strict assumption that no additional imports were needed to run and maintain the factory, the project would have paid for itself after five years, at least if one looked from the ideological point of view of industrialization by import substitution. However, such a calculation, even if often applied under such an economic development scheme, is highly dubious. This would have demanded two completely separated economic cycles, one for the domestic economy and another for foreign trade not intertwined with each other. In reality, such separate systems didn't exist, neither in the Eastern Bloc nor in India.

The Indian planners wanted the Soviets to implement the most advanced blast furnaces that were produced in the Soviet Union and already reliably tested. However, the latest Soviet blast furnaces demanded inputs of coking coal with a very low ash content. This resulted in additional Indian investments, since Indian coal had to be purified to be applied to this process.[131] Furthermore, there were opportunity costs for the project. The harbor at Visakhapatnam had been built to export iron ore. Diverting the iron ore to domestic use for the proposed steel plant meant that large parts of the harbor would have remained unutilized and the previous investments in vain. The discrepancy amounted to several million tons annually.[132] It was clear to the economic planners that Visakhapatnam was not the best suited location for a steel factory:

> The cost comparisons above are intended to show the regional advantages and disadvantages, not to suggest that new-steel making capacity should be located precisely at Bokaro, Bhilai and Paradeep. There are many potential steel plant sites in the Bengal-Bihar-Orissa area. Unfortunately, detailed investigations of these sites have not been undertaken because of the 1970 decision to locate new steel-making capacity in the south. The implication of locating a major steel-making facility in the south at this stage of development will be to increase the cost of production of steel. The loss to the economy by producing steel at Vizag rather than in the eastern region will be of the order of Rs 125 per tonne of finished steel. This means an economic loss of Rs 33.5 crores per annum on the operation of the completed plant. This estimate would not be substantially reduced even if (as suggested) allowance is made for the higher quality of ore to be used at Vizag.[133]

On the 107th meeting of the Public Investment Board on 24 May 1979, the Secretary of Steel brushed the concerns of the Planning Commission aside and stated that further expanding the factories at Bhilai and Bokaro or building a new one in this area was unfeasible, because such a large plant would be unmanageable and not enough raw materials could be transported.[134] He also contradicted the findings of the Planning Commission by stating that the use of higher quality iron ore would make steel production at Visakhapatnam as economical as at Bokaro or Bhilai.[135] The experts of the Planning Commission had clearly stated in their analysis that this would not substantially alter the picture. The Secretary of Steel reacted the same way when asked, if the plant would be prone to tropical storms like cyclones by saying that adequate care will be taken off without naming any details.[136] It was clear that the politicians dominated the economic experts. The factory had to be built, not because it was efficient to do so, but because imports of steel had to be curtailed and the development of the Southern regions advanced.[137]

It is interesting to note that back in May 1979 when the Public Investment Board made its decision, the Janata government under Prime Minister Morarji Desai was still in place.[138] The project was associated with Indira Gandhi's government. Therefore, when the Janata Party came to power, its leadership was not too fond of executing the projects of the former government. But they were experiencing severe resistance from inside their own party. Tenneti Viswanathan, the head of the Janata Party in Andhra Pradesh, the state of the prospective steel plant, wrote a letter to Morarji Desai in April 1977:

> Dear Shri Morarji Desaiji,
>
> I am enclosing herewith a copy of my letter addressed to Shri Biji Patnaik, Minister for Steel about the Fifth Steel Plant at Visakhapatnam. His statements show that he is thinking about shifting the place for which work has been done and money has been spent. Such changes are not good for the country or for its economy. Kindly interfere and see that the work proceeds apace in order to see that our iron and steel are cheap comparatively with the world market.[139]

His letter to the Minister for Steel, Biju Patnaik, was more direct:

> I am sorry to see the statements made by you and some of your officers that the Visakhapatnam Steel Plant would be shifted. The grounds advanced are that the site is not the best; that it was chosen for political considerations and that it was an Election matter. None of the grounds have any base. In the mid term reappraisal of the Third Plan it was suggested that Steel Plants need not be necessarily located at oreheads, they can be located far away; that two Steel Plants were necessary in South India to remove regional imbalances. And according to modern trends of location one should be a coastal based one. . . . Change of Ministers should not mean change in well considered plans and projects.[140]

There had already been a public struggle prior to the announcement of Indira Gandhi's government in 1970 to build another public steel plant at Visakhapatnam.

Agitation to build a steel plant at Visakhapatnam led to riots in the mid-1960s which were stopped violently by the police. Thirty-two people were left dead and several hundred wounded.[141] One of the activists, T. Amrutha Rao, went on hunger strike in 1966 and he threatened to do so again in a letter to the Minister of Steel in 1977.[142] Thus, the costs for the Janata government in Delhi were too high to change course. None of the available documents in East German, Soviet, and Hungarian files show that the full complexity of the projects and its contested political background were known to the Eastern economic planners. Activists like T. Amrutha Rao who spearheaded the slogan "Visakha Ukku Andhrula Hakku"[143] are still celebrated for their dedication to the steel factory.[144]

## Problems in the field

The final treaty for Visakhapatnam was complicated, since so many parties were involved in building the factory, not only Indian but also foreign ones. The East German combine SKET was delivering equipment to India for the steel plant and supervised a small part of the assembly. The treaty was concluded by August 1987 and the CSSR and GDR had to finish their deliveries till August 1989. Afterwards they had to provide services for the assembly and commissioning of the factory till the end of 1991.[145] All in all, the obligations of the East Germans amounted to not more than fifteen million US dollars including the deliveries of spare parts for their equipment and assembly services by experienced engineers. The GDR charged ca. 20 US dollars per hour for its consulting services which was less than a Western engineer would have demanded but more than an East German engineer received as a salary.[146]

The East German state combine SKET was a subcontractor of the Czechoslovak combine Skoda for some of the deliveries, for others it had concluded direct contracts with the Indian state company Vizak Steel that was to build and run the factory or one of its subsidiaries.[147] SKET, however, could not produce all of the equipment by itself nor was it able to procure the equipment it needed from inside the bloc. This could only partially be accomplished by imports from the Soviet Union and Romania.[148] SKET had to rely on imports of West German technology which made up more than 25 % of the money SKET could hope to obtain from the Indians.[149] This represents just a fraction of the complexity of the project, as Czechoslovak and Soviet documents would probably expand the map of suppliers much further. With a certain expression of resignation an East German report on the project stated:

> First plant-typical symptoms like
>
> - delays in delivering the assembly instructions by SKET
> - problems in timely shipping by SKET till 31.12.1988
>
> allowed already back in February to draw the conclusion that we have to anticipate critical and expensive legal consequences again.

> The delays in realizing the object are the fault of all partners involved and are estimated at six months by the HPA [East German trade representation].[150]

Therefore, the minister for foreign trade in East Berlin, Dr. Beil, feared that the East German industry could not abide by the original treaty. The same report on the meeting of the Governmental Commission for Uniformly Steering Import and Export (RKEI) on 9 June 1989 reads:

> Com. Dr. Beil has critically reviewed the hitherto existing results of the management and control of the execution of the object middle steel rolling mill Visakhapatnam/India[151] in responsibility of Com. Dr. Rößner. The special significance of this project lies therein that it is to be realized as a reference object. This demands – as immeditate task – the unconditional adherence to the L/C- [delivery] date 30.8.1989.[152]

Just as in the Syrian example of building cement factories, delays were one problem, disappearing equipment another. Some of the deliveries shipped from Rostock to Mumbai disappeared for unknown reasons in the harbor of Mumbai which led to quarrels with the Indian partners at the construction site, in this case the Mukand Iron and Steel Works in Mumbai, because the equipment was urgently needed for the assembly.[153] Interestingly, the main company responsible for the Visakhapatnam steel plant asked SKET to ensure that the Indian company Mukand Iron and Steel Works would be able to speed up its work.[154] Although SKET and Skoda were responsible for the middle steel rolling mill only, which was just a part of the factory, their deliveries made up 38.8 % of the equipment needed, and 61.2 % were to be produced by Indian companies according to Czechoslovak and East German blueprints and instruction.[155]

The cooperation between SKET and Skoda was prone to misunderstandings and mistakes, as well. SKET needed special plunger pumps for its own designs to be delivered by Skoda. Although SKET and Skoda had concluded the treaty in July 1987, nearly two years before the deliveries had to be made, Skoda could not abide by the treaty but offered to deliver the pumps by late 1990. The representatives of SKET could not convince their colleagues from Skoda to deliver the equipment earlier. They therefore turned to other potential partners outside the bloc and concluded the treaty with an Austrian company. However, this meant payments in Western currency. From a business perspective, the initiative shown by the directorate of SKET was sensible. Since they didn't want to threaten the whole project, they turned to other companies in the market. This angered the RKEI and foremost its head, Dr. Beil, for several reasons: first, foreign exchange had to be spent; second, this would have allowed the Indians and Czechoslovaks to blame SKET if anything went wrong, while otherwise SKET could have blamed Skoda for delays. However, another important reason was that the Indians had to pay with foreign exchange themselves not only once but repeatedly for the spare parts. The RKEI therefore anticipated that the Indian side would have liked the contract with Skoda to remain in place, even if it meant delays. This was the logic of industrialization by import substitution.[156]

## Conclusion

The findings in this chapter underline that with regards to changing the rules and policy objectives of the CMEA and doing business with the Global South the Gorbachev administration didn't undertake a radical departure from its predecessors at least till 1989. This is logical for several reasons: since Stalin's death and the Khrushchev reforms, the Soviet leadership had not been able to command the smaller members of the CMEA and dictate its will. Therefore, Gorbachev could try to convince and to a certain degree push the smaller members by building upon the still important role of the Soviet economy inside the CMEA but he could not make them do what he wished for. This was truer for leaders outside the CMEA. What changed under Gorbachev was that his government gave up the traditional Soviet opposition to market-oriented intrabloc reforms. If this had happened twenty years earlier, a breakthrough inside the CMEA would have seemed within reach. But the other members of the CMEA had changed their position as well with some of them becoming more orthodox in their economic views not less.

With regards to the Global South the Gorbachev administration tried to redirect resources from socialist regimes in Sub-Saharan Africa and the Middle East to India. It could use its influence in the CMEA to convince the smaller members to jump onto the bandwagon. However, this was no radical departure from previous policies, as strong ties between the CMEA and India already existed in the mid-1980s. The Indian government had even begun to negotiate a cooperation agreement with the CMEA in 1975. The Soviet urge for multilateral cooperation inside the CMEA in general and between the CMEA and the Global South in particular was related to the new leadership in the Kremlin as well as to the increasing difficulties of the Soviet economy to sell other products than commodities. The project of building the steel works of Visakhapatnam, which largely fell inside the Gorbachev period, shows that the hopes connected to multilateral cooperation didn't come to pass. This was not necessarily due to outdated equipment but to a lack of managerial capacity, as it proved increasingly difficult for the state combines and foreign trade officials to coordinate their complex economic interdependence and web of relations inside the CMEA and outside of it.

## Notes

1 See Brabant, *Economic Integration in Eastern Europe*.
2 Brabant, 113.
3 Zwass, *Der Rat Für Gegenseitige Wirtschaftshilfe*, 132.
4 Brabant, *Economic Integration in Eastern Europe*, 110.
5 Brabant, 111–3.
6 Brabant, 113.
7 Brabant, 121–2.

8 Zwass, *Der Rat Für Gegenseitige Wirtschaftshilfe*, 158–9.
9 Zwass, 161–2.
10 Tikhonov was replaced by the more energetic and reform-minded Nikolai Ivanovich Ryzhkov in September 1985.
11 Zwass, *Der Rat Für Gegenseitige Wirtschaftshilfe*, 163.
12 Zwass, 168.
13 Zwass, 168.
14 Zwass, 169–71.
15 Zwass, 197–8, 206.
16 Brabant, *Economic Integration in Eastern Europe*, 122–3.
17 Brabant, 123–4.
18 Dannehl, *Politics, Trade, and Development*, 7.
19 Dannehl, 7–8.
20 Westad, *The Global Cold War*, 365–6.
21 Westad, 382.
22 Westad, 382–3.
23 Westad, 383.
24 Westad, 384.
25 Dannehl, *Politics, Trade, and Development*, 7–8.
26 Dannehl, 7.
27 Dannehl, 7.
28 "Information über Regierungs- und kommerzielle Kredite, die die RGW-Länder den Entwicklungsländern gewährt haben, deren Inanspruchnahme und Tilgung per 1 January 1987 und Maßnahmen zur Sicherung der rechtzeitigen Tilgung der Kredite und von Garantien in bezug auf Valutaverluste," dated 29 April 1987, Barch Berlin, DL 2/16975.
29 Ibid (in particular the Russian annexes 2 and 7 to the document).
30 "Gandhi, Due In Soviet, Goes As Friend," *New York Times*, 21 May 1985.
31 Jee, "Indo-Soviet Security Relations," 222–3.
32 "Indians Welcome Gorbachev Gladly," *New York Times*, 26 November 1986.
33 Duncan, *The Soviet Union and India*, 69–70.
34 See on the interwar period also Vasudevan, "Asiatic Orientations."
35 Westad, *The Global Cold War*, 54–5.
36 Westad, 67–8, 80–2.
37 As cited in Westad, 81.
38 Mason, *Development and Disorder*, 269–70.
39 Sukhatme, "Assistance to India," 204–5.
40 Bose, "Instruments and Idioms of Colonial and National Development," 47.
41 Unger, *Entwicklungspfade in Indien*, 8–10.
42 Unger, 20.
43 Mason, *Development and Disorder*, 269.
44 Prasanta Chandra Mahalanobis, 1893–1972, was an Indian scientist who later became a leading member of India's Planning Commission. He spent part of his years as a student in Cambridge, where he met other gifted Indian students like Srinivasa Ramanujan. Back in India he became one of the founders of the Indian Statistical Institute (ISI). He played an important role in masterminding the Indian five-year plans and the industrialization of the country.
45 Bose, "Instruments and Idioms of Colonial and National Development," 53–4.
46 Bose, 54.
47 Mason, *Development and Disorder*, 270.
48 "Austausch der Arbeitserfahrungen über die wichtigsten Fragen der Tätigkeit der AHO im Zusammenhang mit der Gewährung von technischer Unterstützung an Entwicklungsländer beim Bau von Industriebetrieben und anderen Objekten im

Zeitraum vom Dezember 1964 bis April 1965," dated 1965, RGAE, Fond 561 op. 53 d. 13 ll. 59–61.

49 "Informatsionnyi material ob ob"mene mneniiami po nekotorym voprosam okazaniia ekonomicheskogo i technicheskogo sodeistviia razvivaiushchimsia stranam, v chastnosti oplaty okazannogo tekhnichekogo sodeistviia postavkami gotovykh izdelii, sakliucheniia otraslevykh soglashenii o chastichnom razdelenii truda i t.p.," RGAE, Fond 561 op. 53 d. 18 ll. 201–4.

50 "Informatsiia ob ekonomicheskom i tekhnicheskom sotrudnichestve i razvitii torgovli NR Bolgarii s Indiei, Tseilonom i Kambodiei," RGAE, Fond 561 op. 53 d. 27 ll. 49–52; "Informatsiia o razvitii torgovli i ekonomicheskogo sotrudnichestva SRR s Indiei, Tseilonom i Kambodiei," RGAE, Fond 561 op. 53 d. 27 ll. 54–7.

51 Letter by Technoexport Prague, dated 23 September 1967, RGAE, Fond 561 op. 53 d. 31 ll. 95–100. Note that this is in line with a letter by Skodaexport to the Secretariat of the CMEA in the same year.

52 "India's Trade Links with the USSR and Other East European Countries," without date most likely 1977, NAI, List No. 258 S. No. 654 WI/205/5/77 (EE).

53 After the death of Nehru as well as after Shastri's death Gulzarilal Nanda had served as interim premier for a few days.

54 Bose, "Instruments and Idioms of Colonial and National Development," 55.

55 Raghavan, "Between Regional and Global Interests," 332.

56 Raghavan, 326–7.

57 Raghavan, 334–5.

58 See on the political history of the Indo-Soviet relationship Mastny, "The Soviet Union's Partnership with India."

59 "Programma ekonomicheskogo tekhnicheskogo i torgovogo sotrudnichestva na dlitel'nyi period stran-chlenov SEV s Indiei na mnogostoronnei osnove," dated 1973, RGAE, Fond 561 op. 53 d. 47 ll. 22–5.

60 "Informatsiia ob ekonomicheskom sotrudnichestve PNR s Indiei," dated 04.02.1982, RGAE, Fond 561 op. 53 d. 118 ll. 64–6.

61 "Pravitel'stvennye kredity, predostavlennye PNR razvivaiushchimisia stranam po sostoianiiu na 1 January 1982 g.," dated 1982, RGAE, Fond 561 op. 53 d. 118 ll. 123; "Kommercheskie kredity, predostavlennye PNR razvivaiushchimisia stranam po sostoianiiu na 1 January 1982 g.," dated 1982, RGAE, Fond 561 op. 53 d. 118 ll. 124–25; "Informatsiia ob ekonomicheskom sotrudnichestve PNR i Indiei," dated 04 February 1982, RGAE, Fond 561 op. 53 d. 118 ll. 64–6.

62 Directive for the East German delegation to the 27th meeting of the PCTA, dated 1973, Barch Berlin, DL 2/6297.

63 Directive for the East German delegation to the 44th meeting of the PCTA, dated 1982, Barch Berlin, DL 2/6389.

64 "Weitere Präzisierung der Vorstellungen der DDR über eine Beteiligung an der Errichtung der im Indien-Programm aufgeführten Objekte," dated 31 January 1974, RGAE, Fond 561 op. 53 d. 62 ll. 42–4.

65 "Svodnyi Doklad o sotrudnichestve zainteresovannykh stran-chlenov SEV v oblasti okazaniia ekonomicheskogo i tekhnicheskogo sodeistviia razviviaiushchimsia stranam v vyyavlenii i osvoenii vazhneishikh vidov prirodnykh resursov," dated 1974, RGAE, Fond 561 op. 26s/pp d. 52 ll. 26–68.

66 "Spravka po voprosu o sviaziakh Soveta Ekonomicheskoi Vzaimopomoshchi so stranami-nechlenami SEV v 1975 g.," RGAE, Fond 302 op. 2 d. 1521 ll. 2–7.

67 "vstupit' v assotsiatsiiu" in the original document on the meeting.

68 "Zapis 'Besedy Sekretaria SEV N. Faddeeva s Poslom Indii v SSSR D. Dkharom' sostoiavshcheisia 4 aprelia 1975g.," RGAE, Fond 302 op. 2 d. 1303 ll. 40–4.

69 Ibid.

70 Duncan, *The Soviet Union and India*, 70–1.

71 Duncan, 70–1.
72 "Agreement on Cooperation between the Planning Commission of the Republic of India and the State Planning Committee of the Union of Soviet Socialist Republics (GOSPLAN of the U.S.S.R.)," dated 29 November 1973, NAI, List No. 258 S. No. 485 WI/204/10/73.
73 "Zapis 'Besedy Sekretaria SEV N. Faddeeva s Poslom Indii v SSSR D. Dkharom' sostoiavshcheisia 4 aprelia 1975g.," RGAE, Fond 302 op. 2 d. 1303 ll. 40–4.
74 "Ambassadors of India to the USSR and Russia."
75 "India's Trade Links with the USSR and Other East European Countries," without date most likely 1977, NAI, List No. 258 S. No. 654 WI/205/5/77 (EE).
76 "Protokol soveshchaniia nachal'nikov upravlenii ministerstv vneshnei torgovli i gosudarstvennykh komitetov po vneshneekonomicheskim sviaziam stran-chlenov SEV," dated 1983, RGAE, Fond 561 op. 26s/pp d. 111 ll. 2–28.
77 Directive for the East German delegation to the 27th meeting of the PCTA, dated 1973, Barch Berlin, DL 2/6297.
78 Letter by M.S. Pathak to D.K. Barooah and P.K. Dave, dated 23 November 1973, NAI, List No 183 S. No. 68 PAD/1–117/73.
79 Letter by L. Kumar to the Secretary of the Ministry of Heavy Industry and P.K. Dave, dated 26 October 1973, ibid.
80 Directive for the East German delegation to the 26th meeting of the PCTA, dated 1973, Barch Berlin, DL 2/6296.
81 Directive for the East German delegation to the 44th meeting of the PCTA, dated 1982, Barch Berlin, DL 2/6389.
82 Duncan, *The Soviet Union and India*, 78.
83 Duncan, 70–1.
84 Duncan, 76.
85 Duncan, 76.
86 "Protokoll der handelspolitischen Verwaltungen der Ministerien für Außenhandel und der Staatlichen Komitees für Außenwirtschaftsbeziehungen der RGW-Länder," dated 1987, Barch Berlin, DL 2/16975.
87 Directive for the East German delegation to the 52nd meeting of the PCTAC, dated 1986, Barch Berlin, DL 2/16970.
88 Ibid.
89 "Information über die wichtigsten Ergebnisse der Wirtschaftsbeziehungen der UVR zu den Entwicklungsländern im Jahre 1980," dated 02 April 1981, Barch Berlin, DL 2/16950.
90 See the annual reports of the East German trade representatives in Teheran, New Delhi, Damascus, and Bagdad for the concrete numbers, Barch Berlin, DL 2/6342a as well as DL 2/6411, DL 2/6382, DL 2/6359, DL 2/6426, DL 2/6430, DL 2/6401a, DL 2/6422a.
91 "Political Report for the year 1973 Part II – Economic," dated 14 March 1973, NAI, List No. 217 S. No. 333 HI/1011 (25)/73.
92 Unger, *Entwicklungspfade in Indien*, 155.
93 Expanding steel production had been on the agenda of the Indian Planning Commission since its foundation, see Engerman, *Price of Aid*, 81–2. In contrast to Engerman the focus of this chapter lies on a different time span, is more on the economic side and on the archival material of the Planning Commission.
94 Unger, *Entwicklungspfade in Indien*, 158.
95 "Approach Paper on Development of Consultancy, Design, and Engineering Services in India," dated 1982, NAI, List No. 249 S. No. 232 PAD/22–3 (2)/82.
96 Desai, *The Bokaro Steel Plant*, 45.
97 Desai, 18.
98 See e.g., "Soviet Collaboration in Indian Steel Industry, 1954–84," *Economic and Political Weekly*, 05 March 1988, 473–86.

99 Engerman, *Price of Aid*, 131.
100 "Rourkela Sieg der Deutschen," *Der Spiegel*, 3/1966, 68–70.
101 Unger, *Entwicklungspfade in Indien*, 203–5.
102 "Action Committee on Public Enterprises Rourkela Steel Plant – Hindustan Steel Limited Summary of Report," dated 1978, NAI, List No. 183 S. No. 100 PAD/1–206/74; memos of the Planning Commission on the expansion of the Rourkela Steel Plant, dated 28 January 1975 and 29 June 1978, NAI, List No. 183 S. No. 100 PAD/1–206/74.
103 "Debottlenecking and technological upgrading of 1.5 MT stage of Bhilai Steel Plant," dated 1984, NAI, List No. 249 S. No. 328 PAD/22–1 (5)/84.
104 Desai, *The Bokaro Steel Plant*, 43.
105 Desai, 46.
106 Desai, 51.
107 Desai, 52–8, 75–6.
108 Desai, 75–6.
109 See the annual reports of the East German trade representative to New Delhi, Barch Berlin, DL 2/6342a as well as DL 2/6411, DL 2/6382, DL 2/6359, DL 2/6426, DL 2/6430, DL 2/6401a, DL 2/6422a.
110 Duncan, *The Soviet Union and India*, 70–1.
111 Military trade on the other hand was flourishing in the 1970s, see Engerman, *Price of Aid*, 16–7.
112 Duncan, *The Soviet Union and India*, 70–1.
113 Duncan, 74.
114 "Information über die ergriffenen Maßnahmen zur Aktivierung der mehrseitigen Zusammenarbeit der RGW-Länder mit Entwicklungsländern," dated 23 January 1987, Barch Berlin, DL 2/16974.
115 Ibid.
116 "Langfristiges Programm der mehrseitigen Zusammenarbeit interessierter RGW-Länder mit Indien für den Zeitraum 1986–1990," dated 19 February 1987, Barch Berlin, DL 2/16975.
117 "Approach Paper on Development of Consultancy, Design, and Engineering Services in India," dated 1982, NAI, List No. 249 S. No. 232 PAD/22–3 (2)/82.
118 Letter by M. N. Dastur to P. N. Dhar, dated 18 October 1974, NAI, List No. 193 S. No. 697 17/982/1974-PMS.
119 "Fourtieth Meeting of the National Development Council," dated 19 March 1988, NAI, List No. 249 S. No. 32 Q-19012/129/85 RD (Vol. II).
120 "107th Meeting of Public Investment Board to be Held on 24th May, 1979 at 4.00pm," dated 16 May 1979, NAI, List No. 249 S. No. 98 PAD/22–1 (1)/79.
121 Letters by R. Murali advisor to the PAD, dated 29 March 1979 and 25 April 1979, ibid.
122 Letter by R. C. Dutt to the bureau of Indira Gandhi, dated 06 February 1970, NAI, List No. 193 S. No. 368 17/982/1970-PMS; "Protocol of the first meeting of the Inter-governmental Soviet-Indian Commission on Economic, Scientific and Technical Cooperation," dated 1973, NAI, List No. 258 S. No. 386 WI/239/2/72 (EE) Vol. II.
123 "Note for the Cabinet Subject: Setting up of an Integrated Steel Plant at Visakhapatnam," dated 26 May 1979, NAI, List No. 249 S. No. 98 PAD/22–1 (1)/79.
124 Ibid.
125 "Planning Commission Note for the Cabinet Subject: Setting Up of an Integrated Steel Plant at Visakhapatnam," dated 1979, ibid.
126 Ibid.
127 Letter by Brahmananda Reddi to Indira Gandhi, dated 27 October 1970, NAI, List No. 193 S. No. 353 17/933/1970-PMS.

128 "Note for the Cabinet Subject: Setting Up of an Integrated Steel Plant at Visakhapatnam," dated 26 May 1979, NAI, List No. 249 S. No. 98 PAD/22–1 (1)/79.
129 Ibid.
130 "Planning Commission Note for the Cabinet Subject: Setting Up of an Integrated Steel Plant at Visakhapatnam," dated 1979, ibid. 2693.5 crores equate to 26,935 million rupees, roughly 3.2 billion US dollars in 1979.
131 "Note for the Cabinet Subject: Setting Up of an Integrated Steel Plant at Visakhapatnam," dated 26 May 1979, ibid.
132 "Record of discussion in the 107th meeting of the Public Investment Board held on 24th May, 1979," dated 24 May 1979, ibid.
133 "Planning Commission Note for the Cabinet Subject: Setting Up of an Integrated Steel Plant at Visakhapatnam," dated 1979, ibid.
134 "Record of discussion in the 107th meeting of the Public Investment Board held on 24th May, 1979," dated 24 May 1979, ibid.
135 Ibid.
136 Ibid.
137 Another line of confrontation ran between the deputy head of the Planning Commission who was the actual chair of the Planning Commission and the Minister of Steel. The deputy head of the Planning Commission wanted to inhibit the building of a steel plant at Visakhapatnam or at least to downscale it. He lost that issue. See letter by M. Sivagnanam advisor to the PAD, dated 28 May 1979, ibid.
138 The government led by Morarji Desai and the Janata Party in general resembled disparate partners united only in their opposition to Indira Gandhi.
139 Letter by Tenneti Viswanathan to Morarji Desai, dated 30 April 1977, NAI, List No. 193 S. No. 929 17/933/1977-PMS.
140 Letter by Tenneti Viswanathan to Biju Patnaik, dated 30 April 1977, ibid.
141 Letter by Tenneti Viswanathan to Biju Patnaik, dated 22 June 1977, ibid.
142 Letter by T. Amrutha Rao to Biju Patnaik, dated 13 May 1977, ibid.
143 Visakha's Steel, Right of Andhras'.
144 " 'Visakha Ukku' Stir Now 50 Years Old," *The Hindu*, 14 October 2016, accessed September 2, 2019. www.thehindu.com/news/cities/Visakhapatnam/%E2%80%98Visakha-Ukku%E2%80%99-stir-now-50-years-old/article16071011.ece; "Sri T. Amrutha Rao Jayanthi Celebrated in Ukkunagaram," *RINL News*, 21 October 2016, accessed September 2, 2019. www.vizagsteel.com/rinlnews/details.php?newsid=192.
145 "Bericht über den Stand der Realisierung des NSW-Anlagenexportvorhabens Mittelstahladjustage Visakhapatnam/Indien sowie Darlegung erster Erfahrungen in der Zusammenarbeit mit den indischen Unterlieferanten," dated 18 January 1989, Barch Berlin, DL 2/14972.
146 "Abrechnung des Realisierungsstandes 'Mittelstahladjustage Visakhapatnam/Indien'," dated 17 July 1989, Barch Berlin, DL 2/14972; annex 1 to "Bericht über den Stand der Realisierung des NSW-Anlagenexportvorhabens Mittelstahladjustage Visakhapatnam/Indien sowie Darlegung erster Erfahrungen in der Zusammenarbeit mit den indischen Unterlieferanten," dated 18 January 1989, Barch Berlin, ibid.
147 Protocol on the meeting of the Governmental Commission for uniformly Steering Import and Export (RKEI) on 9 June 1989 particularly TOP 5, ibid.
148 "Bericht über den Stand der Realisierung des NSW-Anlagenexportvorhabens Mittelstahladjustage Visakhapatnam/Indien sowie Darlegung erster Erfahrungen in der Zusammenarbeit mit den indischen Unterlieferanten," dated 18 January 1989, ibid.
149 Protocol on the meeting of the Governmental Commission for uniformly Steering Import and Export (RKEI) on 9 June 1989 particularly TOP 5, ibid.
150 Ibid.
151 In the original "Mittelstahladjustage Visakhapatnam/Indien."

152 Protocol on the meeting of the Governmental Commission for uniformly Steering Import and Export (RKEI) on 9 June 1989 particularly TOP 4, Barch Berlin, DL 2/14972.

153 "Abrechnung des Realisierungsstandes des Objektes 'Mittelstahladjustage Visakhapatnam/Indien'," dated 06 June 1989, ibid.

154 "Reisebericht SGD Hauth AHB SKET Direktor WIT, Prof. Schmidt 30.1.-11.2.1989," ibid.

155 "Bericht über den Stand der Realisierung des NSW-Anlagenexportvorhabens Mittelstahladjustage Visakhapatnam/Indien sowie Darlegung erster Erfahrungen in der Zusammenarbeit mit den indischen Unterlieferanten," dated 18 January 1989, ibid.

156 Protocol on the meeting of the Governmental Commission for uniformly Steering Import and Export (RKEI) on 20 October 1989 particularly TOP 3, ibid.

# Conclusion

There could hardly be any truer words than those of the German-Australian economist Heinz Wolfgang Arndt printed in his book on the history of economic development:

> Some readers may come away from the book saying to themselves, with Eccleasiastes, there is no new thing under the sun. This should cause neither surprise nor disappointment, for embedded in the concept of development are all the dilemmas about the human condition and human hopes. It is probably true that almost everything that has been said in the last thirty years about development as a policy objective can be found somewhere in the writings of Adam Smith, John Stuart Mill, Giovanni Batista Vico, Karl Marx, Gandhi, Sun Yat-sen, or Schumpeter. Finding it is one of the pleasures of the historian of thought. But it will be found only because it has been rediscovered, presented in terms relevant to our time, discussed, and made familiar.[1]

Hopefully, his words apply to this book, too. It is tempting to state that the cooperation schemes with the former colonized countries of the South the CMEA member states were embarking on from the mid-1950s onwards were doomed to fail. This would be an unfair assessment. During the 1970s the prospects for East–South cooperation shined brightly and till the early 1980s the economic model of industrialization by import substitution prevailed in most countries in the Global South which provided enough synergies with the planned economies of the East to allow for a variety of cooperation schemes.

Mutual trade was important for both sides. This is not only evident in the CMEA documents but applied to the South, as well. When trade with the East collapsed following the dissolution of the Eastern Bloc, many countries outside the European core of the CMEA lost important suppliers and customers. The dissolution of the Eastern Bloc had severe repercussions foremost for Cuba, Mongolia, and Vietnam that were closely integrated into the CMEA and dependent on investment by and subsidized exports to the European state socialist countries.[2] India, to make a case in point, experienced regional economic disturbances, particularly in the agricultural sector. Indian coffee growers lost a market of 50,000 tons annually in the early 1990s and the list could be expanded to other branches of the economy, as well.[3] Only a fraction of the former economic ties has survived the disturbances of the early 1990s, like between India and the Russian Federation as the main heir to the former Soviet Union.[4]

As concerns question one of the research agenda formulated in the introduction, it is clear that the realms of politics and economics were closely intertwined when it came to economic cooperation between East and South during the Cold War. For the South cooperation with the East could underpin the new-found independence economically and thus served political purposes, as well. Emulating the economic model of the East promised to shield infant industries from global competition, while economic planning promised in theory complete control over scarce resources and their best possible utilization. Eastern technology may have been subpar from a Western perspective, but seen from the perspective of many Southern leaders and experts, it was sophisticated enough to boost the technological and industrial level of predominantly agrarian countries and sufficient to form a domestic industrial workforce.

Therefore, economic cooperation between East and South did not constitute a means to gain political prestige and nothing else, nor was every move driven by a push for maximum exploitation. The state socialist countries of the East may not have been able to provide the other side with the latest technology of the world but the technology they could provide was sufficient for the purposes it had to serve. East German cement factories and Soviet steel plants improved the industrial capacity at their places of destination and equaled "development" in a very basic sense. The question, whether the results justified the costs is in many cases difficult to answer and makes for an unfair assessment, as this question can only be realistically answered by knowing all the information available to the parties involved at a certain point in time. The cooperation between East and South during the Cold War was underpinned by ideological as well as pragmatic political considerations. Many of the elites ruling in non-aligned countries shared some similarities with the Soviet development model in their thinking. The heads of big state companies could conclude deals more easily with their peers from a state socialist country than with the head of an American company, as is evident in the case of the expansion of the Indian steel industry. On the other hand, many Southern leaders saw no problem in putting butter on both sides of their toast by concluding cooperation agreements with Western as well as with Eastern governments.

The internal web of relations prevailing in the CMEA proved more sophisticated than one could assume at a first look. On paper the Soviet leadership was in a strong position to use the CMEA for dictating its will to the smaller members of the organization. Reality resembled more the opposite view, at least in the post-Stalin years when the CMEA gained sizeable importance. Soviet representatives could dictate the agenda for discussion, they could not dictate their outcomes. The smaller member states rarely said no directly to Soviet demands but they could refuse to implement the desired policy changes which equaled a no in practice. This is clearly shown in the example of the Resource-Program, the discussions of which lasted well over a decade and led to marginal tangible results at best. Seen from the perspective of the CMEA, the Eastern Bloc didn't resemble an empire with the Soviet Union at its core but more a zone of Soviet influence with the Soviet Union as a hegemon similar to the role of the USA in Latin America for the most part of the 19th and 20th centuries.

This allows for the conclusion that the nature of the relations between the Soviet Union and the Central Eastern European states had indeed structurally changed during the Khrushchev years. It is therefore no coincidence that the CMEA had played no role during the Stalin years when the Soviet leadership was enforcing decisions made in Moscow and was dealing bilaterally with each member of the bloc without any possibility for them to cooperate with each other multilaterally. The differences between the smaller European member states of the CMEA were felt more strongly when it came to cooperation with partners outside the realm of the CMEA. Bulgarian state companies, to make a case in point, were on more equal footing with East German state combines for projects in the CMEA area with its own pricing and accounting mechanisms. Outside the CMEA, they were more often than not reduced to providing low value-added services, while their industrial products were not deemed good enough to be incorporated in plant designs to be sold outside the CMEA. Bulgarian state combines needed strong partners from inside the bloc to prevail or had to turn to less reliable customers on the international scene like Gaddafi's Libya. The pressure to cooperate with countries like Libya was less urgently felt in East Berlin and Prague.

Obviously, the partners involved in East–South economic cooperation had to gain from one another. The conclusion of ever more treaties over a period of almost 40 years wouldn't have taken place, if every project had proven a failure. There is no evidence that the CMEA member countries systematically blackmailed or forced large parts of the former colonies into cooperation agreements and could dictate their will. Quite on the contrary, as mutual dependencies became stronger, the leverage of the Southern partners of the CMEA increased considerably, since most projects were financed on credit. This meant that the plants and factories were built before they were paid for. Theoretically, due to their supreme military power, the smaller CMEA members together with the Soviets could have made them pay in the way the British and French imperial powers did with the Ottoman Empire during the 19th century or the way Anthony Eden so disastrously tried at Suez in 1956. One could argue that such a behavior was out of question, because both the Eastern Bloc led by the Soviet Union and the West under American guidance had to take the reaction of the opposite bloc into account and hence could not roam the world as freely as Britain did during the Victorian age. However, there is no hint in the available files that such a move was even considered by the CMEA countries. The sovereignty of countries outside the sphere of direct Soviet security reservations was never seriously questioned.[5]

Nevertheless, the problems encountered during the execution of development projects were manifold. They concerned the coordination of imports from different countries from within the CMEA, the partial implementation of Western technology in Eastern designs, communication, and cooperation with partner organizations in receiving countries as well as the funding and settlement of projects.

The recipients in the Global South could more often than not preserve their own interests quite well. They could swap Eastern for Western partners and vice versa with moderate risks, could defer payments or deliveries of goods, or try to play the different CMEA members off against each other. These strategies were employed by close allies of the socialist East and more neutrally minded countries alike. The CMEA countries had remarkably few options on hand to effectively counter such strategies in practice. This holds true in comparison to the West, as well.

By the 1970s, a system of division of labor had developed between East and South that found its expression by a substantial stream of goods and services between the two world regions. While the South delivered mainly commodities to the East, the CMEA countries achieved significant surpluses in their mutual trade relations. What followed was a constant stream of foreign exchange earnings for the CMEA countries that could be used to partially offset the costs of importing Western technology. This came with a significant downside for the East which gave leaders of the Global South a considerable amount of leverage: East–South trade relied on credits handed out by the CMEA countries. If the credits were not repaid, anticipated profits turned into losses for the East. This mechanism played an important role during the 1980s when many Southern debtors went bankrupt or had to defer payments, thereby aggravating the already impending crisis of the East.

When crisis struck most parts of the Global South in the 1980s, a considerable number of the economic partners of the CMEA countries reacted by deferring payments to the East while simultaneously trying to repay the credits handed out by Western institutions. This was no "oriental deviousness" but exemplified the real international power relations, at least in the economic sphere prevailing in the 1980s. The CMEA countries found no remedy for the debt crisis but tried to weather the storm by more, and not by less, cooperation. Western lenders found it much easier to get their loans repaid, because they were able to exert a considerable amount of institutional soft power by controlling the Bretton Woods institutions and the most important currencies, like the US dollar or West German mark. In the end, the CMEA members felt they had to succumb to the same pressure as their Southern partners.

Thus, at the critical juncture of the 1980s, the East came in third behind the West and the South in the economic hierarchy prevailing on the international market. This is the more interesting, since Eastern state combines could still find customers for their industrial products in the late 1980s. However, economic cooperation between East and South had become increasingly difficult by that decade. The technological gap between the European CMEA countries and some countries of the Global South like India and Brazil had decreased considerably by the 1980s. To stay competitive, Eastern state combines had to envision ever more complicated supply chains and partial inputs of Western technology into their designs. Walking down this path was theoretically possible but proved too challenging for socialist managers operating in the framework of a planned economy. As more and more Southern countries turned away from industrialization by import substitution and implemented export-oriented development strategies as practiced by countries like Taiwan and South Korea and demanded by the Bretton Woods institutions, the position of the state socialist CMEA countries deteriorated further as the 1980s commenced and would have done so, if the Eastern Bloc had continued to exist without economic reforms of its own.

There is, of course, a lot more to be said and to be researched on East–South cooperation during the Cold War. Many relevant documents have not yet been disclosed. It would be promising to see detailed Soviet project reports, to give just one example. In India, the Jawaharlal Nehru Memorial Museum and Library (NMML) contains papers of leading figures of public life in India. The collection of the NMML can only become more valuable as an increasing number of papers is made accessible to the public. India is an important, but not the only, country that became independent after the Second World War. It is therefore crucial to include documents from African, Latin American, and other Asian countries, as well. Good research opens more doors than it closes. If this book has created more questions than answers and raised the readers' curiosity for the issues discussed, its quest has been fulfilled.

## Notes

1 Arndt, *Economic Development*, 7.
2 Desai, "East-South Trade," 74–5.
3 Desai, 84.
4 See Vasudevan, *Shadows of Substance*.
5 Afghanistan comes to mind as an exception to this statement, if one doesn't see neighboring Afghanistan as a vital security issue of Cuban importance to the Soviet leadership. However, as the latest research on the Afghan invasion shows, the events tell as much about the fears and militant thinking of the Soviet leadership as they tell about the political pressure certain Afghan political players could exert on the much more powerful Soviet Union.

# Sources and bibliography

## Newspapers

Economic and Political Weekly
The Hindu
Neues Deutschland
New York Times
Pravda
Der SPIEGEL

## Archival sources

Bundesarchiv Berlin (Barch)
DC 20 Council of Ministers
DE 1 Planning Commission (SPK)
DL 2 Ministry for Foreign and Inner-German Trade
DN 1 M/o Finance

Konzernarchiv der Kreditanstalt für Wiederaufbau (KfW Company Archives)
Staba State Bank of the GDR

Magyar Nemzeti Levéltár (MNL)
XIX-A-90-c Commission for International Economic Relations (NGKB Titkárság)

National Archives of India (NAI)
PAD Project Appraisal Division, belonging to the Planning Commission
WI Material of the European and Pakistan Division, M/o External Affairs
HI Material of the Historical Division, M/o External Affairs
PMS Material belonging to the Prime Minister's Office

Politisches Archiv des Auswärtigen Amtes (PA AA)
MFAA M/o Foreign Affairs of the GDR

Rossiskii Gosudarstvennii Arkhiv Ekonomiky (RGAE)
Fond 302 Material of the Permanent Representative of the Soviet Union to the CMEA
Fond 561 Documents of the Secretariat of the CMEA

# Bibliography


Adebahr, Hubertus, and Wolfgang Maennig. *Außenwirtschaft: Außenhandel und Weltwirtschaft*. Vol. 2. Berlin: Duncker und Humblot, 1987.

Ahrens, Ralf. *Gegenseitige Wirtschaftshilfe? Die DDR Im RGW – Strukturen Und Handelspolitische Strategien 1963–1976*. Köln: Böhlau, 2000. https://opacplus.bsb-muenchen.de/metaopac/search?isbn=3412122009&db=100.

"Ambassadors of India to the USSR and Russia." *Embassy of India – Moscow*. Accessed February 25, 2017. www.indianembassy.ru/index.php?option=com_content&view=article&id=47&Itemid=539&lang=en.

Arndt, Heinz Wolfgang. *Economic Development: The History of an Idea*. Chicago: University of Chicago Press, 1987.

Ban, Cornel. "Sovereign Debt, Austerity, and Regime Change: The Case of Nicolae Ceausescu's Romania." *East European Politics & Societies* 26, no. 4 (2012): 743–76.

Bernstein, Thomas P. "Introduction: The Complexities of Learning from the Soviet Union." In *China Learns from the Soviet Union: 1949 – Present*, edited by Thomas P. Bernstein and Hua-Yu Li, 1–26. Lanham: Lexington, 2010.

Besnik, Pula. *Globalization Under & After Socialism: The Evolution of Transnational Capital in Central & Eastern Europe*. Stanford: Stanford University Press, 2018.

Bockman, Johanna. "Socialist Globalization Against Capitalist Neocolonialism: The Economic Ideas Behind the New International Economic Order." *Humanity: An International Journal of Human Rights, Humanitarianism, and Development* 6 (2015): 109–28.

Boden, Ragna. "Das Scheitern Der Sowjetischen Modernisierungsoffensive in Indonesien." In *Ökonomie Im Kalten Krieg*, edited by Bernd Greiner, Christian Th. Müller, and Claudia Weber, 104–23. Hamburg: Hamburger Edition, 2010.

Boden, Ragna. "Soviet World Policy in the 1970s – A Three-Level Game." In *The Crisis of Socialist Modernity: The Soviet Union and Yugoslavia in the 1970s*, edited by Marie-Janine Calic, Dietmar Neutatz, and Julia Obertreis, 184–203. Göttingen: Vandenhoeck & Ruprecht, 2011.

Bose, Sugata. "Instruments and Idioms of Colonial and National Development: India's Historical Experience in Comparative Perspective." In *International Development and the Social Sciences: Essays on the History and Politics of Knowledge*, edited by Frederick Cooper and Randall Packard, 45–63. Berkeley: University of California Press, 1997.

Brabant, Jozef M. van. "1992, the Revolutions in Eastern Europe and East–South–North Relations." *Journal of Development Planning* 21 (1992): 227–57.

Brabant, Jozef M. van. *Economic Integration in Eastern Europe: A Handbook*. New York: Routledge, 1989.

Brabant, Jozef M. van. *Socialist Economic Integration: Aspects of Contemporary Economic Problems in Eastern Europe*. Cambridge: Cambridge University Press, 1980.

Bradley, Mark Philip. "Decolonization, the Global South, and the Cold War 1919–1962." In *The Cambridge History of the Cold War*, edited by Melvyn P. Leffler and Odd Arne Westad, vol. 1, 464–85. Cambridge: Cambridge University Press, 2010.

Bundesstiftung Aufarbeitung Biographische Datenbanken. "Beil, Gerhard." In *Wer War Wer in Der DDR? Ein Lexikon Ostdeutscher Biographien.* Accessed February 14, 2017. www.bundesstiftung-aufarbeitung.de/wer-war-wer-in-der-ddr-%2363%3B-1424.html?ID=190.

Bundesstiftung Aufarbeitung Biographische Datenbanken. "Leuschner, Bruno Max." In *Wer War Wer in Der DDR? Ein Lexikon Ostdeutscher Biographien.* Accessed November 8, 2016. www.bundesstiftung-aufarbeitung.de/wer-war-wer-in-der-ddr-%2363%3B-1424.html?ID=2086.

Bundesstiftung Aufarbeitung Biographische Datenbanken. "Sölle, Horst." In *Wer War Wer in Der DDR? Ein Lexikon Ostdeutscher Biographien.* Accessed February 14, 2017. www.bundesstiftung-aufarbeitung.de/wer-war-wer-in-der-ddr-%2363%3B-1424.html?ID=3326.

Bundesstiftung Aufarbeitung Biographische Datenbanken. "Weiss, Gerhard." In *Wer War Wer in Der DDR? Ein Lexikon Ostdeutscher Biographien.* Accessed December 23, 2016. www.bundesstiftung-aufarbeitung.de/wer-war-wer-in-der-ddr-%2363%3b-1424.html?ID=3745.

Collective of Authors. *Geschichte in Übersichten.* Berlin: Volk und Wissen, 1982.

Cooper, Frederick. "Modernizing Bureaucrats, Backward Africans, and the Development Concept." In *International Development and the Social Sciences: Essays on the History and Politics of Knowledge*, edited by Frederick Cooper and Randall Packard, 64–92. Berkeley: University of California Press, 1997.

Dangerfield, Martin. "Sozialistische Ökonomische Integration. Der Rat Für Gegenseitige Wirtschaftshilfe (RGW)." In *Ökonomie Im Kalten Krieg*, edited by Bernd Greiner, Christian Th. Müller, and Claudia Weber, 348–69. Hamburg: Hamburger Edition, 2010.

Dannehl, Charles R. *Politics, Trade, and Development Soviet Economic Aid to the Non-Communist Third World, 1955–89.* Aldershot: Dartmouth, 1995.

Darwin, John. *After Tamerlane: The Rise & Fall of Global Empires 1400–2000.* London: Penguin Books, 2008.

Deaton, Angus. *The Great Escape: Health, Wealth, and the Origins of Inequality.* Princeton: Princeton University Press, 2013.

Desai, Ashok V. "East–South Trade: Consequences of Economic Changes in the Soviet Union and Eastern Europe." *Journal of Development Planning* 23 (1993): 73–108.

Desai, Padma. *The Bokaro Steel Plant: A Study of Soviet Economic Assistance.* Amsterdam: North-Holland, 1972.

Duncan, Peter J. S. *The Soviet Union and India.* London and New York: Routledge, 1989.

Easterly, William. "The Lost Decades: Developing Countries' Stagnation in Spite of Policy Reform 1980–1998." *Journal of Economic Growth* 6 (2001): 135–57.

Easterly, William. *The White Man's Burden: Why the West's Efforts to Aid the Rest Have Done So Much Ill and So Little Good.* London: Penguin Books, 2007.

Engerman, David C. "Ideology and the Origins of the Cold War, 1917–1962." In *The Cambridge History of the Cold War*, vol. 1, 20–43. Cambridge: Cambridge University Press, 2010.

Engerman, David C. *The Price of Aid: The Economic Cold War in India.* Cambridge, MA: Harvard University Press, 2018.

Frieden, Jeffry A. *Global Capitalism: Its Fall and Rise in the Twentieth Century.* 1. pbck. ed. New York: Norton, 2007.

Fursenko, Aleksandr, and Timothy Naftali. *Khrushchev's Cold War: The Inside Story of an American Adversary.* New York: Norton, 2006.

Gaidar, Yegor. *Collapse of an Empire: Lessons for Modern Russia*. Washington, DC: Brookings Institution Press, 2007.

Gaidar, Yegor. "The Inevitability of Collapse of the Socialist Economy." In *The Economics of Transition*, edited by Yegor Gaidar, 19–30. Cambridge, MA: MIT Press, 2003.

Gasztold-Sen, Przemyslaw. "Cooperation by Ideology? Polish-Syrian Relations During the Cold War." In *Syria During the Cold War: The East European Connection*, edited by Przemyslaw Gasztold-Sen, Massimiliano Trentin, and Jan Adamec, 5–40. Fife: University of St. Andrews Centre for Syrian Studies, 2014.

Gôlan, Galya. *Soviet Policies in the Middle East from World War Two to Gorbachev*. 1. publ. Cambridge: Cambridge University Press, 1990.

International Monetary Fund, The World Bank, Organisation for Economic Co-Operations and Development, and European Bank for Reconstruction and Development, ed. *The Economy of the Soviet Union: Summary and Recommendations*. Washington, DC: World Bank, 1991.

Ivkin, Vladimir. "Skachkov, Semёn Andreevich." In *Gosudarstvennaia Vlast'SSSR Vysshie Organy Vlasti i Upravleniia i Ikh Rukovoditeli; 1923–1991; Istoriko-Biograficheskii Spravochnik*, 525–26. Moscow: ROSSPĖN, 1999.

Jajesniak-Quast, Dagmara. "Polen, Die CSSR Und Die Europäische Wirtschaftsgemeinschaft Während Des Kalten Krieges." In *Ökonomie Im Kalten Krieg*, edited by Bernd Greiner, Christian Th. Müller, and Claudia Weber, 370–94. Hamburg: Hamburger Edition, 2010.

Jee, Jyotirmoy Baner. "Indo-Soviet Security Relations." In *The Soviet Union, Eastern Europe and the Third World*, edited by Roger E. Kanet. Cambridge: Cambridge University Press, 1987.

Jersild, Austin. *The Sino-Soviet Alliance: An International History*. Chapel Hill: University of North Carolina Press, 2014.

Jersild, Austin. "The Soviet State as Imperial Scavenger: 'Catch Up and Surpass' in the Transnational Socialist Bloc, 1950–1960." *The American Historical Review* 116, no. 1 (2011): 109–32.

Karsh, Efraim. *The Soviet Union and Syria: The Asad Years*. 1. publ. London: Royal Institute of International Affairs, 1988.

Kotkin, Stephen. "The Kiss of Debt: The East Bloc Goes Borrowing." In *The Shock of the Global: The 1970s in Perspective*, edited by Niall Ferguson et al., 80–93. Cambridge, MA: Belknap Press of Harvard University Press, 2010.

Lavigne, Marie. "Implications of Reform in Eastern Europe and the Soviet Union for Developing Country Members of the Council for Mutual Assistance." *Journal of Development Planning* 23 (1993): 155–80.

Lorenzini, Sara. "Modernisierung Durch Handel. Der Ostblock Und Die Koordinierung Der Entwicklungshilfe in Der Ständigen Kommission Für Technische Unterstützung." In *Osteuropäische Geschichte Und Globalgeschichte*, edited by Martin Aust and Julia Obertreis, 221–36. Stuttgart: Steiner, 2014.

Louis, William Roger, and Ronald Robinson. "The Imperialism of Decolonization." In *The Decolonization Reader*, edited by James D. Le Sueur, 49–79. London: Routledge, 2003.

Lüthi, Lorenz M. "China and Eastern Europe, 1956–1960." *Modern China Studies* 22, no. 1 (n.d.): 233–57.

Lüthi, Lorenz M. "The Non-Aligned: Apart from and Still Within the Cold War." In *The Non-Aligned Movement and the Cold War: Delhi – Bandung – Belgrade*, edited by Nataša Miškovic, Harald Fischer-Tiné, and Nada Boškovska, 97–113. London: Routledge, 2014.

Lüthi, Lorenz M. *The Sino-Soviet Split: Cold War in the Communist World*. Princeton: Princeton University Press, 2008.

Maier, Charles S. "The World Economy and the Cold War in the Middle of the Twentieth Century." In *The Cambridge History of the Cold War*, edited by Melvyn P. Leffler and Odd Arne Westad, vol. 1, 44–66. Cambridge: Cambridge University Press, 2010.

Mason, Michael. *Development and Disorder: A History of the Third World Since 1945*. Hanover: University Press of New England, 1997.

Mastny, Vojtech. *The Cold War and Soviet Insecurity: The Stalin Years*. Oxford: Oxford University Press, 1996.

Mastny, Vojtech. "The Soviet Union's Partnership with India." *Journal of Cold War Studies* 12, no. 3 (July 1, 2010): 50–90. https://doi.org/10.1162/JCWS_a_00006.

McMahon, Robert J., ed. *The Cold War in the Third World* (Reinterpreting History). Oxford and New York: Oxford University Press, 2013. https://opacplus.bsb-muenchen.de/metaopac/search?isbn=9780199768684&db=100.

Molle, Willem. *The Economics of European Integration: Theory, Practice, Policy*. Aldershot: Ashgate, 2006.

Mong, Attila. *Kádár Hitele. A Magyar Államadósság Története 1956–1990*. Budapest: Libri Könyvkiadó, 2012.

Motyl, Alexander J. *Imperial Ends: The Decay, Collapse, and Revival of Empires*. New York: Columbia University Press, 2001.

Moyo, Dambisa. *Dead Aid: Why Aid Is Not Working and How There Is a Better Way for Africa*. New York: Farrar, Straus and Giroux, 2009.

Müller, Uwe. "Der RGW Als Schlüssel Zu Einer Transnationalen Wirtschaftsgeschichte Des Östlichen Europas in Der Zweiten Hälfte Des 20. Jahrhunderts." *Internationale Wissenschaftliche Vereinigung Weltwirtschaft Und Weltpolitik (IWVWW) – Berichte* (June 2015): 32–50.

National Bureau of Economic Research. "Gross National Product in Constant Dollars for United States." FRED, Federal Reserve Bank of St. Louis, January 1, 1921. https://fred.stlouisfed.org/series/Q0896AUSQ240SNBR.

OECD. "Is It ODA?" November 2008. www.oecd.org/dac/stats/34086975.pdf.

"Official Development Assistance – Definition and Coverage – OECD." Accessed March 4, 2017. www.oecd.org/dac/stats/officialdevelopmentassistancedefinitionandcoverage.htm.

Ottaway, David. *Afrocommunism*. New York: Africana Publishing, 1981.

Owen, Roger, and Sevket Pamuk. *A History of the Middle East Economies in the Twentieth Century*. Cambridge: Harvard University Press, 1999.

Painter, David S. "Oil, Resources and the Cold War 1945–1962." In *The Cambridge History of the Cold War*, edited by Melvyn P. Leffler and Odd Arne Westad, vol. 1, 486–507. Cambridge: Cambridge University Press, 2010.

Pechatnov, Vladimir O. "The Soviet Union and the World 1944–1953." In *The Cambridge History of the Cold War*, edited by Melvyn P. Leffler and Odd Arne Westad, vol. 1, 90–111. Cambridge: Cambridge University Press, 2010.

Pittaway, Mark. *Eastern Europe 1939–2000*. London: Arnold, 2004.

Plaggenborg, Stefan. *Experiment Moderne. Der Sowjetische Weg*. Frankfurt: Campus-Verlag, 2006.

Polányi, Karl. *The Great Transformation. Politische Und Ökonomische Ursprünge von Gesellschaften Und Wirtschaftssystemen*. Vienna: Suhrkamp, 2014.

Raghavan, Srinath. "Between Regional and Global Interests: The Indo-Soviet Treaty of 1971." In *India in the World Since 1947. National and Transnational Perspectives*, edited by Andreas Hilger and Corinna R. Unger, 326–45. Frankfurt am Main: Lang, 2012.

Ramet, Sabrina P. *The Soviet-Syrian Relationship Since 1955: A Troubled Alliance*. Boulder: Westview Press, 1990.

Reinhart, Carmen M., and Kenneth S. Rogoff. *This Time Is Different: Eight Centuries of Financial Folly*. Princeton: Princeton University Press, 2011.

Robinson, Paul, and Jay Dixon. *Aiding Afghanistan: A History of Soviet Assistance to a Developing Country*. London: Hurst, 2013.

Sanchez-Sibony, Oscar. *Red Globalization: The Political Economy of the Soviet Cold War Stalin to Krushchev*. Cambridge: Cambridge University Press, 2014.

Shen, Zhihua, and Yafeng Xia. "Hidden Currents During the Honeymoon: Mao, Khrushchev, and the 1957 Moscow Conference." *The International History Review* 11, no. 2 (2009): 74–114.

Shipway, Martin. *Decolonization and Its Impact: A Comparative Approach to the End of the Colonial Empires*. Oxford: Blackwell, 2008.

Siddharthacharry, Venkata. *Brahmanic Vignettes: Diplomat's Nostalgia*. New Delhi: Partridge India, 2013.

Smith, Arthur J. "Recent Developments in East–West Economic Relations and Their Implications for U.S.-East European Economic Relations." In *East European Economies Post-Helsinki*, edited by Joint Economic Committee Congress of the United States, 152–73. Washington, DC, 1977.

Sobell, Vladimir. *The Red Market: Industrial Co-Operation and Specialisation in Comecon*. Aldershot: Gower, 1984.

Steiner, André. "The Council of Mutual Economic Assistance – An Example of Failed Economic Integration?" *Geschichte Und Gesellschaft* 39, no. 2 (2013): 240–58.

Steiner, André. *Von Plan Zu Plan Eine Wirtschaftsgeschichte Der DDR*. Aktualisierte und bearb. Neuausg., 1. Aufl. Berlin: Aufbau-Verl.-Gruppe, 2007.

Stone, David R. "CMEA's International Investment Bank and the Crisis of Developed Socialism." *Journal of Cold War Studies* 10, no. 3 (2008): 48–77.

Stone, Randall W. *Satellites and Commissars: Strategy and Conflict in the Politics of Soviet-Bloc Trade*. Princeton: Princeton University Press, 1996.

Sukhatme, Vasant. "Assistance to India." In *Aid and Development*, edited by Anne O. Krueger, Constantine Michalopulos, and Vernon W. Ruttan, 203–25. Baltimore: Johns Hopkins University Press, 1989.

Suny, Ronald Grigor. *The Soviet Experiment: Russia, the USSR, and the Successor States*. New York: Oxford University Press, 1998.

Taubman, William. *Khrushchev: The Man and His Era*. New York: Norton, 2004.

Tignor, Robert L. *W. Arthur Lewis and the Birth of Development Economics*. Princeton: Princeton University Press, 2006.

Tooze, J. Adam. *The Wages of Destruction: The Making and Breaking of the Nazi Economy*. 1. publ. London: Allen Lane, 2006.

Trentin, Massimiliano. "Between Solidarity and Convenience: Socialist East Germany and Postcolonial Syria." In *Syria During the Cold War: The East European Connection*, edited by Przemyslaw Gasztold-Sen, Massimiliano Trentin, and Jan Adamec, 41–66. Fife: University of St. Andrews Centre for Syrian Studies, 2014.

Unger, Corinna R. *Entwicklungspfade in Indien. Eine Internationale Geschichte 1947–1980*. Göttingen: Wallstein, 2015.

Unger, Corinna R. "Histories of Development and Modernization: Findings, Reflections, Future Research." Accessed March 1, 2016. www.hsozkult.de/literaturereview/id/forschungsberichte-1130.

Vandewalle, Dirk. *A History of Modern Libya*. 2nd ed. Cambridge: Cambridge University Press, 2012.

Vasudevan, Hari. "Asiatic Orientations of Early Soviet Socialism." *Indian Historical Review* 41, no. 2 (2014): 271–95.

Vasudevan, Hari. *Shadows of Substance: Indo-Russian Trade and Military Technical Cooperation Since 1991*. New Delhi: Manohar, 2010.

Walle, Nicolas de. *African Economies and the Politics of Permanent Crisis, 1979–1999*. Cambridge: Cambridge University Press, 2001.

Wallerstein, Immanuel. "The Rise and Future Demise of the World Capitalist System: Concepts for Comparative Analysis." *Comparative Studies in Society and History* 16, no. 4 (1974): 387–415.

Westad, Odd Arne. "The Cold War and the International History of the Twentieth Century." In *The Cambridge History of the Cold War*, edited by Melvyn P. Leffler and Odd Arne Westad, vol. 1, 1–19. Cambridge: Cambridge University Press, 2010.

Westad, Odd Arne. *The Global Cold War Third World Interventions and the Making of Our Times*. 1. publ. Cambridge: Cambridge University Press, 2005.

Zatlin, Jonathan R. *The Currency of Socialism: Money and Political Culture in East Germany*. Cambridge: Cambridge University Press, 2007.

Zhang, Shu Guang. "The Sino-Soviet Alliance and the Cold War in Asia 1954–1962." In *The Cambridge History of the Cold War*, edited by Melvyn P. Leffler, and Odd Arne Westad, vol. 1, 353–75. Cambridge: Cambridge University Press, 2010.

Zubok, Vladislav. "The Soviet Union and Détente of the 1970s." *Cold War History* 8, no. 4 (2008): 427–47.

Zwass, Adam. *Der Rat Für Gegenseitige Wirtschaftshilfe 1949 Bis 1987. Der Dornige Weg von Einer Politischen Zu Einer Wirtschaftlichen Integration*. Vienna: Springer, 1988.

# Index

For Product Safety Concerns and Information please contact our EU
representative GPSR@taylorandfrancis.com
Taylor & Francis Verlag GmbH, Kaufingerstraße 24, 80331 München, Germany

www.ingramcontent.com/pod-product-compliance
Lightning Source LLC
LaVergne TN
LVHW011124300926
849160LV00008B/508

* 9 7 8 1 0 3 2 1 7 3 6 1 0 *